THE FIRST TIME I KICKED THE BALL WITH MY LEFT FOOT

IMANOL IBARRONDO

Awake the Leader Inside of You

KOLIMA BOOKS

Original Title: *La primera vez que la pegué con la izquierda*
«7Ps» para brillar

© 2015 Editorial Kolima, Madrid
© 2023 Editorial Kolima, Madrid
www.editorialkolima.com

Author: Imanol Ibarrondo Garay
Editorial Manager: Marta Prieto Asirón
Cover illustration: Higinia Garay and Asier Gallastegi
Cover layout: Valeria Hernández

ISBN: 978-84-19495-41-9

The ball came to me a little forcedly, as my left side pressured me, I quickly pushed the ball ahead with my right leg. I kicked it hard with my other leg without thinking. I kicked it almost a hundred feet, relatively high. I aimed it well, right at the chest of the left inside forward, who was waiting for it next to the side line.

What an incredible feeling! At last, I had dared to kick it with my left foot...

...a shame I was already thirty-two.

To my "ama", the best example of generosity, humility and devotion to the service of a team I have never met.

CONTENTS

PROLOGUE

I met Imanol Ibarrondo some years ago, when the *Comité Olímpico Español* (Spanish Olympic Committee) invited him to show us an original and new project that consisted in educating national coaches, trainers and managers of different federations in coaching skills, until then, a discipline virtually unknown in the sports sphere. Imanol rubbed off on us from the first day his irresistible passion for leadership in the service of people, and that also permeates this book.

We soon understood the need to share his project and work together. We, the COE, started hosting small coaching and leadership discovery workshops for all national team managers. They evolved almost immediately into full-day training workshops and finally we started organising an annual edition of the *Máster de Coaching y Liderazgo Deportivo* (Coaching and Sports Leadership Master) due to the demand and great acceptance that these initiatives received, led by Imanol alongside his collaborators, with the backing of the Universidad de Barcelona (UB), in the COE since the year 2011.

In the COE we are fully committed to providing all athletes, coaches and Spanish managers with any help they may need and we may offer to achieve the extraordinary results they daily dream of, for which they sacrifice themselves without rest. In that sense, we have made sure that the skills and competencies Imanol and his work team convey in their teachings –as well as their experience, enthusiasm and energy with which they carry them out and echo throughout the building every day–, turn to an exceptional mixture that undoubtedly pushes the participating coaches to connect with their best version at the service of their athletes.

Because of the recent crisis, we too have been going through rough times in the Spanish sports world, with a drastic decrease in the available economic resources, which limits our offering of teaching possibilities, and that is what makes this book's edition much more valuable now. Through the teachings, articles and reflections that the author shares with us, we will learn skills as easy as they are useful, skills that will help whoever applies them to start their transformation process from boss to leader, whichever their responsibilities may be.

I hope and wish that this book will be a must-have and recommended manual for athletes, managers, coaches and anyone that needs and wants to lead, and also will be of use to spread concepts as useful, meaningful and necessary for our society as they are presence, empathy, being able to listen, compassion, humbleness, acknowledging others' deeds, true commitment, service leadership, the "fruitful insight" (*"mirada bellotera"*) and, of course, the *convers(a)ctions* to create new realities.

ALEJANDRO BLANCO BRAVO
President of Spanish Olympic Committee

"Our deepest fear is not that we are inadequate. Our deepest fear is that we are powerful beyond measure. It is our light, not our darkness that most frightens us. We ask ourselves, 'Who am I to be brilliant, gorgeous, talented, fabulous?' Actually, who are you not to be? You are a child of God. Your playing small does not serve the world. There is nothing enlightened about shrinking so that other people won't feel insecure around you. We are all meant to shine, as children do. We were born to make manifest the glory of God that is within us. It's not just in some of us; it's in everyone. And as we let our own light shine, we unconsciously give other people permission to do the same. As we are liberated from our own fear, our presence automatically liberates others".

MARIANNE WILLIAMSON

I. PREAMBLE

I have always played football, even though I suffered through a delicate heart surgery (so severe that I could not even sweat for a long time) and a femur fracture in a spectacular car hit (another year and a half without being able to move). On top of that, I wore glasses with a patch over one eye. All this happened before I was fourteen. I was discharged the following year after five football seasons. I don't blame them, I didn't look well as a footballer: poor sight, crippled on one leg and with heart issues... Apart from that, everything else was fine. I curiously keep a nice memory of that tough period. At that time the Club informed every player via letter whether they were still counting on them or they were dismissed for the next football season (it was a tense wait), but in my case, it was Iñaki Sáez, back then the Lezama youth team coordinator, who told me in person and did so affectionately. At that moment he made me feel loved and supported beyond that painful disappointment. I felt that I was still a part of the Athletic despite everything. I thank him here from the bottom of my heart.

I changed clubs and teams, new members, other managers, fewer advantages and worse facilities. There was no special reason to keep playing: I did not have a strong will to reach a goal, did not hold a grudge nor desired revenge, nor I was strictly obligated to prove anything to anyone. It had nothing to do with suffering, or working hard and making an extreme effort to be a professional football player. There was none of that. I simply played because I liked playing. Without knowing very well how it happened, I reached First Division the long way, advancing through the categories by enjoying the game and without expecting anything in return. It was then that it stopped being fun. I was twenty-two. I simply lost my way then. I don't know what happened, or how, nor when it occurred... although I do know that the guy that used to go out on the football pitch wasn't me.

Fear[1]

The year is 1990. Barcelona's Camp Nou Stadium. A Saturday evening. 28th minute of the first half, Dream Team 5; Rayo Vallecano 0. While I walk to get the ball from the net for the fifth time, the goalkeeper asks me, teary-eyed on the ground:

–How many goals will they score us?

I tap his head and tell him:

–Easy now

I don't tell him what I'm thinking: "They have scored 5 goals in 30 minutes, in 90 minutes... 15". At that moment an acute feeling of panic took over my mind. I was gripped by that distressing emotion and I could only think about the cat-astrophic consequences that imaginary terrible final score, which I was already taking for granted, would have on my life. Nowadays I still consider the torment I suffered in front of 100,000 spectators to be the clearest testimony of the power that emotions possess to limit or even paralyse mind and body of anyone. I would have paid three years' salary to disappear at that instant.

It is said in the footballers' inner circle that "being a football player is the best life in existence... if it wasn't for the matches". This sentence may seem exaggerated since we are undoubtedly talking about a privileged job, but there are situations, matches, competition phases or even full seasons that are filled with fear. In an increasingly complex and de-

---

1   The article *Fear* was published in the daily *El Correo* on December 2006.

manding scenario a where every encounter is considered "the most important", "it's a battle", "our life is at stake", "it's a life or death match", "it's a final"..., facing simple and daily situations such as playing football generates such anxiety and even anguish levels (and I am not only talking about pros and adults) that these toxic emotions end up strengthening in moods that block athletes' performance and have negative collateral effects on their lives.

According to Catalan writer and science populariser Eduardo Punset, happiness is, primordially, the absence of fear. There is a recurring debate on whether athletes can or even have to enjoy playing. I did not most of the time. Some years ago I would have vehemently defended that it's impossible to enjoy it when playing competitively, although I would be more cautious with that claim today. I have concluded that being afraid made me not enjoy matches. Afraid of underperforming, of people's comments, of not being up to the task, of proving I was not good enough, of making a fool of myself, of criticism, of fear of losing... in short, fear of shame. That absurd and irrational fear is the worst thing that can happen to an athlete (and to anybody) as it paralyses, blocks, and impedes performing based on real abilities, inhibits talent and leads to the impression of lack of enthusiasm, indolence, passivity, little motivation, lack of implication on the football pitch... which leads to stronger negative judgments, more mistakes, more criticism, more trust loss... more FEAR.

Fear makes you face a match as if it was a threat instead of a new opportunity to intensely enjoy your privilege. It's the difference between those who enjoy the match and those who feel so gripped by it that they experience it in anguish, between those who have no fear or shame (what a blessing!) and those who cannot get over it.

I remember how the first time I kicked the ball with my left leg in an official match was, on purpose and unconditioned by the match's circumstances. It was a long pass of around 98 feet (30 meters), directly aimed at a team mate's chest. What a feeling! I had been training with my left leg for months and even though nobody but me noticed in the stadium, the satisfaction and emotion that pass made me feel still lasts as a permanent memory. From that evening onwards, I kicked it many more times with my left leg. I missed more passes than I completed... yet the fear had disappeared... pity I was already thirty-two.

Twelve more seasons passed since that fateful night in Camp Nou until I finally decided to listen to my body that asked me to stop; it had been enough and it was time to quit. A few years later I discovered coaching after overcoming my journey through the desert. It was not a matter of chance. I was searching for something. Something that would help me improve. Like everyone who approaches our training workshops, I did not know well what... and I found myself. An unexpected gift and surprising discovery.

I was 38 years old at that moment and I was in an especially complicated phase of my professional life as the head of a video game company that gave me many headaches. One day my good manager friend told me he was working with a coach and recommended him to me. I resisted for a while: "but, what is he, a psychologist?... I'm fine". A classic and universal response in the sports world. An unfortunate one because it reflects a belief that tags you as someone who suffers from some disorder, instead of thinking of someone who seeks to improve by developing new skills or managing their mind and emotions, or simply, someone who wants to learn to enjoy more his sport and life. A very limiting perspective of life as we will see... But well, that's how I was. Fortunately, my friend insisted and told me that he appreciated the conversations he had with his coach, which inspired and helped him become a better manager. I had nothing to lose, so I gave it a go.

"My Coach"

His name is Julen Ortiz de Murua and I will forever be grateful to him for believing so much in me and for having supported me in such a generous way at that delicate moment. It was a very revealing process for me, to the point that during those transformative conversations he created I felt that, if I had had someone close to me when I was 20 years old that had put into practice the simple skills that Julen applied, I would have played for ten years in First Division. All right... I indeed had my limits: I was technically mediocre, I had one leg and was slow, and would have not been a cracking player or the like, though I saw I could have enjoyed my privilege much more intensely so clearly that this very same second I decided to become someone capable of accompanying others in their improvement processes, growth and development, both personal and professional.

The decision was immediate, although the change of path took a little longer to become apparent. I needed to organize and plan it: a solid training in schools of different visions, ongoing learning in courses, seminars and workshops; reading, studying and reflecting; learning and experimenting with the new skills and competencies I was discovering and integrating; discarding my knowledge; with a lot of practice and personal work; knowing myself more deeply; accepting and besting myself... But there started this passionate course whose ways I have the pleasure to share every day with other searchers like me.

One of the first challenges that Julen gave me was to reflect on my professional experience as an athlete and how it would be to write some articles about it. I had never written anything but I accepted and felt great while doing it. When I sent the first texts he cranked up the difficulty two notches and dared me to publish them. He asked me: "how would it feel to share them?", "what could happen if you did?", "who could they help?"... Casually at that time, First Division Athletic Club was going through a complicated sports situation, and I thought I could hook the articles there, thus, despite feeling a bit uncomfortable with public exposition, I accepted again. Fear was the first article I published in a newspaper, the first step, the first chosen action of a transformation process that I had just begun and which made me go beyond, get out of my comfort zone, explore new places and find out what I was capable of.

Despite the article's title and although we will inevitably go back to fear, in this book I don't intend to understand what it means, or to analyze it, to know where it comes from or what fuels it. On the contrary, we will only listen to it whenever it appears, as it always does with the excuse of protecting us from ridicule and embarrassment, without negotiating or arguing with it, to overcome it until we engage the immense capacity of every human being to learn to be brave, to decide and to choose to be brave, as that is our true nature.

II. CONVERS(A)CTIONS WITH AN "ACORN"

"Seeds sleep in the secret of the soil until one of them comes up with the fantasy of waking up…".
ANTOINE DE SAINT-EXUPÉRY
The Little Prince

Like an "acorn". That is how my coach Julen saw me. As an "acorn" that already has everything inside to turn into an extraordinary oak, everybody is born complete, with creativity and all resources needed to become the best version of themselves, whatever their age, sex, work or responsibility. There is nothing broken or nothing to fix in the essence of any human being whose value is immense. This "acorn metaphor" is not the "truth"; I cannot prove it either and therefore is not a dogma or a doctrine to follow without hesitation. It is a simple and enhancing belief that helps me see the people and teams I work with, not only as they are nowadays, but what they could become. I don't see them in terms of their current performance but of their potential future. There is no need for the time being that you believe you are an "acorn", I only ask you to accept this metaphor for a while, for us to play with it throughout the book and for you to dare to experience it.

> *"Treat people as they are and they will remain as they were. Treat them as they might become and they will turn into what they may be".*
> W. A. Goethe

Like a gardener who knows there is no need to put anything in the "acorn", save simply planting it in fertile soil, watering it, cutting off some branches, being patient and giving it time, leaders' responsibility does not consist in adding but subtracting what is already inside; discovering the essence of each of their followers, what makes them different, valuable, special and unique; recognizing and enhancing it, respecting and easing their learning and natural development; making it grow without pretending to transform it into something else, in what it is not. People's essence, the one we all have inside our "acorn", is never lost; it's always there, in the deepest place... asleep, waiting for someone to help it wake up.

When famous Michelangelo was asked how he was able to create such fine works, he just replied that his task only consisted in uncovering what was already there, hidden below the stone. The leaders' great challenge is to discover the latent treasure wishing to get out of every follower; to be helpers of a transcendental possibility, the transformation from what they are... into what they might be. I consider that finding extraordinary athletes is not as remarkable as finding something outstanding in every athlete (pupils, team members, children).

Coaching is also known as the "art of blowing on embers" (the title of the book by Leonardo Wok), undoubtedly an excellent metaphor to show that people are not jars to fill but red-hot embers that one has to blow on to until they become a smoldering fire. Everything you are and who you might become are already inside of your "acorn", as well as the skills, attitudes, competencies and abilities we need to lead, to take out what already is there and to make it grow, are different to those we usually utilize to try putting in what isn't there and are the ones that fill this book.

Sculptors, gardeners, ember blowers... any of these images are useful to show the invaluable work of those who assume the honorable purpose of daring to shine, illuminating the gift that every follower carries inside waiting to be revealed. If you think the "acorn metaphor" makes sense and it is a "truth" that may be inspiring, I am sure you will make some simple discoveries of immediate use and important and transformative impact in your life through this journey.

Who has seen you like an "acorn"?

Think of someone who saw you in that way at some point. Someone who believed in you and helped you grow and be better than you were until then. Somebody who acted as a leader for you. Consider for a moment the answer to those questions: how did they make you feel? And what exactly did they do? When asking these questions in workshops, we get emotional responses, since the participants dedicate that special moment to honour and thank those who did something for each of them. Many times it's someone who has not appeared in our minds for years, and we suddenly realise the impact and print they left in our lives. The same conclusions appear constantly in the answers: "I felt important", "valuable", "confident", "brave", "respected", "sure of myself", "supported", "renowned", "I felt they believed in me", "I felt capable of achieving anything"... "I felt loved".

When we asked them to summarize what those people did to make them feel that way, they answered: "they played down the situation", "they smiled", "they listened to me", "they recognized me", "they didn't judge me", "they asked me with curiosity", "they were there", "they let me make mistakes", "they strengthened me", "they worried about me", "they challenged me", "they helped me look on the bright side of life", "they put themselves in my place", "they didn't break their promises", "I could always tell them how I felt", "they gave me room", "they were kind and loving"... The truth is that they don't seem to like especially complicated things, nor do they require otherworldly talents, but listening, asking, smiling, pointing out the positives, empathizing, acknowledging, speaking the truth, caring about others, reinforcing... Instead they seem like simple skills and attitudes of practical application and instant effect. Why don't we use them more frequently with others if they were so impactful for us?... Notice that charisma, glamour, style, oratory, looks or sympathy don't appear as prominent leadership attitudes (they never do) as they might be popularity attributes, but in no way define a leader.

Now we have almost answered the classic question: are leaders born or made? The famous Austrian management guru Peter Drucker said that "leaders are born, though, because they are so few, the rest have to be trained". These people are born with a tendency to lead that later they have to work on, polish and apply. Nevertheless, that does not mean that the rest cannot learn it. Leadership is an attitude, it is a set of specific actions, and as such it can be learnt and developed. In fact, I am positive that, when leadership is at the service of other people to help them improve, every one of us has acted a leadership role at some point in our lives and in one or another activity sphere. We only need to do it more consciously, more often, for longer, with more people and more impact. Leading is not an option at the grasp of a chosen few, but a habit that helps all of us to be better than we are now.

Coaching and Leadership

"No leader tries to be a leader. People live their lives seeking to express themselves to the max and they inspire others that identify them as leaders when that expression is valuable. You only need to become the person you want to be and the one you might become to lead".

WARREN BENNIS
Becoming a leader

According to an ancient Hindu legend, there was a time when all human beings were gods but they abused their divinity to such an extent that Brahma, the lord of them all, decided to take their divine power away and hide it somewhere they could not find. The main problem was choosing a suitable hiding place. Then the lesser gods were summoned to a council to find a solution and they proposed hiding the divinity in the world's highest and most inaccessible summit. Brahma refused to, claiming that sooner or later someone would reach that place and would discover it. Hiding it in the deepest chasm of the vastest ocean was rejected for the same reason. After discussing other possibilities for a long time, Brahma found a solution when he was about to give up: "we will hide their divinity in the deepest part of themselves as it is the only place a human being will never consider searching in".

Coaching and leadership are intimately linked. One is not understood without the other. Before leading others I need to lead myself by daring to look inwards with curiosity, love, wonder and admiration, until I find out what I want, what is important to me and what lies in the deepest part of my Being waiting to be unveiled. It is introspection and personal developmental job that I need to carry through to be able to become a model of coherence. An example is the best sort of discourse and the one that uses the least words and every one of us possibly has a pending task until we can transform into someone that deserves to be perceived as a truly positive influence by others.

When I work with managers, I often ask them who they would want to be like. The same names anyone can think of are the ones that are mentioned... always those who win. Then I make them answer what is it that they most admire about them, what is it they would like to steal from them if they could. They conclude that what they want, what the vast majority seeks desperately, is that their players believe them, trust them and follow them "to infinity and beyond". When they express themselves in that way they are no longer talking about training players, but about leading people. It is a big deal. All managers wish to be perceived as leaders by their players, though few are willing to pay the price that entails daring to transform into someone who deserves to achieve it.

I honestly believe that any of us in our best version can be a leader, someone capable of inspiring and strongly connecting with our followers, being worthy of their trust and at their service, helping them to unleash their maximum potential. That talent is there, latent, and I see it constantly every day. Although to connect with it, to develop, strengthen and expand it, it is not about looking outwards but inwards, creating a space of conversations for reflection where suitable questions can pop up to find the best answers. Leadership is not a manager or boss exclusive privilege, nor the leader's main purpose is to have followers, but to create, enhance and develop new leaders among them, being a behavior model that inspires them to be better. We can all be leaders and we can all become the light that illuminates the way for the rest. There are no excuses, and you, in essence, are also a leader.

> *"Only the good ones want to improve.*
> *That's why they are good".*
> Nick Faldo

When I am asked at whom the coaching is aimed, I usually reply it is for the "good ones". I know some are bothered by this statement, but for me, the "good ones" are those with courage and bravery wanting to improve and not settle for being what they are. Those who know that they can give much more and don't know how to do it; those tired of being afraid and always searching for excuses, others' fault and justifications; those wanting to stop playing the victim card and wishing to take the reins of their lives; those aspiring to offer a valuable contribution that gives a purpose to what they do for their teams, families, companies, community or the world. In short, coaching is a powerful resource for all those daring to lead and shine to enlighten others. The truth is that we all have been, are, or will be "good" at some point… though maybe not everyone at the same time. If you're reading this book, it may be because this is your time.

If facing calmly a process of this kind would be recommended for anyone, athletes need the support of managers and leaders that make it easier for them to permanently live connected to that possibility. Their sports life ends in the blink of an eye and this is their moment. Later, soon, they will become part of the club of "ex-athletes" in which they will train, either with the unrivaled sensation of a deep appreciation for everything experienced and enjoyed or with the uncomfortable and bitter feeling of having been able to do much more, of not having dared, of not having taken advantage of their opportunities, of having let others and circumstances define who they were, of not having devoted themselves to the sport, of not having made a compromise, of having complained too much and blamed others, of having suffered more than enjoyed and of having let go off an amazing opportunity to discover their true Identity. This is their time, now!... and they need your help. They need a leader at their service. Are you ready and available?[2]

Leadership and Convers(a)ctions

If you are indeed ready and, in case this was your first contact with the world of coaching, it may be convenient for you to be offered here a simple and brief definition of the term. For the time being it is enough to approach Sir John Withmore's vision, a worldwide example on the topic. He summarises it in two words that encompass and synthesise the essence of this meaning: "conscience" and "responsibility". Starting from this idea, coaching would be a "process of transformative conversations that increase everybody's and teams' conscience and responsibility, motivating them to transform into their best version to achieve extraordinary results".

These are "transformative conversations" because they create new realities and other possible futures that we were not able to think of nor see before the conversation. Efficient leaders know well that language generates new action possibilities that did not exist until we created them in our conversation. Language is not only descriptive, but also generative, action in itself and, therefore, normal conversations turn into *convers(a)ctions* that helps us reveal and modify the sort of

---

2   I will refer permanently to managers as the people who basically represent leadership in sports. I invite my dear readers to replace the word manager, based on their task or responsibility, for directive, teacher, parent or boss, as well as the words athlete or player for collaborator, student, or child, adapting to the unique situations or circumstances of the sport that are told at every moment for their own activity or scope of activity.

reality observers we are at that moment. By changing our way of observing people, life and circumstances, we redefine our Identity and coordinate and design new actions to transform ourselves and reality, in that way creating another desirable future for us, our followers and our teams.

"The new paradigm doesn't lie in knowing the sport, but in knowing the athletes". These are the words of Paco Seirulo, the people responsible for the methodology of Barcelona FC. The deepness of your technical/tactical/physical knowledge won't be taken for granted like courage in the military nor will make a difference between your success or failure as a leader; instead, it is your ability to strongly connect with your athletes, to care for them, to make them feel listened, understood, capable, important and valuable, and to be worthy of their trust so that they believe in you, follow you and pledge to you. You know well that it is not enough to exercise the power that entails working as a manager or boss for them to follow you, as it will only get you their obedience at most. Instead, you need to be a tireless generator of transformative and binding conversations, a *convers(a)ction* creator.

What do managers and leaders do in reality? Although they have many planning and analyzing tasks to deal with, as well as decisions to make, most of the functions and responsibilities that they have to take care of in order to exercise their leadership role are developed through conversations. Individual and collective, public and private, along with their players and staff, with executives, when training or while in the locker room, in interviews and press conferences, in addition to those talks they have with themselves and they will learn to manage properly before any other as we will see throughout the book.

Think about it! To lead we need to learn to generate high-quality transformative conversations based on a superior level of connection and communication; *convers(a)ctions* through which to seduce and positively influence, to require, demand, and set limits; to co-create an exciting vision and share common values that get everyone involved; to pose challenges, to express and transform moods, to create petitions and to offer feedback, to enhance and recognize, to reach agreements... and also to face those pending conversations that we avoid because they are difficult and make us struggle, for which we never find an appropriate time and they scare us believing that we can lose something valuable, we can be hurt or hurt someone, because our authority may be at risk or because we want to elude the intense emotions they might unleash and that make us uncomfortable.

True leaders know that the others (their followers) will have to acknowledge and accept them as such since their influence ability and authority do not come with the job and cannot be imposed, unlike the boss or manager's power. Leadership is a relational phenomenon based on the potential followers' perception of the leader, and the quality of this relationship will be directly determined by the quality of their *convers(a)ctions*. These are the ones that will finally define the efficiency of their transformative leadership. Leaders are artists who build relationships that work; and, for that, aside from being exemplary in their behavior, they have to talk to their followers, not only talk with them. *Tell me how you talk to them and I will tell you who you are for them.*

III. «7PS TO SHINE»

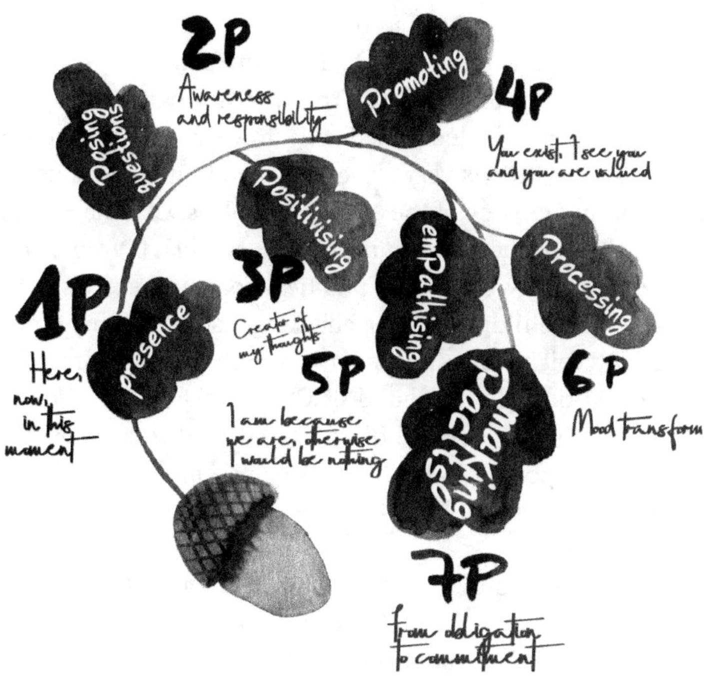

These are the "7**P**s to shine" book, the training in coaching and leadership skills you need to design *convers(a)ctions*, created by Incoade (*Instituto de Coaching Deportivo* [Sports Coaching Institute]) as a synthesis of the Coaching and Leadership Master we have been teaching every year since 2007 thanks to reference Institutions such as the RFEF (*Real Federación Española de Fútbol* [Spanish Royal Federation of Football]) and the COE (*Comité*

Olímpico Español [Spanish Olympic Committee]), endorsed by prestigious universities like the *Universidad Francisco de Vitoria* (in Madrid) or the UB (*Universidad de Barcelona*). Numerous national coaches of different sports disciplines, technical managers, executives, professional managers and elite athletes have attended our courses and they guarantee the quality of this pioneering training in Spain.

Curiously, both the "7**P**s" original format and its first editions were oriented specifically towards the parents, a responsibility that is very close to us and that worries us especially (in fact, one of the "7**P**s" facilitators, Claudia Bruna, has just published *Descubriendo a Matías* [*Discovering Matías*], a lovely book with practical coaching exercises for parents and children). After checking its great acceptance, we adapted it to the sports world where we have provided tens of editions by the hand of CSD (*Consejo Superior de Deportes* [Superior Board of Sports]), the Mexican Football Federation and the INEFC of Barcelona among others. The "7**P**s" are now available for the education, enterprise and politics sectors.

If we understand leadership as the ability to be at the service of others influencing positively on them, you being a father or mother, manager, teacher or boss, the essential skills and competencies needed to generate *convers(a)ctions* with your family, athletes, student body or collaborators are the same and they are the ones we experience intensely in the "7**P**s" workshops.

What is needed is learning to be present and connected to listen and understand (1st **P**); overcoming fears and limitations that only exist in your head and theirs (2nd **P**); creating your thoughts and designing new realities for your team and you (3rd **P**); discovering and connecting with your true values, with what you are and with the best you can offer

(4th **P**); walking in someone else's shoes to be a humble and compassionate leader at their service (5th **P**); developing your emotional intelligence to transform states of mind (6th **P**); searching in yourself until you declare your commitment with a vision and purpose that inspires you to transform into your best version (7th **P**). In short, you need to reach a valuable expression of your life before being perceived as a leader worthy of being trusted by others.

These are the seven powerful ideas on which we reflect in each of the seven workshops that complete the "7**P**s to shine". They are simple concepts to understand and of immediate use in your relationships and life until you finish 28 hours of practical, intense, exciting training, full of energy, fun and great learning ready to be put to action.

Hundreds of people from different fields and responsibilities that have already enjoyed these workshops daily confirm that it's a profoundly transformative experience. This has pushed me to share in this book some of the discoveries and learnings of this surprising and magical training.

From now on, as you may have guessed, we will develop the "7**P**s" in-depth, one "**P**" per chapter:

1. **Presence:** That is the access door to a superior level of connection and communication with people you want to lead. When, at last, you manage to live in the present, you will be amazed by what you can do… and how well you do it. There are no *convers(a)ctions* without Presence.

2. **Posing questions:** you will find out that powerful questions wake up your conscience and increase your responsibility, as well as those of the people you have influence over. Face your fears, jump over your "saboteurs" and… fly!

3. **Positivising:** "reality is explainable". Deeply feeling the impact of this claim is what will give meaning to your *convers(a)ctions*, as you will now be the creator of your thoughts and you will learn to design your reality, choose your attitude and generate new possibilities for your team and yourself.

4. **Promoting:** you will discover how to make visible those who you are honored to lead, helping them to connect with the best they have. "You exist, I can see you, and you are valuable" are key messages from transformative and helpful leaders. The "fruitful insight" will change your whole life.

5. **emPathizing:** if being at others' service is needed to lead, maybe humbleness is the leaders' fundamental value, and empathy its loyal squire. "I am because we are, otherwise I would be nothing" is the best team definition. You need to lead at service to all, even those you dislike.

6. **Processing:** if our mood is what defines our horizon of action possibilities, how valuable are leaders capable of creating a safe space to identify, name, express, sustain, accept and transform emotions and moods? After this "**P**"... You will be able to!

7. **Making a Pact:** cocreating the relationships you want with your followers and helping them to take responsibility for solutions, going from obligation to commitment. Nobody can force anyone to commit, you have to earn it by becoming a trustworthy leader who deserves it... Do you dare to?

I will share with you, when developing each "**P**", my personal and professional experiences as a footballer, coach and trainer, pieces of training and discoveries that have helped me through these years; some published articles, as well as some stories and fables that inspired me. I will also propose several practices for your reflection, and others so that you train your new version with other people, on top of a summary at the end of each chapter in the form of 7 pills, in the hope of offering you a useful introduction to the astonishing opportunities that the simple typical skills of this exciting discipline may provide those who are in a search process. You do not have to become a manager, I only hope you enjoy and feel enthusiastic while you discover an exciting world full of new possibilities through this window.

"Enthousiasmós"

"He who carries a god inside" is the meaning of the Greek word *"enthousiasmós"* (ενθουσιασμός). In Ancient Greece, it was believed that gods entered their bodies using them to manifest when they gave in to excitement. Those who acted like that deserved respect and praise because they were possessed by a divine spirit. This is an inspiring thought! Starting from the etymology of "enthusiasm", I have not found a better-updated definition of this intriguing word than the one in Andrés Ubierna's blog:

"Enthusiasts are tireless dreamers, project inventors, strategy creators that pass on their dreams to others, and who are neither blind nor irresponsible people. They know there are difficulties and obstacles, sometimes unsolvable. They know that nine out of ten initiatives fail. However, they do not give up. They start again, they renew themselves. Their mind is fertile. They continually look for ways and alternative paths. They are possibility creators. The enthusiasts are aware of the weakness of men, they know evil exists, and they see maliciousness. They have suffered disappointments and yet they have decided to focus and base on the good. They appeal to the most creative and generous side of those around them. They stimulate them to use this enthusiasm, to make it bear fruit. They force them despite themselves to be better than they would have been. And it is so that their potentialities sprout, they make them grow. They drag them along proving that everything is possible by acting with energy, optimism and generously".

I find it an excellent definition of what transformative and obliging leaders are. I picture them like adventurers, lonely at times and with an explorer's soul, hunters of treasures buried in the depths of their "acorns". Enthusiastic dreamers, visionary creators of new realities they share with their followers, sometimes energetic, inspiring, enthusiastic, showing the way to the rest of the pack. Other times they stay in the background, silent, serene and wise, but always accompanying them in their *convers(a)ctions* and challenging to transform into the people and teams that they deserve, to achieve that vision, that land to conquer, that new possible and desired future.

If leadership is nourished by enthusiasm, by the creative energy you are capable of generating in you to rub it off on others, you will hardly be able to motivate others if you are not. I declare myself an enthusiast, I have decided to be that, it is a conscious choice at the grasp of every one of us, and helps me to believe we can all be better and transformative, and I need to do it daily to genuinely be at the service of the people I care about, in any personal and professional area alike.

I seek in these pages to pass on to you the passion I feel for this art, shedding light on your path for the time being, and helping you discover what you would be capable of doing if you dared to live as if you had a god inside.

PRESENCE

*"Do not run, do not worry. You are only visiting here.
Stopping to smell the flowers is worth it".*
WALTER C. HAGEN

A classic Biscayan football manager, ingenious and ironic as no other, and with whom I never shared a locker room, said that I should earn four salaries per match: as a player, as a manager, as a referee and as a linesman. I took this comment as a compliment until I discovered the **Presence**'s impact on performance. I took it differently afterwards. I was convinced at that time that my hyperactive behaviour in the field made it easier to have control and influence over almost everything. But the effect was the opposite: I paid attention to everything... save the thing I had to be focused on –being connected to the match. That is if we understand **Presence** as the way athletes have total control over their attention. No thinking, only feeling. Letting their body be. It is clear now that I was barely present. It is a shame not having known this when I was a footballer.

(Pr)esence

There is a concept in the sports world that defines great defenders, called defender's toughness, and it is intimately linked to wanting to defend, knowing how to do so and enjoying it. In football, it means giving your best in every defensive action until the last consequence, as if every play was the most decisive in the match. This quality is recognised in those defenders who do not let a centre shoot from the sideline without stopping it; in those who do not allow an easy pass or stop turning to the opposing team with ease. It is seen in those players that do not commit easy fouls –not to mention penalties–, do not lose sight of the ball nor turn in fear at a shot, who give it all to stop a shot, who do not allow a shot nor a dribble without opposition, who do not lose a dispute without fighting, who win individual duels and enjoy taking back and stealing balls. In short, defenders who do not give the air the forward players breathe. Defending mostly consists of an attitude that demands a high determination and **P**resence level in the game apart from excellent physical qualities.

My Youth Division manager, the legendary Jesus Garay, the fabulous center-back of Athletic Club and Barcelona FC during the 60s, used to scream "planes!" at me so that I paid attention. I, being thirteen, did not think much of it. But there appeared with absolute clarity one of the hallmarks of my sports career: my difficulty to maintain **P**resence and a connection with matches. Airplanes that landed and took off in the old Sondika airport continually flew over the field and I observed their low-level flight, losing sight of the training. "Indian!... Planes!" screamed Garay, and I paid attention for a short while.

It was not until some years ago that I did understand the concept of **P**resence. At first, I linked it to being concentrated, but **P**resence is a lot more than that. Nobody can be forced nor obliged to be present, nor does it have to do with thinking a lot about something. It is quite the opposite. Being present is not thinking. It is feeling. **P**resence is a relaxed and effortless state of concentration in which the mind is absorbed in the here and now. There is neither tension nor need to control when you are present. It is about letting it happen, not making it happen. It is something like telling your body "do what you know to do" and trusting it, without interfering with your thoughts. It is permitting you to flow with the match. It is about connecting with serenity, with the inner silence, with the deepest part of your Being, where the best you are and possess dwells.

Presence allows accessing your full conscience. Having total control over their attention is a sign that athletes have made it, as they only pay attention to the stimuli they need, those from the match, and they avoid distractions (external and internal) as long as necessary. We all have a limited and short attention span; the difference is that some are capable of intentionally focusing it as an energy beam in a concrete activity, and others, we scatter it in a bunch of random movements (or thoughts). The shape and content of life –and matches– depend on how we use our attention, and energy without which we cannot work. That energy being under our control is the most powerful tool to improve the quality of our experience, of any experience.

Players focused on matches manage to attract and cause the **P**resence of their teammates, as well as notably improve their performance. Carles Puyol, a Barcelona FC legend, has been an eloquent example of **P**resence throughout his career, as his attention and connection to matches were such that he exerted a contagious effect over those who played by his side, connecting them as well with their own best version. Puyol's (**Pr**)esence summoned his teammate's Essence. His **P**resence made them better.

You seem like a magnet that pulls all balls when you are present, and then football seems easier and simpler. You flow so well in the matches that you can almost foresee what is going to happen at every moment. You can feel as if everything that happened in the field was under control without any effort or need to think, just by feeling. That is the **P**resence's effect. It is like a perception booster and helps compensate for your shortcomings, since it allows you to anticipate plays, accurately measure distances and trajectories, feel the passes, falls, and rebounds... and that gives you extra time to decide the most suitable technical action to execute it conveniently. You are a better player by being present. I felt that way sometimes.

The rest of the time my mind used to get distracted and sabotaged me shamelessly instead of helping me be focused on the match by keeping the necessary tension and concentration as it was its task. My mind occupied itself by broadcasting the match as if it were my worst enemy, saying things such as "you'll probably miss", "what a hell of a day", "you'll lose the ball" "do it this or that way", "why do you ask for the ball when you are going to lose it?"... and other lovely things. Otherwise, it simply started to think about other stuff that had nothing to do with the match itself. All this made me lose confidence and assurance, it lead me to get blocked and inactive for fear of the negative predictions of my whimsical mind.

Presence in matches is like power during a great storm –it comes and goes. The challenge consists of learning to maintain it for as long as possible, since football is an un-predictable game and the decisive action may happen at any time; that instant requires you to be connected, on, focused... Present. In some team sports, everything boils down to a one-on-one, where you stake everything against the oppo-nent despite the collective tactic's importance. Having your mind 100% on your side is vital to gaining that yard or that tenth of a second that makes the difference between success and failure while heading, tackling, disputing, dribbling, clashing, anticipating, scoring or strategizing. In the end, it is you against your rival. It is a duel and you must win a piece of play by a piece of play, yard by yard until the other players give up and you drive them out of the match... or they drive you out.

Finding out on time the **Presence's** impact on players and managers may change the course and career of any athlete.

The Great Confusion

One of the first and most important discoveries at the start of my coaching training was becoming aware of a great confu-sion that limited a lot my performance as a footballer. I was convinced that it was I who controlled my mind up until that moment. I identified myself with my thoughts since I believed I was the thinker –how wouldn't I!–, to the point of being fully convinced that I only was what my hypercritical and uncontrolled judgments said. Those complaints, those useless and negative thoughts that my mind generated over and over were so harmful that my body eventually gave up and made its pernicious expectations a reality by becoming what my mind was thinking of and driving me away from my true potential. A real shame and a classic occurrence in the sports world.

Proving that this limiting belief and identification of my Self with my mind was just a fake and perverse illusion was very liberating. I am much more than my thoughts. It is very confusing to believe that we possess our mind when it is the mind that includes us most of the time with very negative consequences on our physical and emotional state.

Eckhart Tolle, writer of the bestseller book *The Power of Now* claims that this compulsive thought, this impossibility to stop thinking is a terrible disease which we are not aware of because most people suffer from it. It is considered normal. If this situation is harmful to anyone, it is lethal for athletes.

Thinking is bad and thinking a lot... even worse!

The brilliant Real Madrid forward Karim Benzemá, when asked in an interview about his game's transformation and what he had changed after winning the 2014 UEFA Champions League, he replied: "Now, I am confident in myself". This sentence may be one of the handiest athlete replies when they are asked about the reasons for their success after overcoming a negative or low-performance phase. It is as if Benzemá and the rest of us had two beings inside: one who is confident (me) and the other who receives or not that confidence (me myself). These reflect the eternal and unconscious struggle in the sports world between the thinking mind that says and decides how things have to be made and the body, which is the one that knows they have to be made... although the mind does not let it, as it is constantly interfering.

According to Timothy Gallwey, writer of the book *The Inner Game of Tennis* and one of the worldwide coaching references, once, while playing a veteran tournament, he used a simple trick against a rival that was thrashing him with his service. Gallwey asked him to share how he did it after praising his extraordinary service while lane changing. His flattered rival started explaining it in detail, with technicalities and demonstrations. That was the beginning of the end. The rival's double faults started piling out in the next sets. Many brain research studies by neuroscientists prove that the best recipe for failure is questioning the technique details during the activity. We lose concentration and our performance notably decreases when we start thinking about what we are doing. Or even worse, how we are doing it. The thinking mind's interference at that moment causes higher energy consumption, slows down movement and makes it less efficient. It is like having the enemy at home.

From this perspective, I claim that thinking is bad and thinking a lot… far worse for athletes. Thinking disconnects you from the matches and yourself. It takes you out of the **P**resence and forces you to make a needless effort to do what your body knows how to do perfectly. This is so because of the thousands of training hours, and it does not need the "help" of a controlling mind with a desire to be the protagonist when its role is just to be a silent secondary character in the play. Your mind needs to relax and trust.

Thinking and "worrying one's head off"

I believe there is confusion between thinking and "worrying one's head off", a catastrophic mistake with fatal consequences for athletes. It is infuriating to spend so much time, effort and resources to achieve the best shape to compete at our top level when we allow most of that energy we sacrificed so much to escape uncontrollably, and unconsciously be transformed into useless, negative and even self-destructive thoughts ("you are the worst", "you're useless", "you're not up to the task", "walk away"...) Too many times we are hostages at the service of a capricious and unfocused mind that acts as an organ without control, dedicated to reacting instinctively to everything that happens, keeping us away from the present, the only moment we can influence and do something differ-ent to change things.

We should reexamine the belief that claims that think-ing is free. If we were aware of the amount of energy we waste daily on "rubbish thoughts", and if someone would put a mental counter on us quantifying how much energy we waste, we would possibly be much more careful with our thought management. We would pretend to be at home, switching off the light when a room is empty or using timed switches or low-energy light bulbs... Some days in the evening I come back home exhausted, without the energy to do anything. I can only watch something on TV, not paying much attention. Notwithstanding when I stop to go through the day, I realize that I have done nothing to be so tired, except of thinking... thinking a lot. The only thing I have been doing is "worrying my head off", which dreadfully wears me out.

Of course, you have to think and define goals and ob-jectives, plan and organize, analyze situations and search for solutions, get busy in actions, in concrete tasks and set off causing small changes that will add up to big transforma-tions. However, "worrying one's head off" is something else that makes us worry, wears us out and wastes energy without moving an inch, paralyzed and trapped by our minds. This state is similar to when computers crash and freeze. The only thing we can do then is to reset them, pushing the button and starting anew. We can do the same with our minds. We can stop and break free.

You are the observer

Before the London Olympics, I was privileged to work several times with the male Spanish selection of grass hockey, where I recognised a great leader at everyone's service: their captain, Santi Freixa, an athlete devoted to his sport and his teammates, full of highly contagious happiness, light and passion. He's currently working at a consultancy firm in Holland at the same time as he plays hockey there. Some months ago he sent me this email:

> *"I've just got home, but today's training has left me speechless... and I wanted to share it with you. I've started the pre-season for the league and the World Cup we will play this summer (2014) in Holland. After a hard day in the office, I wasn't very motivated to go for a run in that nasty weather. The thought of "you'll train tomorrow" was already working on me, so I decided it wouldn't be me who would go for a run that afternoon, but my body (I know it sounds really weird, but it did!)*
>
> *I've let my body take control over rhythm, stride, and breath... and I've become a silent observer. At times I felt like I floated over the park, light as a feather as if I weighed nothing. That feeling was so pleasant and surprising... I often think of things that motivate me when I'm running, but eventually, tiredness prevents me from thinking and I suffer a lot... This time has been different!*
>
> *Now, while writing this email to you, I have become aware that I was thinking of nothing, I just felt my body, my legs, my heartbeats, every step, my breathing...*

there were no objectives, no times, no special purpose to keep running. At some point while running, two of my usual negative thoughts appeared: "you're not cut for this anymore" and the other one, the most painful one, "after six surgeries, the best thing to do is to retire". It was amazing, they only lasted two seconds... I thanked them for wanting to protect me and for worrying about me, and I told them I was busy, doing what I wanted to do, being who I wanted to be and intensely enjoying the privilege of being able to be that guy. I looked ahead, I smiled and they disappeared not to come back nor bother me for the rest of the training.

When I got home, I took off the device that calculated distance and speed... and I couldn't believe the mark, amazing for the first day of preseason training. My body is tired, but my energy is intact. I feel much better than before going out for a run. I feel happy, calm and confident. I discovered a space and place where the body performs with Japanese efficiency and Buddhist mentality. I don't know what it's called, but I've felt it and I want to make it a regular habit for my last hockey months".

You must know your thoughts are a part of you... but they are not you! You are not what you think of; you are the observer of the thinker (like Santi), the observer of your thinking mind. Observe what it thinks of and listen to its voice, but do not judge it, just look at it. You are a more present conscience, you are the light that shines over everything and makes it visible. You are the Self that is behind looking at your thoughts, emotions, memories, states of mind, roles, and what you are or should be... You are the observer that dwells in the stillness, in serenity and who, at that moment, was feeling the deep happiness of being there, connected to your essence, further and bigger than our conditioned, repetitive and too often distressing thoughts.

The gift

> *"The past is history, the future is a mystery and the present is a gift".*
>
> Anonymous

Our controlling and usually uncontrolled mind spends most of the time travelling... to the past to complain, blame, regret or justify, and to the future, which gives us anxiety, worries, fears and distress. Our mind only affords short visits to the present, the only thing we have. If reversing these proportions (more **P**resence and fewer trips to the past and future) would be advisable to improve our health and well-being, staying in the present as long as possible in the athletes' case would be a strategic objective to train permanently. Its true gift is being able to live and enjoy intensely connected to that privileged moment, practising, playing, competing... flowing, within a quiet and serene mind.

In the recommendable film The Peaceful Warrior, based on the real story of US gymnast Dan Miller, there is a final sequence in the culminating point of the rings event, while the protagonist replies to the three questions that echo in his mind right before performing his last and decisive exercise: Where are you?... "Here". What time is it?... "Now". Who are you?... "This moment".

Presence, relaxed concentration, is exactly that —quieting your mind, muting it and putting it at your service. Be connected to what you are doing and you no longer will differentiate between thinking and feeling. When you are present, it is as though the thought felt and the feeling thought, as Dante said.

Muting the mind is no easy task, as its natural essence is wandering (Daniel Goleman, Focus), which means that it does its own thing-nonstop thinking, focusing on deep thoughts and worries that cause discomfort, stress and above all, it drains most of the energy we need to be present, control our attention and focus it in the activity we are developing at every moment. The great difficulty of being present is that the mechanisms and neuronal resources needed to control our attention are the same that the wandering mind needs to do its own thing, scattered and rambling about past or future. The biggest challenge to being Present is realizing you are not. Although paradoxical, at the precise moment that you become aware of not being present, you already are.

Don't judge me!

"The main battle I fight in every game is against the voices that I hear inside my mind".
RAFA NADAL

If even Rafa Nadal, known worldwide as the embodiment of mental fortitude, has this inner struggle, how are the rest of us mortals not going to be affected! Although Nadal has an advantage over us since he seems to know that the voices inside his mind are not himself. He has realised that and, thus, can get down to work and solve this awkward situation. Once we are aware of this limiting internal dialogue, we need a new way of linking body and mind. We need to reach an agreement to "trust ourselves" as Benzemá said. The mind disrespects and distrusts that body who knows how to and must play. It goes overboard with critical comments, permanent pieces of advice, insults, and belittlements. I am sure it intends to help, but, if anyone but me dared to say the things that my mind tells me, we would undoubtedly have a grave altercation.

Perhaps our mind could start acknowledging the immense grandness of this incredible machine it pretends to control, admiring its huge potential and inexhaustible capability to learn naturally, showing a little bit more humility that way, decreasing the stream of thoughts and judgments, and keeping a respectful silence that would allow our body to feel the necessary peace to do, or learn to do that it is amply capable of. To achieve that we need an activity for the mind, something it can focus on, focusing on like the here and now, and thus silence its chatter, stay calm and not bother when we are busy.

Stay busy!

One of my pupils, a football manager, shared in class a revealing and surprising experience for his whole team who played in 2nd B during that season. They were playing a ball possession game in a reduced field, and losses and errors were piling up. His anger grew accordingly as he saw that his players were not focused on the task, and he decided to apply what he had learnt in the classroom regarding **P**resence. He proposed a dynamic modification. He asked all his players to focus on the ball-hitting sounds and to hear a tac every time the ball was hit. He did not want to listen to any voices, just to have them play and focus their attention on that sound.

Ten minutes later, the exercise quality reached such an execution level that the gathered and silent technical staff could barely believe it. All players' flow sensation and connection with the game were such that they could only smile and marvel at the surprising effect of the **P**resence. At that moment, an overjoyed player screamed: "we look like the national team" and the spell disappeared. Someone hit the ball badly, others laughed, two players got angry, another one replied... and the carriage turned into a pumpkin. Attention is awareness, focused and concentrated on objects, sounds (tac) or sensations, always here and now. That way we avoid our minds wandering, scattering, making us lose focus or interfering in the activity's correct development.

When Nadal starts his peculiar and complex routine before executing his service, it is neither mania nor a superstition, nor a sacred ritual. What he is doing is focusing his attention on a sequence of tasks that allow him to disconnect from the previous and following points, focusing only on the present. He stops thinking about the sensational two-handed backhand that he has just executed, how well he is playing, in his next competitor, the points he will score if he wins... how his knee hurts, if he is risking too much, what will happen if he loses the number one ranking, if he injures himself again, that he may not get back to his former level... or many other things that have nothing to do with the here and now.

That way Nadal builds a moment without past nor future, only the present and the point at stake, avoiding that way his mind disconnects him from the match, wandering, judging and interpreting what has happened or what his mind imagines is going to happen. Those thoughts would take a great amount of the energy he needs to neatly grasp what is going on here and now in the match. With this sequence of actions before the service, Nadal controls his attention again and he focuses it on the present moment while he keeps his mind busy counting bounces, pulling his shorts, and removing his sweat... he keeps it interested, occupied and without interfering in the match.

Practice!

Presence is also a skill and can be learnt, practised and developed. There are ancient techniques like meditation, or more focused and modern, like mindfulness, adapted to the Western lifestyle demands. They are all excellent training to live more connected to the present moment. Sports psychologists and coaches are also experts in using tools and resources to focus attention and stop negative thoughts. On top of all this, in our daily lives, there are many situations to experiment with and training moments of intense **Presence**.

We can use some routine activities we normally pay no attention to with the purpose to transform them into an end in themselves when they are nothing more than ways to achieve an end. From the morning shower in which I focus my attention on feeling the warm water sliding down my body, the water stream on my back and my head, on feeling how my muscles relax instead of thinking of the day ahead. Eating an apple and paying attention to my jaws chewing, to my teeth biting into the fruit, to its juice, taste and smell. Washing my hands before meals, placing all my attention on the senses, in the smoothness, aroma and texture of the soap on my skin, and the rubbing of the towel when drying myself. We could say **Presence** is making our senses play and leaving the thinking mind on the bench.

Everyone will know what daily activities to transform into experiences to train the **Presence**. I can share a few, like walking upstairs: I live on a walk-up third floor, and what used to be a tolerable annoyance or a nice daily exercise, has become an objective in itself because, as I pay attention to every step, every move, I feel my hips, my knees, my feet, I connect with my breathing... I can almost feel how every fiber of my calf muscles —even my tendons— stretches when I focus on them.

Another situation I consciously work on my **Presence** in is in cycling class. In the past, I used to switch off and I just pedaled and sweated while my mind wandered off, far away from the room. I heard the instructor from afar as if he was a buzz, and I more or less followed his instructions. Now I let myself get surrounded by the music, I feel the rhythm, I strongly connect with the drum that echoes within me (boom boom boom...), I sway my body to the music's rhythm, I dance on the bicycle, I pay attention to my posture and my breathing, I listen to the beating of my heart, I go all out. I end up exhausted... yet happy. On occasions, if I find out that my mind has wandered off... I do not blame nor do I judge myself. I smile, I connect with the drum again (boom boom boom) and I start feeling, I start feeling myself.

There's a classic resource, universal and very effective, which can be used at any time in the field, on the court, and outside as well, training and competing. It consists of paying attention to the breathing, which is always with us, even when asleep, and never leaves our side. Breathing does remain in the here and now without a change. It is not about controlling it, only watching air go in and out of our lungs, though. Our mind goes silent and achieves calm when it connects to the breathing rhythm.

1750 steps

This is how long the beach of the town I live in is, and this is what I do when I walk: I count my steps. Barefoot, leisurely and with the water over my ankles. I do not think, I only count. Whenever thoughts come to me I do not cling to them, I observe them and I let them pass... and I keep counting... I do not care that I may have missed many steps or that the counting is not adding up... I keep counting and, if I do not remember the number of steps I have taken, I start over again.

Other times I decide to match my breathing to my stride and I number the steps I take when inhaling (...four, five, six) and exhaling the air (...five, six, seven, eight). I walk like an emperor, head up, straight back and square shoulders... and I smile until I connect with a deep feeling of serenity and peace. I walk every time I can, especially when upset or angry because by doing so I know my emotions will transform and I will end the stroll happy, calm, and thankful. Sometimes I do it at night, admiring the sky's immensity and the starts, humbly assuming the briefness and frailty of my existence while I become aware of the insignificance of my problems and worries, and that provides me with the peace of mind I need for my thoughts to clear up. It is about creating **Presence** windows in which we can feel the stillness and happiness created when we connect with the true essence of the human being, quite remote from the compulsive thought that overwhelms us.

In those moments of intense **Presence**, now I can think and efficiently use my mind at my service, and if I am in the field, on the court, training or competing, I totally and exclusively focus it on only getting those relevant aspects and pieces of information of the match that I need, engrossed in what matters, the here and now, freeing my body from thoughts and distractions, letting it do what it knows to do.

Presence and Convers(a)ctions

According to different neuroscientist and cognitive psychology studies, the activities that ease the **Presence** and exercise control over attention are, in order of importance: having sex, playing and doing sports. Taking this Top 3 into account, it seems clear that adult athletes are in very good conditions to enjoy a life of intense **Presence**... Managers and bosses also have the possibility of practising the fourth activity on the list to develop this skill: conversations.

I have a handicapped friend who claims that the worst question he can be asked is: how are you doing? He never knows for sure if they want the short or the true answer. There lies the difference. When you are present in a conversation, the other fellow perfectly perceives that you want the true answer and then... things happen. Worries and fears, wishes and dreams, judgments and beliefs, goals and challenges, emotions and moods, excitement and hope are shared in these *convers(a)ctions*. That way we discuss relevant matters that affect people's realities, their way of acting and behaving, their way of looking at life and those circumstances that finally define the way of being in everyone's world.

As in the pitch, on the court or managing the team from the bench, my (**Pr**)esence is also an infectious conversation and it summons other people's Essence. Our **Presence** is like an invitation, a deep and authentic call for their Essence to emerge to the surface from the depths of their Self, to dare to look out to the space we have created and to value if that place is respectful and safe, if it can show itself or, on the contrary, it senses it is going to feel judged, interrupted, guilty, ashamed, ignored, misunderstood, incapable... If that was the case, it would quickly return to its hiding place, it would put its armor and protective mask back on, and would reply to the uncomfortable question my friend referred to with a simple "fine, thank you". The conversation would have ended almost before it had started with no transformative qualities.

Generating a *convers(a)ction* requires designing, building, facilitating a safe space, although not necessarily comfortable, in which the other fellow feels we are present and available for them. **Presence** is the key to creating that privileged moment in which two people can find each other. It is hard for anything meaningful to happen without **Presence**. A conversation may happen, but it will not be a *convers(a)* *ction.* When I am present I have full control over my attention and I can focus it on the person before me, focus on listening to them as if there was nothing more important for me at that moment.

Listening to someone means suspending for some time absolute "truths", certainties and opinions, postponing judgments, keeping quiet and respecting the other person's space, without giving advice nor finishing their sentences or telling them our "story" (our replies and solutions), and without hogging the conversation by interrupting and forcing them to listen to our "war stories" that are much more interesting (ironic mode ON) than whatever they were trying to unsuccessfully tell us before we cut them off in mid sentence. I am sure you are not the kind of person who does this... even though I mention it here in case you know any "conversation hogger" who has not realized it.

In general, we believe we know how to listen, yet what matters is not that you think you are listening but the other feels they are being listened to and understood. When we feel that way, we can freely and confidently express ourselves and, as we keep talking, we start organizing our ideas, recognizing and accepting our emotions, freeing them and identifying and facing our fears by slowly finding new possibilities and our answers... which makes us feel more capable and valuable. Perhaps listening is the most sublime leadership competence as it gets you involved and shows generosity and respect.

For the other fellow to feel listened to, you need to be present and connected, not only feeling what they are telling you and how they are doing so, but also identifying what judgments they are expressing, and listening to what they are not telling you –the emotion, whatever matters to them, and whatever is inside their "acorn" that wishes to sprout. Listening in silence would be a good start.

In silence...

"The pupil asked the teacher: 'master, where does wisdom's essence lie?'. The teacher closed his eyes and kept quiet".
Anonymous

How hard it is to be quiet during a conversation! Listening in that way is much more than listening without speaking, only waiting for the other person to finish for your turn to start and bring up your speech. It is not about listening with the intent of speaking, but doing it with the intention of understanding, and that causes a radically different attitude in whoever is listening. Listening in silence, creating a private space, feeling genuine curiosity and admiration for the greatness of the human Being we have in front of us, before whom our silence reveals a deep acknowledgement, respect and acceptance of what they already are, without needing them to turn into someone else.

There is nothing wrong with Human Being's essence. There is nothing broken, nothing to fix. You do not have to fix people's life, nor solve their problems, just believing and trusting that these unique and incomparable Beings that are in front of you, are complete since birth and possess all the resources they need to transform into what they want and can be. Your responsibility is not to tell them what they have to do nor how they must feel or what their attitude should be. You have to help them discover themselves by turning them into better observers of themselves and their relationships, connecting with that inexhaustible energy that comes from the deepest part of the Being when they feel acknowledged, valuable and lined up with what is important for them, and inevitably pushes them into action. From that "fruitful belief", when we listen to people in that way, in respecting silence, we help create a serene, trusting and safe space so that they can reflect on their current situation and what they want to, what is important, what is happening to them, how they are interpreting it, what is difficult for them, what they are not daring to do, what would be possible... From the calm of silence, we help them increase their responsibility and conscience level.

We can only offer that silence space if we can do it for ourselves too. Only if we observe ourselves and silence our minds, if we suspend for some time our judgments, emotions, opinions, suggestions, advice, truths, interruptions, reasons and interpretations of what the other person is telling us, and we use our serene beginners' minds to respect their space, then and only then, we can generate a *convers(a)ction*.

Listen to me!

"When I ask you to listen to me and you start giving me advice, you haven't done what I asked you to do.

When I ask you to listen to me and you start telling me why I shouldn't feel that way, you don't respect my feelings.

When I ask you to listen to me and you feel the need to do something to solve my problem, you are not tending to my needs.

Listen to me!!! All I am asking you to do is to listen to me, not to speak or do anything. I just need you to listen. Giving advice is easy. But I am not incapable. I may feel downhearted, but I am not hopeless.

When you do for me what I could do instead and do not need to do, you only contribute to my insecurity, though, when you simply accept that what I feel belongs to me, no matter how irrational it is, then I don't have to make you understand, but starting to find out what is inside of me".

R. O´Donell

It is not always about listening with that level of **Presence**, but about knowing how to do it whenever you need it. I know very well that among the tasks and duties of a leader are those dealing with ordering, establishing limits, being demanding and instructive, pinpointing what does not work, what needs to be improved and be done; making decisions, being executive, achieving goals and the results that will finally be the scale by which the efficiency of their leadership occupies a prominent spot. What I am suggesting is that you forget for a second all about your analytical abilities (nonetheless, basic to manage things) when you want or feel the need of generating a *convers(a)ction* with a player or with your team, and you decide to be at their service to lead people.

If you have made it this far, you may have been able to notice that I have had some difficulties with my **Presence**. I still have them since my impulsive, anxious, impatient, vehement and passionate nature does not facilitate this skill. I admit that achieving silence spaces is hard for me and others, but I enthusiastically face the challenge of improving every day that key aspect of my life and my job. I have discovered that seeing people and teams I work with as "acorns" is a radical perspective change that helps me keep quiet. This "fruitful belief" has a great impact on my behavior, as I feel it awakes a curious need to discover who is the people before me, what are they capable of, what makes them unique, different and special, and what would be missing in their team if they were not there, what makes them essential. To the point I become a fan of the people I work with; sometimes I believe more in them than they do, while I accompany them in their awakening process and they find out they can transform into what they truly are.

Practice!

Like any other skill, we can only learn it, dominate it and integrate it if we practice repeatedly. If you want to train active listening as we have discussed, you only need a quiet place, without a phone or distractions of any kind, and someone you trust and whom you can ask to tell you something for ten minutes. It does not matter whether it is a story, what they have done that day or random thoughts. Let them speak of what they want at that moment. You will tell them that you will not interrupt them nor speak, that you will not say a word until the exercise ends.

Your task consists of listening in complete silence (including non-verbal communication), without interruptions, connected and present. Focus your attention on listening closely and, when you realize you are judging what you are hearing, you want to say something, or you think of something else, go back to focus your attention on them and observe their voice rhythm, tone and cadence, their non-verbal language, what they are transmitting, the emotions... You will likely feel very uncomfortable the first time you do it. It will be difficult to remain silent and focus on listening. It is normal, it is a muscle we have not worked on and needs training. The more you do it, the easier you will find it and the more surprising the results will be.

If you want it to be more fun and useful, I suggest practicing it with your partner, your children, your mother, your best friend... And then the other person will listen to you in the same conditions. You will likely start to experience the transformative effect of listening to someone with no judgments, without wanting to speak, and eager to understand them after training a couple of times.

How many people listen to you in that way?

We asked in the classroom how many of the participants had someone close in their surroundings, who listened to them the same way they had experienced during several **P**resence and Listening dynamics and exercises. Very few, barely anyone, raised their hands. And when we asked how it would be if you were that someone capable of listening in that way to your players, collaborators, and family, the silence was total. There is a revelation, a powerful learning, a "eureka moment" in which they become aware of who they would be if they did that, what would be different in their relationships, what their conversations would be like, what the impact on those surrounding them would be, how their leadership would be, and who they would become... Just by applying **P**resence and Listening, only with the first "**P**".

From now on, you are in shape to start generating *convers(a)ctions* and you will enjoy greatly accompanying people and teams in their transformation to become their best version, inspiring them to get going and to define stimulating challenges, greatly connected to their brave essence as you feel how they improve, grow... and sprout until they become what everyone is —an extraordinary oak tree.

Presence in 7 Pills

1. **Presence** is silencing our minds and putting them at our service while keeping control over our attention, which allows us to be fully connected to the experience, here and now, on the pitch, on the team bench... or in a covers-action.

2. **Presence** in the sports ground consists of letting it happen, not making it happen. It is trusting your body without thinking or judging, without need to control, connected to serenity and stillness, with internal harmony and silence, and with the deepest part of your Being.

3. Our (**Pr**)esence, highly contagious, turns into an invitation that invokes the other's Essence so that it dares to come out and share real things in that safe and confidential space we have created.

4. Uncontrolled and compulsive thoughts take us out of the **Presence** and they disconnect us from the experience and ourselves. The other people feel that when we stop being present, the connection is lost and the communication level and quality decrease immediately.

5. Being present in a *convers(a)ction* means building a special moment without past or future, suspending truths, judgments, opinions and interpretations for a second, and focusing attention on actively listening to deeply understand.

6. From the **Presence**, listening means respecting other people's space, without interrupting nor giving advice, quietly, connected and feeling not only what we are being told but how they are saying it to us, their judgments, what they are not saying, their emotions, what matters for that people and what there is inside their "acorn" waiting to be revealed.

7. Leadership is a rational phenomenon that cannot be imposed as it is based on your potential follower's perception of yourself. It will be your **Presence** level in your *convers(a)ctions* which will start defining their quality, thus determining your relationships' strength and your leadership's efficiency.

POSING QUESTIONS

The moment "Nino" Lema got a yellow card I knew my moment had come. It was his fifth, and he had to stay out of the field for a match. I had been waiting for months for an opportunity but the team had been on an impeccable streak of 6 consecutive matches won since the arrival of the new manager. I felt well, the previous manager did not count much on me, and I was looking forward to my chance. In addition, we were playing in Éibar, half an hour away from my home. I excitedly trained that week and, on Thursday, I knew for sure one of the training bibs Camacho was handing over for the match in which the titular team was already showing off was for me. What a moment, the handing of training bibs! You are there, warming up and touching the ball, like nothing, looking out of the corner of your eye and waiting. The manager passed by my side and handed it over to a teammate. I felt blocked, paralysed. I stopped warming up, I looked down and I started crying... inwards, holding the tears in, but feeling distressed and anxious.

I was so sure that this was my moment that I was going to make the most of it, that it was going to be different from that day onwards, that after over a year of barely playing, at last, the opportunity I needed so much had come... I fell apart. I cared about nothing in the match. Camacho noticed and he sent me to take a shower. He did it with love, he was not angry, I guess it was not an easy decision for him either. He placed an inside-left in my central defender spot... Argenta, a great fellow. Despite all that, I had been called and sat on the team bench. Five minutes later, Miguel Hernández, the other central defender, who had suffered from muscle discomforts for days, told us he was not feeling well and I got up and started warming up. I thought maybe fate was on my side and that I would finally have my chance. There was no swapping in the first half of the match, I kept warming up in the break, and throughout the second half. In the 90th minute, I was still on the sideline... warming up. I did that for a hundred minutes, possibly the lengthiest warming-up of football history. You cannot believe how warm I was feeling inside.

It was an intense sequence of emotions, which started with excitement and hope of playing and went from the nerves and anxiety of going out in the field as time was passing, to anger, frustration and rage because I was not going out until I reached absolute disappointment and despair. We won 0-1. Much later I thought it could have been worse. They could have got me out to waste time...

I felt so humiliated I did not even use the permit that I had to stay in Bilbao for two days. I wanted to be alone. I got on the bus and spoke to nobody. I spent the next five hours flooding my mind with thoughts of the sort: "if you haven't played today, forget about doing it for the rest of the year"... "your contract is going to end and they are not going to renew it"... "nobody is going to want you"... "where are you going to go as a 25-year-old with almost two years on the bench"... "you will have to stop being a football pro"... "you are not going to be able to pay rent"... "your flat is going to get impounded"... "what an embarrassment!... what are they going to think"... "you are a loser"... " you are useless"... "what are you going to do now"... "nobody is going to want anything to do with you"... " you are going to die". That was my line of thought. Devastating. This sequence was repeated over and over, with a few variations that did not change the dark omens.

There was also another plot line that overlapped with the other one and had to do with the manager. It said something like: "this bloke wants to break you down"... "he has it in for you"... "he publicly humiliated you, in front of your family, your teammates and your friends"... "it's obvious he doesn't trust you"... "you are nothing but filler to him"... "he is taking advantage of you because you are nice and friendly... you have to be a bastard"... "he hasn't even apologized to you"... "he doesn't give a sh*t about you"... "you are not going to play for a minute in this season"... "the truth is that you are bad"... "you are not up to the task"... "you are not good enough"... "you are going to be thrown out"... "you are going to die". I ended up dead anyway.

I remained like that for the following week. I got little and poor rest, I trained badly, with a sour face, worried, angry, lonely, disconnected and exhausted. The following Sunday I did not even have a place on the team bench and I sat in the grandstand (as the famous self-fulfilling prophecy had foretold: it was clear the manager disliked me). It was the natural conclusion of a pitiful sequence I had not been able to stop at that time. I spent almost two months without being called until I started respecting myself again and I won my manager and teammates' respect, started getting called again, playing from time to time and feeling a part of that promotion.

Saboteurs!

"Being scared isn't the same as being a coward. Fear is an emotion, but cowardice is a behaviour and, between the two, lies the human being's ability of choice to be brave".
JOSÉ ANTONIO MARINA

"Saboteur" is the name given to those thoughts that limit us, block us, belittle us, paralyse us, inhibit our talent and send us far away from the athlete we could be if we were not so scared. "Saboteurs" are the fruit of an uncontrolled and feverish mind that devotes itself to boycott internally and takes us in the opposite way of what we really would be capable of being and doing, of our true potential, if we became aware of it.

There is a sequence that I find very revealing to understand the transcendence of being able to carefully observe what I am thinking of at every second.

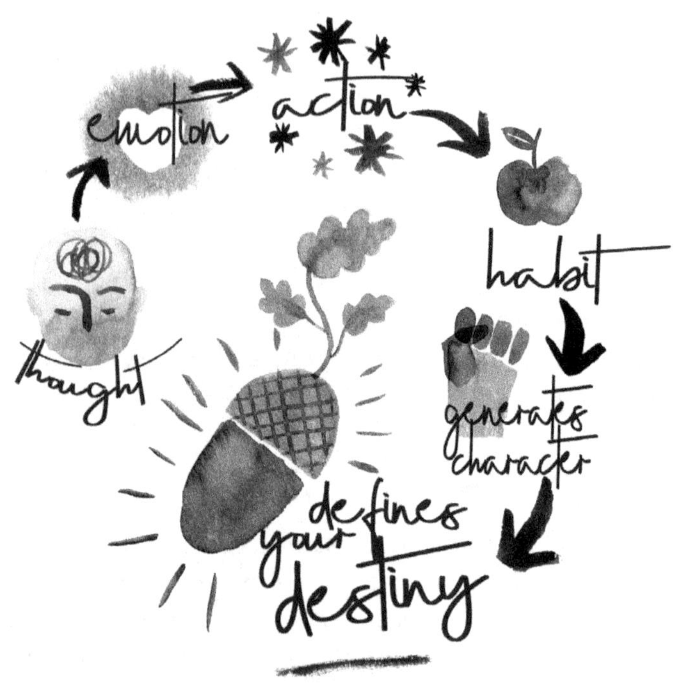

"You sow a thought, you harvest an action. You sow an action, you harvest a habit. You sow a habit, you harvest a character. You sow a character and you will harvest destiny".

ARISTOTLE

Some attribute this reflection (as many others) to great Aristotle, and others attribute it to the 19th-century Scottish doctor and writer Samuel Smiles. I have read it with a small variation in other places: *"You sow a thought, you harvest an emotion"*. It is about time we start paying attention to emotions, take them into account, become aware of how we feel and find out what their impact is on us.

Those emotions I felt on the bus on the way back to Madrid, as a result of a shameful thought sequence, had me emotionally "gripped" for too long, to the point where I was unable to change my fate that season. All those negative and irrational thoughts, all those "saboteurs" generate fear, anxiety, and anguish, they wear us out and steal our energy, and, although those terrible predictions may not take place, the harm is already done.

It is the thinking mind, the mind that reacts automatically, exaggeratedly and inadequately to what is going on (too) many occasions, yet it is the body that feels the emotion and suffers those aggressions as if happening. The extent of loss of distrust, insecurity, sadness, apathy, disconnection, happiness and enthusiasm that those feelings cause radically limit our action possibilities, which conditions and directly impacts our behavior. Our behavior is what defines our character, how we react and how we are in every situation. Again we turn to Aristotle to finish the thought-provoking sequence that illustrates the image: "We are what we do every day, thus excellency is not an act but a habit".

If everything starts with a thought, we should get used to asking ourselves more often: *"What are you thinking about?"* (Several people I know have written that sentence as their *WhatsApp* status), especially in difficult moments, to become aware of who is in charge, since letting our "saboteurs" manage our mind is like letting a monkey drive a Formula 1 car. Destined for disaster.

I could have relaxed under the warm shower (a cool one would have been better) for five minutes in the Ipurúa restroom, looking at my out-of-control thoughts from a distance, feeling which emotions in that sad situation were acting on me and what impact they were having on my body in Éibar. If I had done that, if I had created that small conscience space under the water, I might have been able to calm down my anxious mind and value other actions and different possibilities instead of the stupid decision of choosing to restlessly and needlessly whip myself, giving up the opportunity to spend the weekend with my family and friends.

Perhaps, in that moment of clarity, I could have thought of calmly asking my manager to have a conversation the next week and I could have asked him his thoughts on what I should have improved, how he saw me, what I had to work on, what I was doing well or what good he could see in me, what he disliked, what he believed I could provide more to the team than I already was, what he needed of me, what concrete behavior he thought I should correct. Pay attention, my dear reader, especially if you are a manager, as this is about getting over that limiting and absurd belief that persists in team sports. A reserve player usually replies to the question *Has the manager talked to you?* with statements of the sort: "I never ask for explanations when I play or when I don't play". When you are playing you are already getting feedback that you are doing things reasonably well, that is why you are playing, but, when you do not, you need to know where you should focus your attention to improve, or what behavior you must correct to have more possibilities of playing. You may be answered that you are doing well, that they are happy with your attitude and that you should continue like that until your moment comes. Perfect. Or they may break down the matters that, in their opinion, you need to improve. It is not about demanding explanations but receiving the information you need to be busy and stop worrying.

Athlete "Saboteurs"

So many "saboteurs" flood the suffering minds of athletes that it would be convenient to identify them, stop for a minute, get our mind going from automatic to manual, and assume control to become aware of what we are thinking about a situation and us. What is your saboteur recurrently telling you, what repetitive argument it is using to crush us every day and, whether what it is telling us is helping us or limiting us, who we are with that thought, whether it opens up possibilities or takes them from us, if it gets us closer or farther away from the person or athlete we want to be. You must know that the "saboteur" undoubtedly represents your worst version.

These are some of the "saboteurs" that appeared every working day with the professional playing staff of any football club under great media stress when going through a complicated sports situation. All those that appeared were classic and universal. Anyone who is working or has worked in sports may have identified with some of them: "you suck", "you are not up to the team's level", "you don't score any goals", "the club doesn't value you", "you are dead in the water", "you are an embarrassment", "you are invisible", etc.

These were so many, so harsh and, in some cases, so cruel, that I could feel the pain when put into words. Training and playing with so much crap, so much noise, and so much fear in your head was torture. A scenario very far away from the silence and stillness we need to be present and connected to the game. What a paradox! *Playing…* football, that is what it is called. *Playing* becomes suffering and torment in that way. It is impossible to do it.

Manager "Saboteurs"

Of course, managers also have their own "saboteurs", and they are a pain in the neck. We can point at these among many others: "the players don't believe you anymore", "you are not up to the task", "you are a square", "they don't respect you", "it doesn't matter what you do", "they are going to throw you out", etc. It is very complicated being connected to the enthusiasm and confidence they need to offer the best they have with thoughts like these, making noise in their anxious minds.

When talking about manager "saboteurs", I sometimes give the example of a conversation that might have happened when Guardiola was offered to coach Barcelona in 2008. It is a three-way imaginary conversation between Laporta, Guardiola and his "saboteur". There are several possible narrative threads. The first one could be something like this:

Laporta.- "Pep, we thought you could coach the first team". (Before replying, Guardiola has an internal dialogue with his "saboteur".)

"Saboteur".- *"Pep, you are too young", " you are not experienced enough", "you are not ready yet", "baby steps", "you have a lot to lose", "take it easy" "what will happen if you fail (the most logical outcome)", "you have an image to maintain"...*

Pep (after listening closely and heeding his "saboteur").- Thank you, Mr Laporta. Your confidence flatters me, but I am not experienced enough to accept this challenge; I have only coached a third-division team for a season. Besides I am too young, I am only 36. If it is alright with you, I would prefer to stay with the B team, which we have just promoted to the second division, then two more years in second A to gather experience, then a couple of seasons in First Division, and I believe I will be better prepared to coach Barça's first team as a 42-year-old manager, very young still.

Laporta.- Ok, Pep. Thank you. We'll talk again... Bye.

Nobody can deny that the "saboteur's" arguments were not true. It tells him that he is too young because he is only 36 years old and he lacks experience, because he has only been a manager for a year... and that is correct. However, these arguments are only a part of reality, of *truth*. There are many more things that, when we pay attention to the "saboteur", we are not even able to discover, explore and know how they connect with what matters to us, with our true skills and competencies, and with what we essentially are. Much more than our limiting and scared thoughts.

Whatever your "saboteur" tells you may be true or not... I do guarantee that it is not all the *truth*. It shows your fears, insecurities, doubts and uncertainties. You can hardly connect with the emotion, passion and determination you need to face the new challenges that force you to grow and become the person capable of deserving and achieving them.

It seems clear that Guardiola did not surrender to his "saboteur" (although he probably had one), seeing how the situation went down. I can imagine how Guardiola's "true Self" may have replied to his "saboteur" after listening to his limiting arguments:

"True Self".- *Thank you for your concern. What you say is true: I am young and lack experience, although what I am about to tell you is also true. I have been in this club since I was a ball boy, I know the tiki-taka style, I deeply believe in it and have lived it intensely. I have been a Barça cap-*

tain in all categories and I have had the privilege of being an outstanding pupil under Cruyff. I have absolute faith in this great idea and contagious enthusiasm for football. I know that I strongly connect with players and I passionately transmit what I am and what I believe in. There are former teammates in the locker room that will help me, who I trust and can rely on. I have a lot of energy, great working capacity and overflowing enthusiasm. I know it will be a Herculean challenge but I have a spectacular working team that deeply believes in me, and I am looking forward to putting everything I am and have at the service of my players, my club and football.

Guardiola replies to the President's offer with a: "thank you, Mr Laporta, for this great opportunity. I am ready and willing to undertake this challenge and I wish to start working now" after having the conversation between his "saboteur" and his "true self". Guardiola did have "saboteurs", he faced them and beat them by connecting with what truly was important to him, with whom he may be if he dared to, of what he would be capable of and what may be possible if he did it.

My "saboteur" is not me

This discovery was very liberating for me, like finding the key to stop being a prisoner in my mind. Understanding that the "saboteurs" were only thoughts fruit of my untrained mind, as decisive to define who I was as a freckle on the tip of my nose, was revealing, and it was even more enlightening to understand that I could change them and replace them for others until I became the creator of my thoughts. If you let your mind sow "crap thoughts", do not be surprised you reap no fruit, as their quality will be determinant in the quality of your actions. It is in your hands to stop being a slave of these limiting and will-gripping "saboteurs", and to choose who you want to be and how you want to behave before future challenges.

If I had known this as a 20-year-old, I could have taken care of my mind by visualizing what player I wanted and I could become, using every circumstance and situation to grow, dealing with bravery and enthusiasm in my improving areas, polishing my strengths, enjoying and progressing through every training session, every match and every season, until I reach my full potential.

Conversation between SR4 and his "Saboteur"

Sergio Ramos gets closer to executing his kick in the penalty shoot-out to decide the 2012 European Championship finalist between Spain and Portugal, and, while I admire his courage and boldness to assume again this huge responsibility after his recent error in the UEFA Champions League semifinals against Bayern Munich, I completely give up as I see he is going to dare with a maximum risk Panenka style kick.

As the sounds of mockery, humiliation and public jibe that the Andalusian center forward was subjected to still resonate (multiplied in time and amount by the anonymous social media loudspeaker), SR4 tremendously raises the stakes. How? I could almost hear his "saboteur" from my home's sofa, advising him to be cautious, sweet-talking him with sentences like "you have played excellently today", "you have done your share", "you have been better than CR7", "you are the best centre forward player in the Tournament", "you don't need to do more", "let others assume their responsibility now", "they already punished us enough when we missed the penalty kick against Bayern Munich", "they are still laughing their arses off", "CR7 and Kaká, who also missed (Golden Ball award each) got away with it and we suffered every possible humiliation", "relax, don't shoot the penalty, we don't need it, cover your back, move aside, forget about it".

The conversation got heated when the "saboteur" realized that Sergio had no intention of heeding its words and still wanted to shoot. Then it changed its approach and increased its critical tone by using less nice and condescending comments: "are you stupid?", "you don't listen to me and you screw up", "I warned you too during the match against Bayern Munich", "what on Earth are you doing?", "don't shoot!", "you are not ready", "you are going to miss for sure", "you are not a specialist", "if you miss again we'll have to leave Spain" and all sorts of nasty comments.

The "saboteur" went insane when he realized SR4 had decided to kick a Panenka-style penalty!". It almost fainted at that moment. His laments were grief-stricken: "please, don't do this to us!", "it will be terrible!", "your end as a footballer!", "we will never be able to walk the streets again", "your family's reputation will be tarnished", "they will tell mean jokes to us in Cadiz", "we will be kicked out of the team", "you will end up in the national team's black list with Cardeñosa", "we will be mauled for years on *Twitter*", "please, please, please, don't do it, you're going to sink us", "what an embarrassment!".

It may look dramatic or even comical, but this conversation takes place in a couple of seconds with a devastating impact. Fortunately, SR4 took over control, stopped working on automatic and turned to manual mode, sowing other thoughts that filled him with energy, confidence and determination to do what he did. He calmed his mind and became aware that *he was that moment*. There was nothing else, no past, no future, only present. *Here and now*. When the match ended he declared he was looking forward to that situation happening, he was thankful for that opportunity, he had pictured it on many occasions, practiced in his mind, and he had even talked to his teammates that he would shoot that way if he had the chance. His courage did the rest of the work when facing his "saboteur". He may have asked himself at some point:

"Who do I want to be now?", "what's the challenge for me here", "how would it be to dare to shoot it 'Panenka style'?", "what would change if I did it?, "how would it help my later shoot-out takers?", "what would be the message for all that are seeing me right now if I did it", "what sort of value I would be living?, "what kind of player would I become if I dared to?", "what would I be capable of from this day onwards?" Yes, I know that SR4 possibly did not ask himself any of these questions, but I am going to make the most of this example to leave some tips that may be used by any athlete to connect with the bravery they will need to overcome their "saboteurs" when they appear... and they will.

It is said that what SR4 did was an act of madness or thoughtlessness. I do not think so. I have lately concluded that these ingredients are also necessary for a meaningful life, to grow and aspire to undertake new challenges. After defeating his "saboteur" so brilliantly, I only have one question left: Where are your limits now?[3]

Practice!

I propose you stop here for some minutes to reflect on what they are telling you, your "saboteurs", at this point of your life and what their impact is on your attitude and behaviour. I encourage you to do this exercise because you need to have jumped over them and connected with the energy needed to set off before helping others to do the same. You need to find out if it works. You need to experience it.

---

3   Article published in DEIA on July 2012.

As I guess I am the closest thing you have to a coach on hand, I volunteer to accompany you in this process. After **P**resence and Listening, the skill to create questions is the most powerful resource we have to generate *convers(a)ctions*. Questions will be our essential companions in every "**P**" from this chapter until the end of the book to increase our speakers' awareness and responsibility.

We will only listen to what the saboteur is saying while keeping in mind that what it is saying is not what you are in this *convers(a)ction*, so that you jump over the "saboteur". Your "true self" is a thousand times more powerful than your fearful "saboteur". We do not seek to dig into its origin, nor analyze or criticize it; we will not get involved with it because we would probably lose and it is not our task anyway. We have no particular interest in knowing how this "saboteur" came here or knowing the details of the situation. We only need to feel its impact, for you to land in your reality and become aware of how you are now, how it is affecting you and what is the price you are paying for letting it control your thoughts, emotions, actions and life before you can jump over it.

I will ask you questions to make you feel, reflect and think differently about the topic, objective or situation we are talking about, focusing more on the possible solutions than on the difficulties. Being in "saboteur mode" is like looking at a painting with your nose on the canvas. You cannot see anything since it is a very limited perspective of reality from which we see little. You will be able to step back a few feet and acquire some distance to increase focus with the questions, to see the painting from other angles by changing the kind of observer you are. This will help you change your reference frame, and your perspective; redefine the problem and turn it into a challenge, and re-frame to discover other interpretations of reality that connect you with the energy you need to keep going.

We will jump over the "saboteur" and we will completely ignore it with our answers to discover, describe and feel where you want to be, how the ideal situation would be without it and who you would be without it, searching and finding the resources you have at your disposal inside your "acorn" and which you need to get going. You need to design an action plan that helps you change the limiting habits that are keeping you from being the person and athlete you could be if you moved in the direction your dreams show you.

If we were to divide the time of this particular *convers(a)ction* in percentages for this exercise, we could spend 20% of it to become aware of how impactful the "saboteur" has been on your attitude, 60% to imagine what would be possible if it did not exist, connecting you with another emotion and with the energy you will need to start those little changes, and 20% to define your action plan. There will be many more *convers(a)ctions* in which we will spend a majority of the time specifying new courses of action, as learning and true transformation reside in action. Therefore, we need to spend as much time as necessary to come up with a truly effective plan.

Shall we begin? To properly do this exercise, I need you to get a pencil and a sheet of paper. A notebook would be better. Do not read further...

....

Do you have them? No? Come on, get them! Make this small effort. I assure you it will be worth it. Remember that coaching consists of *convers(a)ctions* to drive you to action! It is not about reading and understanding, but doing and transforming, and you need to spend some time to take conscience of all this. Try it!

Are you ready now? Let's begin! Choose a "saboteur", a recurring thought that you know is harming you, limiting you, tiring you and taking energy and confidence from you (and do not tell me you have neither because… you don't believe it). A thought that is paralyzing you and keeping you away from your best version, of what you would be capable of if it was not always there bringing you down with its dark omens.

Done? Write it down! In the second person, as if it was bluntly talking to you. A "heavy saboteur" does not say "I think you need to lose some weight" but, "you are fat and you don't deserve to be loved". It does not tell you, "you need to improve your communication skills" but "you don't transmit anything. You better shut up". Kind of harsh, is it not? On the other hand, it is a very needed and liberating exercise. Writing it down helps a lot, taking it out of your head decreases its influence and, on paper loses a lot of strength. Personifying can even be fun, naming it, facing ft and even voice, as we did once with the Spanish synchronized swimming team.

In May 2010, we had the pleasure of working with this select group of swimmers thanks to the trust of the national team manager Anna Tarrés. An extraordinary mermaid team that has won an enormous amount of medals in international championships and Olympic Games, absolutely disproportionate for a country with a few hundred federates in this demanding sports discipline, which reflects their talent's quality and huge sacrifice. We had the intention of developing numerous dynamics and activities, but, when we started speaking, we realized there was a special guest in the room we had to deal with first before focusing on other matters. This guest was a massive collective "saboteur" that was greatly affecting every one of them. Once they identified it, they played with it, and gave it a face, a voice, and even a name, Gertru, before managing to jump over it and greatly reducing its power.

Four years later, Clara Basiana, a national team member, sent me these lines from a post titled *Our Great Friend*

Gertru, published in their excellent blog *Among a Thousand Bubbles*:

> «...*whenever we have one of those dark days when all this negative energy is following us, we say 'our old friend Gertru has visited us' (we discovered and named her during an unforgettable day with Incoade). Gertru is a horrible presence that gets in your head and tries to sabotage your training sessions so that everything goes wrong and you keep wallowing in misery. When she visits us, Gertru spends her time reminding us of the long list of unpleasant things about our sport, and attacks us with her classic and harmful comments "you are on your team's level", "you are tired and can't go on", "you better quit", "you won't make it", "you are too tired", "you are fat", "give up!", "you'll never beat the Russians", "this much effort is not worth it".*
>
> *However, as we have already identified her, we know how she is and somehow we manage to whip out her mass destruction weapons and send Gertru far away, somewhere between Sebastopol and Kuala Lumpur, by sharing what she does to our team members, to their help and will. She always comes back, even though every time we have more resources and strength to deal with her power and charm. Our skills help us improve without barely realising it! That is the magic of sport, us being able to transform obstacles into objectives that, once overcome, allow you to grow and keep going. Thank you, Gertru!»*

Let's leave Gertru and come back to you. Have you written what your "saboteur" has told you yet? Let's have a go at it! We will start with some questions regarding your current situation. Choose whichever drew your attention. Take your time to reflect on each one, feel them and write the answers down in your notebook. Here they are:

What is your "saboteur" telling you? How is it speaking to you? When does it appear? How is it limiting you? What is it costing you? What are you missing out on because of it? What is making it hard? What is the worst? How do you feel when it is in control? How is your attitude (on the field, court, team bench, at home, at work...)? What is your behaviour? How are your relationships from there? Who are you being?...

I insist. We are not talking about the problem, but about the effect and impact these thoughts have on you. The fact of uncovering the "saboteur", recognizing it and verbalizing it drastically reduces its power over you. Now we will "get away from the painting" to discover new perspectives that help us overcome it in the remaining 60% of the *convers(a)ction*. We will seek to change emotions and connect with what matters, with your desires and their ideal situation. I am going to ask you to imagine there is no "saboteur" anymore, so that you feel it more intensely. I will ask you these questions about a hypothetical future in a striking present to ease this sensation. Take your time to feel them and calmly reflect on each of them:

How does (whichever situation it is) it feel without a "saboteur"? What are you doing differently? What is different? What is better? What are your advantages? Who are you being? What are you daring to do? What is possible for you now? What are your energy and enthusiasm levels? What are you capable of? How are you behaving? How is your attitude? How are your relationships with your players, children, helpers, friends or partner? How are you feeling? What value are you living intensely? Who have you become? What have you found out? What is your impact on your colleagues, players or family now?"

How did it go? If we have worked well in the previous phase, you should already be feeling inside the energy you need to start doing different things, daring to look straight ahead and jumping over your "saboteur". I call *energizol* this energy that comes from the connection with the deepest and most essential self of everyone. It is the secret that allows us to connect with our brave nature and what we need to cross the bridge that links reason and desire, from what I am to what I want to and could be. It is inexhaustible energy that is always available, is free, and will not test positive although it would give that impression because of the visible symptoms of enthusiasm, optimism and confidence in those who give in to this possibility.

When you plug into your *energizol* tank through the questions, and you stop listening to your "saboteur", it weakens to such a degree that it ends up hiding in the back of your head as if it was background music. It is there but it does not bother us, it does not affect us there, we hear it without paying attention, almost like when we smile at childish pranks. We are now looking forward to taking action.

Once fully loaded with *energizol*, the last 20% of the *convers(a)ction* has to do with designing a plan of action. We will go more deeply into the plan of action, the key to successfully facing any transformation process, in the last chapter of the book. It is enough to bring up the sort of questions that can be used to specify it for the moment:

What could you do differently this week? What are you going to do? Which are the first steps to making what has been explored a reality? What do you need to do it? When are you going to do it? From 1 to 10, how sure are you that you are going to do it? How will you know you achieved the objective? How are you going to celebrate it?...

All these questions are obviously out of context and I only pretend they guide you to generate a new *convers(a) ction*. "Powerful questions" are born of the connection you generate with your Presence, of your true nature to help others to unveil what is hidden inside their "acorn" and the *convers(a)ction*. It is not about having a battery of questions or a questionnaire for that effect, even though I hope you can use them as a reference for the sort of questions that can be asked to jump over the "saboteur".

What are the "powerful questions" like?

As you have seen, those previous questions are brief, they could be made with less than seven words to avoid the temptation of hiding and including our judgments among too many words, they are open (they cannot be answered with a "yes" or a "no") and neutral (I do not ask, *are you mad?* but, *how are you feeling?*). They are questions that give others power, and are aimed at the observer, not at what is observed. "Powerful questions" do not focus on the problem nor pay attention to the "saboteur", but on the solution, and come from the genuine curiosity that comes from my "fruitful belief" to help you reflect and go farther than you can go on your own, until revealing the questions that will connect you with the *energizol* needed to start going.

It could be argued that the questions we usually pose to others are basically for us, to complete our information, obtain data and increase knowledge, or to examine, evaluate and assess situations or people, to diagnose and offer solutions. But these "powerful questions" are not for me, but for others, for them. They are not questions I already have answers for (that would be shoddy manipulation), nor are meant to be answered to me. Instead, their purpose is for them to answer themselves, to help them reflect, find themselves, search and find their resources inside their "acorn". It is unlikely that it will be a "powerful question" if they barely stop to think of the answer.

Why not ask "why"?

"Powerful questions" begin with *what? Which?, How?, What for?, Who?, Where?* I have not posed any questions with *why?* When we start a question with *why?* it looks as if we need to understand in detail someone's "problem" to offer them a solution and that is not our function. We do not need to get in their reference frame, nor stick our noses to the painting as the question is doing, nor do we want them to get tangled in their limiting interpretation of reality ("saboteur"). We need to help them discover new perspectives, new lenses to observe reality and, *why* is not a powerful question for that.

Almost all *whys* can be replaced with *what for(s)* that connect you to the future, with the sought or ideal situation, and with the possibilities you are unable to see in the current situation. Those *whys* tend to trap us with the reason why, dragging us into the search of excuses and justifications. Those who are asked those questions may feel judged and get defensive. The "saboteur" takes the reins in these situations, decreases the energy level and, thus, a disconnection between the speakers happens. End of the *convers(a)ction*.

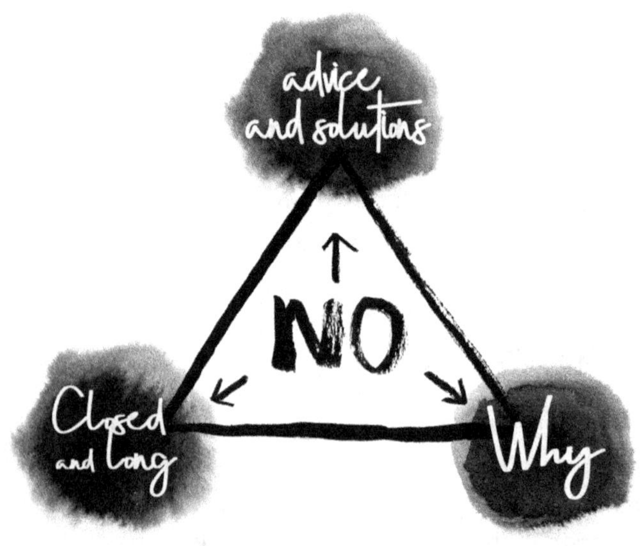

"Book saboteur"

In January 2014, in the "7**P**s" workshops where we work on "saboteurs", just before starting to write this book, I volunteered so that the participants practiced the "powerful questions" with me. I brought up a situation that referenced my trouble starting the project of writing this book, since it was taking too long and was causing me some discomfort. I gave them context before we started and I explained what my "saboteur" was telling me about it ("you are not prepared", "you are going to be crushed", "you were a nobody as a footballer and you have nothing to teach", "you are not a writer", "it's a waste of time", "you will change nothing"...) and other nice comments of the sort.

After sharing my "problem" they asked me questions I did not answer, although I did mark them from 1 to 10 depending on how impactful they were and where they led me. If they were too long, had implicit advice, offered solutions, were closed, manipulative, only sought information or connected me with my "saboteur" (*Why don't you write it?...* pfff), I marked them down. On the other hand, if they led me to places I had not reached on my own before, connected me with what was important, with true stuff, essential, with values, energy; if they reduced the "saboteur's" power, if they helped me change the sort of observer I was in the situation, if they searched inside my "acorn", then I would score them high.

I received truly "powerful" questions that helped me reflect and go deeply into the book's topic, although there were two that clicked inside of me. The first one was: *What would have been like to read that book at 22 years of age?* I gave it a 9 after feeling it. The second one, even better than the first one was: *What would have been like to have your manager read that book?* I gave it a 10. I admit that question immediately connected me with my purpose to expand the goodness of this fascinating discipline and I started writing the book that week.

The man who gifted questions

I will reproduce here a text published in *Cartografía Emocional*, which I read and saved some time ago, and helped me become aware of the transformative power of the powerful questions.

> *"He came loaded with questions for everyone. Questions that lit up the seed of curiosity in our hearts. Questions that led us towards the search for answers, even if we had to face the beliefs that had stopped us from finding them. Questions that invited us to explore the world around and the world inside of us.*

From then on, everything started to change. We began creating, innovating, building, and doing stuff to improve our lives, relationships and community. His questions gave us wings to travel through time, helped us understand our past better, connect with the best of us, with what gives us life and lets us grow and be better. They also helped us dream, think of better futures and build scenarios full of possibilities so that our lives were fuller and were worth living.

We connected with our power. We found a great source of energy inside of us that we used to change and do things that got us closer to the world we dream of, since from that question we found those paths that turn dreams into realities.

When he left we found out that we had become better people. We had learnt to connect with the best part of us. We understood the value of our lives. We became aware that there is a part of us that maintains and feeds them, even if we have to change, adapt, grow and evolve in the direction our questions point us in".

A farewell letter to fear

In 2009 I signed up for a training program whose title caught my attention. It was called "Fear Workshop" and was imparted by a female doctor. They were two full days for eight people, no theory and full of experiences, becoming aware of "saboteurs", talking like them, listening close to our back and feeling how they drained us of our energy. We turned things around the second day, and everyone connected to their essence, vitality, bravery, and Lourdes, the teacher, invited us to write a "farewell letter to fear" before leaving and as a closing exercise to the workshop. This was my letter:

"I have the great pleasure of informing you that you are made redundant. I know I have been aware of everything I do for years, protecting and saving me pain so that nobody hurts me, intensely working to offer a comfortable, safe and risk-less life.

I have always felt you close, too close, you were always on time every time I had to face important challenges. You claimed you did it to prevent me from looking ridiculous or prove to everyone I was not that good. I know you wanted to protect me from what people may say, from failure and, above all, from embarrassment. I also know it could seem we agreed, but I simply did not know you. Every time I have slid down the ramp of failure, you have always been there to tell me you had warned me and that I should have taken you seriously, that you had already told me it was madness, that it was very difficult... but it was all fine since I would have learnt not to even try it and to listen to you more next time. It repeated again and again. Always the same. Your shadow, bigger and longer every time, to the point of being unable to distinguish between you and me on many occasions.

I now am aware that when you did not let me say "I love you" or ask for help or forgiveness or say "I don't know", it was not so that I did not look weak as you whispered to me, but to prevent me from building up the strength to feel humble, powerful and full. You were worried I would find out your true nature and you locked me up in a castle that seemed safe and comfortable. Although it was isolated, the drawbridge was always up. Inaccessible and superficial. Yes, of course, you were very friendly. So humorous! So pleasant! Once again, it was you. That mask stopped me from showing my emotions or feelings and always used subtle irony to prevent anyone from getting too close to me and dis-

turbing our peace. That skill to de-dramatise even the saddest situations and make them seem superficial and insignificant. Once again to not feel, to not go deep and to protect me from the pain. Unable to seem vulnerable and connect with all my resources.

At last, I have stopped, have turned around and have seen your face. Your rhetoric is repetitive, obsessive and absurd. You are pathetic. It is all over now. It will be different from now on. I will work to live connected to my true values, which you cannot reach. There is no room for you there. The place where I resonate is full of light and you have no place there. You are darkness and any small ray invades you and defeats you no matter how little it is. You are out. I am going to put up an advertisement to search for a replacement from this moment. Someone who trusts me. Someone who looks at everything good I have to offer, someone who helps me name my dreams and who gives me the strength and energy I need to run after them as if they were the last evening bus.

Hold on, I got it! I do not need to search further. I have found them: it's me. I already have all that. I am making room so that the small light that has always been inside of me finds its place and ends up banishing you at the same time I am firing you and opening the door to let you leave.

I say farewell to you forever by telling you that, although I know you will always be there, I will never talk to you again and I want you to know that, when I feel you behind my back (since you never show your face), I will stop, turn around, look at you in the eye, and I know you will disappear because you are a coward".[4]

---

4   Article published on the 30th of May 2008 in the blog *Píldoras de energizol* (*Energizol* Pills).

Asking in 7 pills

1. We ask to help others realise the reality observers they are, so that they can discover new interpretations and possibilities, to connect them with what is important, with what they want, with the best they have, with what touches them and with the energy they need to go into action.

2. We increase their awareness and responsibility with our questions, we help them explore more deeply, and we accompany them to search where they are unable to reach on their own, until they find their resources, solutions and replies inside their "acorn".

3. "Powerful questions" are short, open, neutral, non-judgmental and interpretation free. The *what fors* are more interesting than the *whys*, and we will not have a ready inventory of questions, they will instead be born of my genuine curiosity at the greatness of the complete, creative and resourceful human being I have in front of me.

4. Questions are not for me, they are not an interview nor an exam I have the answers for; they are for others and they do not seek nor have an immediate answer, but they need a silent space so that they can reflect until finding their answers.

5.

6. "Saboteurs" are useless and negative thoughts that fill our minds and block us, paralyze us, belittle us and inhibit our talent from connecting us with the worst version of ourselves. They are not *you* and we do not negotiate with them, we only listen to them to overcome them and reduce their power over us.

7. We ask to make others feel and reflect differently on the topic, objective or situation that worries them, not to get information about the "problem" nor their "saboteur", nor to understand nor go deep about them, but to help people find the reality observer they are and redefine the "problem" until it becomes a challenge.

8. We call *energizol* that vitality and inexhaustible energy that comes from the connection with the deepest and most essential Self. You have industrial amounts of *energizol* inside of you waiting for you to discover them and connect with them to cross over the bridge that links what you are now with what you could be.

Positivising

"Everyone has to make the most important decision of their lives: do I live in a friendly or hostile universe?".

Albert Einstein

Some years ago, I was at a series of training days with Jim Selman, a referent in transformative and organisational leadership, and I heard him make a claim that shook me. He said: "Your past is only a story you tell yourself, it is not the truth. You could tell other stories to yourself and they would also be true". At first I thought: "Such nonsense. My history is what it is and cannot be changed". It took me a while to accept it. I started going over my story and telling it to myself differently when I understood the implications of such a statement. I started searching for new interpretations of past events and finding another sense or meaning to experiences that were limiting me.

It is not about cheating, about not accepting facts or twisting them until they become unrecognizable. On the contrary, it is about finding a fresh look that lets us make amends with our past, assuming the appropriate responsibilities and repairing what is necessary, if possible, or demanding these reparations if that was the case, but observing everything with love and appreciation.

To go deep into this revealing possibility's importance and to put the third "**P**" (**P**ositivising) into context, we need to go over some basic philosophical notions (I apologize in advance to experts in the field due to the brevity and subjectivity of this summary). I only need a few pages to explain where this inspiring idea of *convers(a)ctions* comes from, as it is not an "enlightener's" idea but the most valuable tool at the service of transformative leaders. It appears as a result of the numerous discoveries carried out in many disciplines of human knowledge in the last century.

Parmenides versus Heraclitus

Almost 25 centuries ago, these philosophy titans started a debate in Greece that lasts until today. Parmenides defended that nothing changes: the "Self is static, fixed and immutable" and his rhetoric could be summed up in an immortal phrase we use, listen to and suffer daily: "I am like that". A six-lane motorway with no speed limit towards excuses and justifications for not doing, not daring to do or not change. The perfect sentence is blaming others, not taking responsibility for one's actions and keeping playing the victim that makes us feel comfortable but harms us so much.

On the other hand, Heraclitus postulated that "we are in a constant flux process, everything is permanently transforming, changing continuously, like a river. Nothing is immutable". Our possibilities of action and transforming reality increase exponentially according to this perspective. Changing is possible. We can be different and better. We can take the reins of our lives, assume the protagonist's role and act consequently.

These conflicting visions lived together in the dawn of philosophy, each with its followers. It resulted in a sort of tie that was solved due to a "technical KO" in Parmenides' favor a few centuries later.

Socrates placed absolute "truth" as a model that even transcended human life in his tireless search for virtue and the meaning of life. Knowledge was the only way mankind had to access truth. "Truth" is what it is. Socrates became a follower of Parmenides and reason started getting ahead as the only valid tool to reach the truth. Sometime later, his outstanding disciples Plato and Aristotle picked up their mentor's postulate and focused on the search for this "transcendental truth" that went further than the physical and human world (metaphysics), as humans only live in a semblance of truth since it is not in their reach, it is bigger than them. This "truth" was placed in the realm of abstract, universal and immutable ideas. Thus started the empire of reason.

The cartesian paradigm of "reality is what it is"

A paradigm is a concept that defines the scientific community of an era and determines a way of perceiving the world and reality. It conditions the human being in their way of behaving and reacting to the various circumstances life presents. It becomes the "truth". For instance, it was established that the Earth was the centre of the Universe, and that was the truth until centuries later Copernicus forced a change in the paradigm by proving that the centre of the universe was the Sun, and faced a violent and intense resistance on the part of the "wise men" who defended the old paradigm. He changed the "truth".

René Descartes, 16th-century French mathematician and father of the modern philosophy tendency that names the Cartesian paradigm, confirmed reason's supremacy as the only way to knowledge and understanding of the absolute and immutable "truth" and "reality". He was only interested in the concrete, material and measurable. Only what could be perceived with the senses and accurately measured was real. *Thought was* the base of the Self and *reason* was what made us humans. Emotions, feelings, intuition and anything related to the heart were invisible and did not exist because they could not be quantified. Blaise Pascal, a fellow countryman and contemporary of Descartes, a fabulous mathematician, physician and at the same time, philosopher and theologist, was the exception that opposed this radical and harmful division between reason and heart, between mind and spirit. This was reflected in one of his famous quotes: "The heart has reasons that the reason does not know".

Thus, until a century ago and for almost four hundred years, this Cartesian "truth" of the "I think, therefore, I am" was consolidated as the only way of interpreting reality. It imposed on all knowledge spheres and had an enormous influence on the development of fundamental disciplines for the progress of humanity, such as medicine, biology, physics, chemistry, psychology and mathematics. In turn, it caused a poor and limited understanding of the human being, abandoned to its fate, and with no real possibilities of transformation. The only alternative left was to adapt to what there is, what is and how things are; to "truth".

The new paradigm: "Reality is interpretable"

A new paradigm started to rise in the previous century. A more global one, an overall view that opposes the analytical and mechanical Cartesian vision that only perceives and recognises a minuscule part of reality. A vision that returns the human capacity to interpret the world we live in, to transform it and transform ourselves, to build ourselves and be better in a continuous transformation. A Self that builds itself after every experience, which can change, improve and grow permanently, until reaching its best version on every occasion.

Thus, after more than twenty centuries knocked out in the ring, the legendary Heraclitus gets on his feet strong, boosted by the new scientific discoveries in diverse fields such as physics, biology (now directly linked with the new philosophical tendencies), neuroscience (which proves that our brain is plastic, a flexible and living system that learns through neuron links that are in permanent reconstruction and, thus, us humans are in continuous transformation). This way the metaphysical program installed more than two thousand years ago in our DNA is being diluted alongside its interpretation of a "reality", a "truth", a "Self", fixed, unique, stable and immutable. However, its practical implications still are very present in our way of being in the world.

It is not anymore only about understanding, describing and interpreting the world or the Universe as the metaphysics proposed, but of transforming it, intervening in it, of making it better. Whatever the field we are working in (managers, parents, family, work...) we can choose who we can be and what kind of reality we want to create for ourselves and others. We can co-create it since this reality will be the result of our relationship with the world that surrounds us, with the observer we are being at every second and with the *convers(a)ctions* we have chosen to transform it.

"I change, everything changes"

One of the starring scientific protagonists in this new paradigm was Max Planck, a German physicist, founder of quantum theory and Nobel prize in 1918. He was a scientist in need of visible, measurable and concrete facts who reached this surprising conclusion: "We are unable to separate reality from the observer. Things change when I change my way of seeing them". That is the same conclusion a former international football player and manager, now sporting director of his club. Some years ago he was dismissed mid-season due to his impulsive character and authoritarian style, on top of the bad results that did not support his method. Since his contract included a season and a half more, the board of directors entrusted him with the task of making reports on opposing football players and teams, with the probable intention of him being as less annoying as possible. During those weeks after his dismissal, we happened to meet at a manager lecture I gave in his city. I was surprised he was in the auditorium as I did not think he was very interested in coaching and leadership matters. Wrong. He came to me when the lecture was over and, after a few minutes of conversation, he accepted the challenge of enrolling in the next edition of the *Máster de coaching y liderazgo deportivo* (Coaching and Sports Leadership Master) we were going to hold a few weeks later in the RFEF.

Due to him being the club legend, his situation in the sports city he worked in daily felt complicated and uncomfortable since he had no office and had very few tasks or responsibilities. Despite this, his attitude during the lecture was of openness and curiosity, intensely enjoying every day and proving his great courage, generosity and sensibility with his fellow course mates.

During the ninth or tenth day, he asked for permission before the lesson started to share something that was happening to him. He whispered to us as if he did not want to be heard, that everything had changed in the sports city since the Master began. He said that they were nicer, more open, friendlier with him and, both the atmosphere and relationships had notably improved. I remember that we all went quiet, we looked at him and then, in a surprising WOW! discovery moment, he declared: "They have not changed. It was me. I have changed and everything has changed". He had more than enough reasons to feel aggrieved, offended, humiliated, and abused. Many reasons to justify his emotions and defensive behaviors, but he chose another interpretation.

He decided that space would be the perfect laboratory to experiment with his recently acquired skills, to start trying and offering his new version (he called it 5.1.). He had just had his 51st birthday and he was connecting to his true values, to another energy, with a more confident look and leaving room for happiness and hope to create a new and better possible future, for himself and others. And that is what he did. He hung up a "sports coach" poster in a boot warehouse, he got a table and a couple of chairs and he started having *convers(a)ctions* with everyone he crossed paths with in the corridors. He did not mind who the other person was or what they did: first-team players, managers, youth players or any other employee he asked him.

One morning he invited me to the sports city to show me his facilities and as we walked them together, I confirmed how he greeted everyone, genuinely, as if they all were valuable and important to him. Gardeners, kit men, physiotherapists, he was affectionate, close and accessible to all of them. Different. He told them: "glad to see you!", and I could feel how his new energy, happiness and illusion caused a radically different impact on the system. I confirmed that he was right: everyone had changed.

Tell me what you see and I will tell you who you are

"Reality is interpretable" is one of the principles of the book *Ontología del lenguaje (Language Ontology)* (a highly recommended book by Chilean philosopher Rafael Echeverría). It means that we do not have access to absolute "truth" even if it exists. We live in interpretative worlds and every one of us is a different observer of reality depending on our "perception filter". However, nobody has the certainty that things are as we say they are. We can only observe "our truth", a tiny part of reality that we perceive through our limited senses. The truth is that we do not describe the world as it is, but as how we are.

Beyond the simple truths understood as consensus in language regarding basic matters that we all accept and ease our lives, the fact that "reality is interpretable" means that nobody is completely correct or we may all be correct in some way. I might be thinking something different about what is going on (with me) and that might also be true. And it means that if I am thinking about something that is not helping me, I can choose to think of something else. As writer Viktor Frankl said in Man's Search for Meaning, "the last human freedom is choosing our behavior before any circumstance".

I can also choose who I want to be before every situation, choosing my answers, actions and behaviors despite the weight and influence of social and cultural contexts, heritage and genetics.

I can define my character and create my Identity time and time again, using every experience to go forward in the fascinating process of my permanent transformation towards the utopia of my best version starting from this paradigm. Always out of my reach and at the same time closer every time, challenging me and pulling me.

Facts and interpretations

"When our son Álvaro was born (he has Down syndrome) we asked ourselves: why us? Shortly after, we asked ourselves: and why not? Now and since long ago, we ask ourselves: how could we live without him?".
VICENTE DEL BOSQUE

Life and sports are "things that happen", they are circumstances, events, and facts. They are also neutral, neither good nor bad, they just are. Defeats, lesions, victories, replacements, relegations, titles, sanctions, dismissals, losses, accidents, illnesses. Even death is happily celebrated for days in some cultures because they believe the dead's soul changes clothes at last to start their way to their definitive liberation. Until recently in Spain, the widow had to dress in black when her husband passed away and she had to mourn him almost like a living dead until her last day. This fact, death, is the same but the interpretations are different. Both are the "truth" for someone. The previous image illustrates this process. Something happens, a fact, because there is always something going on, but the interesting thing is becoming aware of *how I interpret this fact* and how it impacts me. That is what will define my attitude.

Epictetus, one of Heraclitus' followers, wrote: "We are not affected by what happens, but what we tell ourselves that has happened". If the interpretation you are doing of the fact helps you go forward, achieve your objectives, do what you must, not stop, if it opens possibilities of action, if it provides you energy and power to think, then, go ahead! If it is a positive though, a seed that will give good fruits. If, on the contrary, that thought brings you down, drains you, blocks you, takes power from you and keeps you away from the person you want to be, if your "truth" is not working for you, there are other possible interpretations that can also be true for you. You can choose to think differently!

Yes, I know what you might be thinking: it cannot be that easy. And you are right but do not tell me that it is not liberating to become aware (the previous and essential step to change anything) that there are other available alternatives for you. You do not only have the option of reacting automatically to every situation, depending on how you think you are and how you think things are, but you could also be depending on how you behaved. I claim that it is in your hand to choose an adequate answer that brings you close to the person you want to be, instead of it being an instinctive reaction that keeps you bound to who you are, but not to whom you want to be.

He humiliated me!

He furiously entered my office. He said he was fed up and could no longer deal with it. He considered being taken out by his manager to waste time in the overtime of the last match to be contemptuous. It was very clear the manager disliked him and did not respect him. On top of that, the manager reproached his behaviour publicly in the restrooms during those five minutes: "Instead of apologising for humiliating me, he gave me Hell". He was angry and sad.

I asked him what he wanted to do about it after letting him vent, if he needed help to change the observer to see things he might not have appreciated and thus search for new interpretations of reality that would help him transform his mood. I asked him what the "fact" was. He replied that the "fact" was the humiliation of being taken out in the overtime to waste time. I told him I reckoned that he was mixing the fact with its interpretation and I asked him again what the neutral and true fact was. After a couple of seconds of silence, he replied: "change in the 90th minute".

Since he had clearly expressed what his interpretation was at the start of the conversation, I asked him how his belief of "playing the overtime is humiliating" made him feel. He was able to identify and name the awkward emotions that thought caused him, as well as to describe in detail what impact it was having on his behavior. It was a Thursday and he told me how he had trained the three previous days: angry, without talking to anybody, thinking the manager ought to apologize to him, indolent, apathetic, unpleasant and unfocused, worrying his head... He wanted to prove to his manager how upset and hurt he was. I asked him what the worst part of the situation was, what he was missing out on due to his behavior, if it helped him in any way and who he was turning into by acting in that manner. He was honest and brave enough to admit that he was uncomfortable feeling and training like that. His anger decreased as he reflected and became aware of what was going on with him and the impact his thought was having on him.

After deeply exploring his current interpretation, I asked him what other things he could think of about the same fact (change in the 90th minute). He discovered another alternative that made him feel different after analyzing some alternatives ("he punishes me because of my poor performance", "he wants me to feel a part of the victory", "he gives me a warning to wake up") that were less harmful than his first interpretation but still did not fully convince him. He thought that his manager trusted him not to waste time but to use his quality and keep the ball possession during those five minutes of overtime and ensure victory with the score of 0-1. He lost all the balls he touched and did not fulfill his duty, to the point that one of his losses led to a great opportunity for the opposing team to score.

This new interpretation helped him calm down and feel a bit ashamed of his immature and selfish initial reaction. He did not only think that the manager had it in for him but what the manager had done was trust him to close the match. The *fact* remained the same but this new and chosen "truth" immediately changed his emotion. He already felt calmer, happy and satisfied due to his learning and discovery, due to him having been able to turn the situation over and due to him having been able to change his mood to the point of deciding that the next day he would talk to all of his teammates before training and he would apologize for his behavior during the match and that week's training sessions. He would also do that with his manager. He left my office after the *convers(a) ction* more aware and responsible, smiling and full of energy.

Beliefs

> *"A man was putting flowers next to a relative's grave when he saw a Chinese woman doing the same with a bowl of rice in a nearby grave. The man addressed her and mockingly asked: Do you believe the dead will eat the bowl? Yes, when yours returns to smell your flowers, she replied".*
>
> Anonymous

Our greatest hardship is our habit of mixing facts and *interpretation*. Actions or responses, reactions more likely, appear automatically. They are an unconscious process. It is undoubtedly more comfortable, faster and sometimes necessary, but we must get used to taking the reins of our thoughts and going from automatic to manual control. It is necessary to learn to separate *facts* from *interpretation* and become aware of what we are thinking, and whether what we are thinking drives us away or closer to the people, managers or athletes we want to be.

We call this "perception filter" *beliefs*, beliefs that everyone applies to every fact, something that finally determines our intellectual, physical and emotional reaction to everything that happens to us. Beliefs are like a rucksack that we carry around, that we have filled since our childhood with lots of elements that come to slowly define the reality observer we are being, determining our way of being in this world. Lived experiences and genes occupy most of the space, while education, family, religion, environment, friends, values, moral and ethical principles; social, sports, economic and cultural context; trends, tribes, and topics complete this personal and non-transferable filter that defines everyone's truth.

On the other hand, it seems rather absurd, arrogant and vain trying so hard to impose our "truth" over other people when taking into account the many variables it has that distort the already limited perception of reality our brain can process. What matters should not be arguing to be in the right, but discussing to achieve the goal.

The difference between *beliefs* and *ideas* is the fact that the former are unconscious but so true to us that we are unable to question them. They start revealing themselves through our language, decisions, actions and behaviors, and we declare them as if they were undeniable truths accepted by everyone. If it is the truth we are talking about, how can they not see it? We can contrast our ideas with others, we can even discuss and change them, but not the beliefs that control all our actions from our deepest mind. We could say that "I have ideas but my beliefs have me".

All my beliefs, including my language, depend on the sort of reality observer I am being. I need to learn to be a different observer, go over how I tell things to myself and how I explain reality to myself, check my perception filter, and my reading "glasses" if I want to change them. I need to break down my limiting beliefs, full of these baseless judgments, topics, collective prejudices, false claims and common places we too often go to feel a part of the mob, to feel normal and accepted by the tribe. Many times we often spend thinking of what others have thought before, saying what others have said before; we make them ours and we believe it. We often become slaves to our limiting beliefs, to our "truths" that make us suffer. It is time to take them apart, redefine and transform them so that they help us jump over the pit that separates what we are being from what we could be.

"You are going to get kicked out!"

Once a manager shared his worry with me at a decisive point of the season. He felt his time as a manager was running out, his players did not trust him anymore, and the results were not favourable. To make matters worse, the board of directors had just ratified him, the previous step to dismissal according to the implicit football laws. He was anxious, restless, obfuscated, disappointed and sad. He was suffering. After listening to him talk about his "issue" for a long time, seeing how stressed he was due to uncertainty surrounding his future, how he punished himself for what he could have done and did not, how he mercilessly blamed and harshly judged himself, complaining about everything and everyone, completely blocked, I could only tell him: "they are going to sack you". "It may be in a week, nine months if you do well or even in three years if you are really lucky, but what seems inevitable is that you will be kicked out sooner or later like the vast majority of your peers. It might sound a bit harsh but it can be truly liberating".

I believe that, unconsciously and unfortunately, the question all managers ask themselves (which we would all ask ourselves) in truly tense situations like the one my friend was experiencing is: *what do I have to do to not get fired?* It does not look like a very inspired or thought-provoking question and is not at all powerful. On the contrary, it seems desperate. The answer seems obvious and, unfortunately, it does not depend on you. "Winning!" is the only answer that echoes in their blocked heads.

The same belief appeared again and again in our *convers(a)ction*: "winning is the only thing that matters". This "truth" immediately connected that manager with his "saboteurs" ("you will not find another team", "you are a loser", "you are not up to the task", "you are good for nothing") and also with loss, anguish, worry, fear and unhappiness. He only saw issues, enemies and plots everywhere; people or collectives who were being unfair to him ("the public never realized your value", "the press is after you", "the players are scheming your downfall", "ungrateful!", "the board of directors have no idea"). A dark scenario that caused him great suffering. His way of observing reality kept him blocked and firmly stuck to a truth that made him feel distrustful, insecure, frightened and isolated. There was also room for resentment and bitterness that placed him in the role of victim, innocent but powerless, and totally took him out of the current time and connected him to his worst version. He was already fired in these conditions and he had not even realized it.

This *convers(a)ction* was not about arguing whether it was true or not that this belief ("winning is the only thing that matters") was the origin of all of his "saboteurs" (who are those that voice the limiting beliefs). That was not the point! There are probably 1,500 arguments in favor and another

1,500 against it. I did not want to be right! That was not my goal, I did not want to convince him that he was wrong. I only needed to help him find how his truth was affecting him and who he was from that point, exploring and taking apart his limiting belief until we found another available truth.

A different question appeared after going over it deeply: *who do you want to be while you are there?* WOW! Silence. An immediate change took place in his emotions, corporal language and energy. A new, until then uncharted scenario just opened up, a world of new possibilities that connected him to his brave and true nature. And to everyone's nature. It was the discovery that it would be him who decided who he was going to be as long as he was in charge. He would commit to living the experience intensely, without tiptoeing over it, being open and accessible, offering everyone the best of himself and facing every moment with courage, happiness and enthusiasm, rubbing them off on his players and staff until his last day, whichever that may be.

The question of *who do you want to be while you are there?* connected with him what really mattered to him, with the privilege of being and feeling like a manager, keeping him plugged to optimism, excitement and hope. He decided that circumstances would no longer determine his reactions, but instead, it would be him who would decide to face that situation as a challenge, as a life challenge to find out what he was capable of, bravely choosing the answers that got him close to who he wanted to be, to who he really was, to his best version.

Doing (behaving) by reacting to fear, distrust, or insecurity is not the same as *doing it from the Self.* The actions' impact that appears from the connection with the deepest and most authentic part of everyone is absolutely incomparable. It connects you with your best version, with the helpful leader you have inside and who is itching to get out and take control of this fascinating journey from which you will return transformed. Whatever happens, it will have changed your life, others as well, and your outlook. And you, *who are you going to be while you are there?*[5]

Beliefs and suffering

Too often, being unable to separate fact from *interpretation,* which are automatically linked in our minds, makes it hard for us to accept and we fight and we suffer because we cannot change it. We need to learn to accept facts, without mistaking them for an unconscious and thoughtless interpretation that blocks us and stops us from deciding and correctly replying as the person we want to be or the leader our team needs.

Juup Heynckes, after winning the Triple Crown in June 2013 (UEFA Champions League, Bundesliga and DFB Cup), declared that the turning point of the new dominating and model Bayern Munich was the 4-0 defeat against Barcelona FC in Camp Nou in the semifinals of the 2009 UEFA Champions League. Despite the elimination with a crushing score, the Bavarian club owners did not take it as a humiliation nor searched for scapegoats inside or outside the club. They did not cut any heads off nor passed any bucks trying to avoid responsibilities. On the contrary, they decided to take that difficult experience to begin the team's football transformation, from what it was to what it could be. They took the style of the best Barcelona and adapted it to its vigorous, fast, strong and energetic style, making it evolve until they reached their best version. Four years later, they returned the favour to the Catalan club with a 7-0 score as a global result in the semifinals of the 2013 UEFA Champions League in their glorious Treble season.

---

5   Article published October 2013 in the blog *Píldoras de energizol.*

I do not intend to say that a 4-0 score does not hurt, because it does! Whoever has played professional sports, knows how hurtful a defeat is no matter their level. Buddhist monks or zen masters may be able not to feel disappointment, disgust, disillusion, rage, frustration, impotence and other similar emotions before a similar result. It would be silly of me to suggest that you should not feel bad or painful when you lose. It might even be worrying that you did not feel that way. What I suggest is that you feel the pain, observe it and, if it was convenient, express it properly to unload your body and free yourself. But do not stay that way too long, suffering without need.

Andrés Iniesta, right after the defeat and elimination of his team before Atlético de Madrid in the 2014 Champions League quarter-finals, declared: "pain may last today and tomorrow. Then we will think that this is football, it is a sport and we cannot always win". Pain is inevitable, although suffering is optional, with all due respect to people that suffer. It is an unconscious decision on many occasions, but optional nonetheless.

There is a theory linked to Quantum physics that psychologist Carl Jung called *synchronicity* and described as an organizing and collective intelligence that is everywhere. A unified reality from which everything emerges, to which everything returns and in which the whole exists in every piece. It is said that near the end of their lives, elderly people often find out that every fact experienced had a meaning as if in that clairvoyant moment all puzzle pieces fit together allowing them to see the full picture that was hidden before.

Being this the case, if everything that happens, happens for some reason, willing to get carried by "synchronicities", without judging the Universe and trusting that everything that happens is convenient, is precisely what we need for achieving what we desire at the deepest level. It would help us to calmly accept things that happen (to us) and stop fighting facts. To stop suffering, we may relax and humbly accept that we cannot control nor accept everything, but opening up to other possibilities and interpretations of reality that remained inaccessible until that moment is what we have to do.

I feel that the majority of the managers I have had *convers(a)ctions* with want me to help them see things they know they are not seeing, change the observer they are, go over their beliefs, find other interpretations to transform their moods and keep being excited, dealing with and leading at the service of their teams instead of being in anguish, in pain, worrying, lamenting, pitying themselves, complaining and blaming themselves.

José Mourinho said: "the youth of today have nothing to do with John Terry or Frank Lampard, and I cannot judge them for that. I know that, if I want to be a manager in the future, I need to understand the world of these 20-year-old kids. If even Mourinho, "the special one", accepts the fact he cannot change and admits he needs and can transform himself, so can you!

You can access another competence level when you stop feeling angry or sad because of certain events, when you stop fighting them and, instead of clinging to what it *should be*, you accept what *it is*. You can see the situation as a challenge to your leader's aptitude, as a master that offers to show you who you have to become, what you have to learn and change in yourself and what you must dare to do to keep going in your transformation process, given that it is not fate but a path.

I recommend seeing every issue, whatever kind, that your life and sports cause (both are things that happen), as a challenge to your growth, finding out what Life, the Universe, God, the Source, the Energy, the Whole, the Self (choose whichever) expects and needs of you anytime. It is not about pretending you are all right in difficult situations, but you dare interpret it as a challenge so that you discover who you are and what you are capable of. It is to feel well for real, fully present and connected to all your resources and the best you have; to keep growing, shining and leading with energy, confidence and happiness at the service of those you care for.

Limiting beliefs in the sports world

> *"Either if you believe you can or if you think you cannot, you are right in both cases".*
> Henry Ford

For a hundred years the incredibly limiting and deep-seated belief in the athletics world was that nobody would be able to beat the mile run in less than four minutes. Some doctors and scientists of the time remarked that the heart could burst, and muscles and bones would break. No one even dared to imagine it because of such dark omens. On the 6th of May 1954, Roger Bannister, a young English athlete and Medicine student, and future neurologist, shattered that belief and finished an extraordinary race that was known as "the miracle mile", running that mile in three minutes and fifty-nine seconds.

Bannister wrote in his diary: "I carefully prepared. I tried to set the record with the attitude of the 'now or never' behaviour because I knew that, unless I was successful, I may miss the chance by giving in to the very common mental reaction amongst athletes: thinking that there will always be another opportunity to try, that maybe this is not the day for trying".

Being himself a student of the human body, he knew he could do it and he did it. Although this story is nothing special because records are constantly broken, and some just take more time than others, the shocking fact is what happened in the following weeks. Only six after Bannister's record was set, the Australian John Lundy lowered it by a second. Six months later, 40 athletes had run it in less than four minutes. Six years later, the number of athletes who had achieved it was over 200. Sir Roger Bannister paved the way for his competitors by not giving up, believing it was possible and accomplishing it, transforming that unbeatable barrier into a manageable challenge.

There is a multitude of beliefs in any field or activity. We live surrounded by them. I shall share some of the most extended ones in football that are also interchangeable in other sports. "Truths" assumed by the vast majority appear constantly. I do not claim that they all are limiting for everyone, but I do believe they are for many.

"Football is like that", "all referees are mean", "football is for smart people", "if you have never been a footballer, you will never become a professional manager", "you train where you play", "I do not ask the manager when I play nor when I do not play", "journalists are bad people", "if you shake hands with football players, they will try to take advantage of you", "the manager must always have a solution", "any good team begins with a good defense", "the young nowadays have got a nerve", "you have to be distant with the players", "if you do not manage the other football you are not competitive", "winning is all that matters", "win, win, win and win again", "the young nowadays do not commit", "don't even give water to your enemy", "nobody remembers the second best", "showing vulnerability is a sign of weakness", "it's impossible to become a pro", "women cannot train as elites", "everything is fair play to win", "the directors have no d*mn clue", "all footballers are selfish", "being a manager is really tough", "the money they make!", "the budget defines the classification", "everything has already been thought of in football", "nothing can be changed overnight", "I am like that", "it is what it is", "you must earn your respect", and "you have to be a bit of a bastard to be respected".

You may be thinking "they are true!" as you are reading them. All right, whatever you want. However, they are "true" just for you. By this point in the chapter, you already know reality is interpretable and the question is not whether they are true or not, but knowing what they provide you, what they take away from you and who of those "truths" turn you into. If they help you move forward toward your goals, then persevere, keep learning, feel useful and valuable, open up to new possibilities, keep achieving your best version with excitement and happiness, and become that helpful leader that your players need. If they power you up with *energizol* and enthusiasm to enjoy the process, go ahead. These "truths" are empowering.

If, on the contrary, you suspect that some of these beliefs are not at all helping you to give your best, and, if you know they are limiting you, I encourage you to choose one of them to look at closely.

Practice!

I suggest you read them over again, all of them. Slowly. Feeling how everyone bounces inside of you, discovering how you cling to some of them. You may have realised that some are not on the list, that "truth" that has always been with you and which now may not be helping you a lot. You can choose that one to work on it. Again, pen and paper! I challenge you to dare go over it, and feel it, and later take it apart and discover other worlds that will open up surprising and, until now, uncharted possibilities. Only by questioning and reinterpreting your own beliefs, will you help others transform their reality.

I like the sentence attributed to Confucius that says "I read and forget; I see and understand; I do and learn". That is why I ask you to stop. Think about it! This book will have a purpose if it helps you to change something, to do something different than what you are doing now, to transform into someone. This is the perfect moment to face any of your non-negotiable "truths". I assure you that, if you just read it, you will only find it "interesting" but nothing will change. It is not reason but heart that connects you with action. *Reason* is useful to understand, but emotion is what moves you. Again, I do not ask you to believe me, simply for you to experiment and for that, I need you to choose a belief and write down your reflections, feelings and answers to the questions I will ask you.

Dismantling beliefs

If you have already chosen your belief to work in it, I offer you some questions to help you go deep and become aware of the impact this "belief" is having on you. I want you to feel it and write it down. I propose that we become explorers together, pioneers of new territories. Choose the questions that echo in you and give yourself time to answer every one of them. Slowly, we are not in a rush.

If it helps, think of a particular fact or situation you automatically link your belief to and whose effects and results stray from what you would like to achieve. For instance, imagine you did not sign up for that cool training workshop you were recommended because, deep inside of you, you shared that widespread belief that "everything has been done in football". What would happen to you if that "truth" determined that and other decisions? What effect would it have on your future? How would it be limiting you? What would be your curiosity to keep learning from everything and everyone, searching for new solutions and answers, and to innovate during the training sessions? Who would you be? How would you become a reality's transformative leader if everything had already been done?

The point is not trying to convince you otherwise, nor prove you wrong, but become aware of what sort of impact it has on you, where it leads you and who this "truth" turns you into in the first part of this exercise. I hope you bring this unconscious belief to light, put it forward to observe it, distance yourself from it, pay attention and reexamine those generalizations ("everyone", "always", "nobody", "never", "it should be", "never", "I have to", "it is obvious", "the natural thing is") used to express the belief you turn into "truth", as well as the judgments you use as statements, and the claims on which you base it. Remember it is not about judging it, just realizing who you are from there.

Let's go and explore your beliefs!

How is this belief helping you? How do you think it is improving you? What do you think it is giving to you? What is taking from you? Is it limiting you in any way? What are you missing out? What is the worst part? What are you afraid of? What are its effects? What results are you achieving? How do you think others perceive you? How do you behave according to that belief? What is your attitude? How do you feel? How is it affecting you? How do you see yourself from here? Who are you being? How are you interacting with your players based on that belief? And with your helpers, press, directors or family? Who are you being now for them with that "truth" of yours? How is your presence level? In what way do you talk WITH (not TO) your players? Where are you speaking to them from? What is your openness and availability level? How brave are you? How are you impacting them? What is your leadership like? What is your daily level of energy and enthusiasm? What are you not daring to do?

Discovering new worlds

Once we have explored and reviewed it in-depth, once you have felt how it is taking power away to act, and who it is turning you into, we start to qualify it, de-dramatise it and relativize it. We respectfully challenge it to open up new perspectives and alternatives, and discover new possibilities, other possible worlds that can also be "true" to you. We seek to reinterpret your reality, retag this limiting belief until you can change it for another empowering one (another "truth"), chosen by you so as to send the old one away. To find this other truth, we keep asking:

How would you nuance this belief? What other things could you think of? In what situations does it not come true? What other things could also become "true" in this situation? What would your "true self" say? With what personal value would you be able to connect? What would a character you value a lot say? What would they do in this situation? What could be different? What would you do differently? Who would you be? What possibilities would open to you? What would you be daring to do? What are you committing to from this new interpretation? What are you agreeing to? What aren't you? What are you choosing? Who are you being now? To what personal value are you connected now? What sort of leader are you being to your players? Which are the first steps/actions? What are you going to do this week? How do you feel now?

As we keep reflecting on and taking our limiting beliefs apart, suffering starts disappearing and we start seeing other possible words. Other "truths" that connect us with what matters, with our brave nature and new possible actions, generating the energy and mood that mobilizes us and drives us to the action and transformation we need, answering instead of reacting, and choosing who we want to be at every second.

"Tag"

It was the typical Saturday training session before Sunday's match. The field was soft since it had rained the whole week and we sneakily entered the municipal park near the stadium, as the gardeners were not there, to finish the training session without setting foot on the field. It seemed as if the manager felt playful that day, a completely unusual event, and one of the games was playing tag. It was fun. One has it and has to tag another one in a limiting but sufficient space to run and move properly. The moment the first catches the second, they both hold hands and try to catch another player, player that joins the chain without breaking contact. It only ends when everyone becomes a link of the chain.

That day, I guess that thanks to my excellent, marvelous flexibility and agility (ironic mode ON as I was extremely clunky at 9:30 am, and because that heel tendinitis forced me to crawl to the bathroom after I got up from bed), I was nimble and I remained free until the end. In the last round, when everyone was already chained and had closed the circle until there was no escape left, I decided to toss myself at everyone to end the game with some laughs. Bad choice.

A thunder struck at that moment. We all heard his scream (I can still hear its echo): "I knew it! You are a loser, you are not competitive! You have never been and never will!". That was his sentence. I won the game but lost a lot that day. How true is that reflection on leadership that claims we can forget everything a manager tells us or does, but we will never forget how they made us feel. I can still perceive the impact it had on me that crushing declaration, echoing like a shot in front of all my teammates. I felt humiliated. I spent a lot of time without understanding how he could say something like that. I understand it now and I feel pity for my manager from the perspective of the years I have spent and the experience I have amassed.

He was right in a way. From his point of view, I was not being competitive, although his sentence was as definitive as unfortunate. *To be* is not the same as *being*. We use the first one to tag others and we erase the option of them being able to change, correct, learn and improve. The second expression allows us to create a space so that others can do it and even help them achieve it. Tags are harmful to everyone, but they are even worse for you, the leader. This simple change of *"you are"* for *"you are being"* opens many possibilities of establishing new *convers(a)ctions*, being curious, listening and asking, helping the other become aware, discovering, learning and growing; and, above all, keep believing that is possible to change and build our future, as well as helping others do the same with them.

Now I know what my manager was expecting when he unleashed his rage on me during that "tag" game. He was hoping that I would not give up, do everything I could to overcome that obstacle, not lower my arms, keep fighting, be present in the game and focused until the end. For me to not leave the game. He trusted me, but he was unable to show it. Hence his frustration, disappointment and rage. He was disgusted because he checked I reacted the same way as I did in the field —that I sometimes left the match and gave up when things got complicated. I lowered my arms and disconnected myself from the match, letting the "saboteur" take control of my body.

Being competitive does not consist of wanting to win, we all want that. If wanting to win was enough, I would be as good as the best player, because I was as enthusiastic as anyone about it. It is not that simple. Competing is wanting to win by sacrificing, persevering, being optimistic, passionate, determined, disciplined, enthusiastic, having the wish to improve every day and grow nonstop on top of being talented. Now things get complicated. Only a few chosen ones accomplish this. Are some born with competitiveness in their blood? Possibly. I know a couple of close cases. Can the rest of us learn to be competitive? Sure! Of course, it is easier and more comfortable to tag people as "non-competitive" than to help them.

I do not know what you would have done in my shoes, but I do imagine the great Puyol as the last one standing in the "tag" game. I can picture him trying to climb a tree, tossing over the bushes, jumping over everyone or under the legs of an absent-minded player. I can see him not giving up, fighting until the end, present and connected to the game, watchful to any possibility, happy but highly alert, as an attitude example for all of the chained ones in his team. I picture him exactly as I saw him in the field.

Athletes like Puyol remind me of Joe's story, the old fighter who dreamt of defeating Jack "the destroyer", the great champion. His trainer was against letting this combat take place because he knew Jack was a master of a special hold that defeated all of his rivals. However, Joe insisted so much that he at last managed for that fight to happen. Just as the fight started, "the destroyer" jumped at Joe and immobilized him with his unbeatable hold. At that moment, his trainer closed his eyes thinking the worst and remained that way until he heard a loud noise in the ring, followed by the cheers of the public. When he opened his eyes expecting to see the disaster, he saw Joe enthusiastically celebrating his victory. Unbelievable! He had managed to break free and defeat the champion.

When they returned to the restroom and still in disbelief at the surprising result of the fight, the trainer asked Joe what he had done to achieve such a miracle:

"I was head down with my waist between his arms, folded over, in a knot, and barely able to breathe. I was going to admit defeat when I suddenly saw a pair of testicles in front of my face. I knew then that it was my only chance to break free and I bit his lunchbox since it was at my mouth level" Joe explained.

"Wow! Congratulations. Even though it may not have been elegant, it has been effective for sure" replied his trainer.

"Yes, it is amazing what a man can do when he bites his balls" concluded Joe.

Jokes aside, I was unable to act like Joe in that situation. A manager with these simple skills we are discovering would have had an excellent opportunity there to help me get something out of that experience. A great learning to take to the field and growing two inches as a person and player. He could have used that opportunity to give me feedback about my behavior, increase my awareness regarding my reaction's impact on the team, and who I was becoming by acting like that, giving in. Who I was being when I gave up without fighting until the end, what I was giving in with that behavior, what could have been different if, I became aware of what was happening to me to offer a better, decided and chosen answer, more positive and beneficial for me and my team next time I perceived these situations during a match. He could have asked me what particular training situations we could work on to improve this side during the week and what I was committing to with that solution. Yet he preferred venting his frustration. I felt insulted, shamed and scorned. In my opinion, his choice was even worse than mine[6].

---

6   Published in the blog *Píldoras de energizol* on September 2013.

Tagging

"He isn't competitive", "he's lazy", "he's fearful", "he's self-ish", "he's stiff", "he's nervous", "he's slow", "he's clumsy with the ball", "he's cheeky", "he's fat", "he's not in shape", "he can only run", "he's not a winner", "he's soft", "he's terrible", "he doesn't know how to read the game", "he's a layabout", "his feet game is bad", "his attitude sucks", "he doesn't care". We start sentencing people without noticing that we are tagging those that need our leadership, as if they were things that had to be classified and categorised. We slowly start boxing them, with their belonging stickers, and we are at a risk of believing we already know what they are and who they will be in the future. Our mind is quite obedient and it will make sure she is right if we sow a limiting tag regarding anyone. Our mind will also make sure you only see what confirms and reinforces this thought from then on. Whatever goes against that tag will be invisible to your eyes.

Tagging is comfortable for whoever does it, and, sadly, it is also easy for those who suffer it because they only have to fulfill those poor expectations from that point onwards. They all know who the tagged ones are and with time they will convince themselves of that identity, blocking all their learning and transformation possibilities. They will simply be content with being what they already are. This is the extent of Parmenides' reach, twenty-five centuries later, to impose his "this is how I am" dictatorship, an immutable being that cannot change.

We behave dangerously unaware, ignorant and shameless when we tag someone. We dare to reduce the human being's greatness and their inexhaustible possibilities of permanent change to four limiting judgments regarding some behavior that confine, box and lock them up. That is what we do every time we judge our players (students, children, or helpers), instead of giving them positive feedback about their tasks and behaviors, albeit taking care and respecting others to the max. It is possible to be at the same time a demanding teacher but respectful with the human being. It is necessary, not just possible.

We need leaders at the service of their followers that do not tag them but convince them that they can change for the better. Leaders who make them feel able to transform and who push them to find out who they could be if they dared to overcome the limits and take off those stickers accumulated for years. Leaders who inspire and help them decide and choose their own stickers. Leaders who do not lose patience nor hope to keep believing in them, even when their progress is not as fast nor clear as they would want. We need conversationally competent leaders, creators of new possibilities who dare to believe and create other and better possible futures for themselves and their teams and players.

Creating other possible futures

One of the postulates of *Ontología del lenguaje* (Language Ontology) by Rafael Echevarría, that works as a philosophical base of this new and emerging paradigm of "reality is interpretable", claims that language is active and creates new realities. It is not only useful to talk about things or describe the, it also allows us to participate and mould the world we live in, making things take place and creating other desired futures, as long as we dare to commit to them, declare them, live them and be the change, making it possible and real.

In the world of sports there are very significant cases of renowned leaders who have managed to create new realities where there were no signs that showed it was possible. In football, for example, there was Johan Cruyff with his unforgettable dream team that forever transformed the Spanish game play. Arrigo Sacchi and his intelligent and unbeatable tulip Milan. The passionate Guardiola who evolved football until achieving an unsurpassable level of efficiency and aesthetics. The hypnotic and incomparable Bielsa who left behind a legacy of limitless bravery, sacrifice, nobility and respect in Athletic Club. Or the untamable Simeone who reflected his unbreakable determination of living every day connected to a powerful and inspiring vision in his Spartan philosophy of "match to match", which changed the reality of a victimized club that was known as "the boo-boos team" until his arrival.

These are transformative leaders, visionaries, passionate and brave people able to create a new reality where there only was a remote chance, who declare their commitment to a fiery vision and transform it into their life purpose from the first day, even when lacking any guarantee of success.

A manager who I admire, two months later after finishing his "7Ps" training, took his first team in Second B in 2013 after the directive solved a couple of doubts regarding his capabilities for the job due to his youth (36 years) and inexperience (2 seasons as a manager). They finally trusted him and, despite having a successful start, the team had a bad streak that led them to lose eight matches in a row. Dismissal rumors grew stronger until his fate depended on winning the next Sunday. I talked to him and asked him how he felt during those days. I was delighted by his reply: "I feel very calm and I have intensely lived this experience. I feel surprisingly well and very present. I often talk with the players and seeing how they train flat out every day touches me, so I hope for the best this Sunday". That is how he felt. I dropped by the stadium to watch the team and they were losing 1-2 against the Noja in the 88th minute. I could feel him on the sideline, very connected to his players and the game itself. They leveled the scores in the 90th minute and they scored the third goal in the 93rd minute. They then won the next six matches and the club was promoted after brilliantly beating the three play-off qualifying rounds.

They started the following season with mediocre performance and the category's lowest budget. I asked him how he saw his players halfway through the season and his answer surprised me again: "I am worried, I can only see 'acorns' running on the grass" he replied with a big smile on his face. I thought the "acorn" thing was getting out of hand, though he was excited. His team became champion and they were promoted after a spectacular second round. He was not afraid to choose seven football players that had been promoted from the Second B team as regular first-team players during their debut in First Division and they won the Derby against Real Sociedad. Gaizka Garitano, Eibar's manager, is creating a new reality for the club and for all those humble teams that thought it was impossible. He has managed to compete in an exemplary manner in the most unequal League in the world with the cheapest playing staff, supported by the huge excitement generated in a small town of 25,000 inhabitants. He has achieved this by sprouting and growing every one of his "acorns" and dignifying the profession he loves while making the most of the experience and sharing it with all of his followers[7].

In short, if according to Jim Selman my past is only a story I am telling myself, not the truth, the future is pure possibility, a choice that I daily take in every one of the *convers(a)ctions* I have with myself and others in the present. We can all be creators of possible futures. The ambivalent and transformative leader is a simple person, like you and me, who dares to stop at some point in life and reflects to design, create and commit to a new, different and better future for themselves and their followers.

From that point on, they declare, build and live their vision on a daily basis in the present, making it be their *raison d'être*, with a sense of urgency that reflects a deep desire of achieving it. They slowly managed to win over followers thanks to a highly infectious enthusiasm and determination that sprout from the connection with the deepest part of their Self. They accompany their followers every day with their *convers(a)ctions* in their growing and developing process, inspiring them to transform into the people and teams that deserve to achieve this new reality, this new desired future.

---

7   Just before closing this book's edition, they were playing as a visiting team against Espanyol. When questioned due to the important losses his team against to face this match, he replied: "Yes, they are important losses, but I am not concerned. Instead, I am glad I can offer this opportunity to other players that also deserve to play. Reality is interpretable. They won.

Positivising in 7 pills

1. "Reality is interpretable" and, even if it existed, we would not have access to the absolute "truth". We live in interpretative worlds, and things change when you change your way of seeing things. You change, everything changes.

2. Life and sports are *things that happen*, neutral and facts. Our beliefs, each person's perception filters, are those that define what the "truth" is for us. They make up the reality of observers we are and determine our behavior. They are the lenses we use to interpret the world. We can change them if we do not see properly!

3. If your "truth" is not helping you, you not only have the option of reacting to every situation depending on how you think you are and how things are, but you could also be according to how you act. You can choose your answer! "I am like that" is not a valid option for you anymore. You can change! You can be better!

4. Taking apart limiting beliefs means exploring them to discover how they impact you, whether they open possibilities to you or they close them, if they grant you the power to act or take it away from you, if they fill you with energy or drain you of it, if they get you close to the person you want to be or take you away of them.

5. We need leaders who do not tag those who work under their influence or responsibility. Leaders who understand that their players (children, students or helpers...) *are being* but not *are*, that changing and transforming oneself is possible, that they believe it and make them feel capable of achieving it.

6. We need conversationally competent leaders who are aware that in their *convers(a)ction*'s quality resides the power to transform Identities and build teams. New possibility leader creators, dreamers of new realities, who dare to declare them and believe in them.

7. **P**ositivising is taking the reins of your mind and life, assuming the responsibility of deciding what you want to think about, not doing it automatically. It is about revising and adapting your beliefs to adequately reply, controlling your behaviour and choosing who you want to be before every challenge life puts in front of you.

Promoting

"The greatest gift we can offer others is not showing them our riches but making them see theirs".
Johann Wolfgang Von Goethe

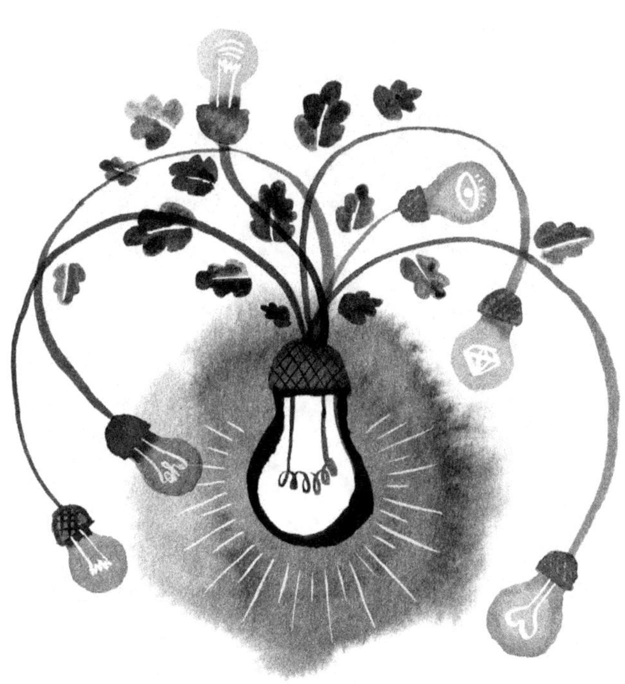

My "true self"

I was nervous. I had been playing bad for a few weeks and criticism was starting to get worse. It was night-time and there were a couple of minutes left before the match started. I felt it may be my last chance to be a regular player. The opposing team had an aggressive (violent at times) Argentinian forward centre who scored many goals and was in great shape. He was my dance partner for that evening and the duel was not looking good for me.

The match began and I found myself getting close and personal with him until he intentionally hit my face with his elbow during an air struggle for a ball. Not even fifteen minutes had passed when blood started to fiercely pour from my nose. I saw the manager gesticulating to swap me while I was on the sideline, having trouble breathing and being checked by the doctor. At that moment, when I was already accepting an honorable defeat (first place loss due to lesion), something deep inside of me rebelled, demanding me to go back to the field at once. I do not know the reason, I did not have time to think, even though I told the doctor to somehow put my nose back in place because I was going back.

From that moment onwards, all my being focused on the ball, on the 9, on my teammates and on the match. I was connected 100% to that moment. Nothing drew my attention away. No referees, no complaints, no cheating, no dark prophecies, no useless thoughts in my mind. Just interior silence and an incredible and unknown feeling of calmness and stillness while I played.

I finished my best match of the season. My feared rival disappeared and was replaced by his useless contribution. Everyone congratulated me when it ended, but I felt a very special emotion. It was not just satisfaction for the job well done or happiness for an important victory. It was not about the relief of having saved us from a match ball or the peace of mind for having secured my place for the following weeks either. It was something different, deeper and more unknown. It was as if, during that match, I had discovered something hidden that was very important and, until then, I had never felt with so much strength nor have been aware of it. That evening I intensely connected with "my true self" while playing football, my authentic me, and with the game's essence. That evening I achieved a moment of plenitude without realizing.

Game's essence

> *"You know a man better when playing for an hour than talking for a year".*
> Plato

One can often hear others talk about sports values. I do not think that sports have values: sports provide the context, the rules, the rivals, the scene, the competition... However, it is the people who practice sports who have the privilege of using this space to discover and play fully connected to who they are. The game's essence has no name, it cannot be defined. We can only try to explain the emotions athletes feel when connected, in a state of grace, when they flow connected to the game, without distractions, and when they are *present*.

There is sacrifice, a will to win and challenge in the game's essence, as well as humility, generosity and cooperation. Rules, referees, rivals and games are respected. So are courage and bravery. Risk and responsibility are also values in the game. There is leadership, passion and service, friendship and cooperation too. There is bliss, happiness, fun and enjoyment, as well as seriousness, formality and discipline.

There is competition and cooperation, nobility and loyalty, solidarity and dedication, aggressiveness and challenge. There is creativity, innovation and imagination, and also trust, honesty, simplicity, determination, serenity, perseverance, patience, integrity...

There is, however, a value that is always present in high-performance athletes and teams, a value which lacks a word that exactly defines it and I suspect we all agree, that it is undoubtedly transcendent not only in sports –"coompeting".

"Coo(m)peting"

Every time I watch Rafa Nadal playing a final that starts to get complicated, I confirm in awe to what extent his figure grows when he faces the most unfavourable situations. Where the vast majority of athletes would negotiate an honourable surrender with their rivals, he displays an incomparable determination. He puts himself at risk, growing and surpassing his limits again and again until he becomes the legend he already is.

While rereading Timothy Gallwey's book on tennis, I have concluded that Rafa Nadal has found out the true meaning of competing. He is very aware that his worth as a person is not at stake in defeat or victory. He is not hostage to that limiting belief for athletes, under whose perspective what you are depends on your results and you will only achieve the respect and love you deserve if you win.

Thus, athletes despair when they lose. Not because of the defeat itself, but because of the link they create between defeat and identity. If I lose, I am not good enough and they will not want me. Crushing. A widespread belief in the sports world and installed in our hard drive since our childhood, when you came back home from a match and the first thing you were asked was: *What have you done?* Winning started to become the most important thing about playing. If I win they get happy, they congratulate me and I feel respected, special and loved. If I lose I am disappointing them, I am not meeting their expectations, I am not up to the task, and they do not love me. This is the origin of an absurd and irrational fear of not being valuable, of not being good enough and not deserving the love of those that matter to us.

That may be the reason why sometimes the fear of winning takes over us during the ultimate free kick in the key match because we unconsciously think we are going to inflict the same pain to the rival team that defeat causes us and we feel guilty and we miss. It is not a conscious thought, but it is there and it dominates that moment in the back of your mind. It is not the fear of losing that blocks you in that decisive moment, but the fear of winning. It is not the darkness that paralyzes us, but the light.

Nadal belongs to another species in that sense. You only need to listen to his exemplary statements after his victories and his defeats, the exquisite respect he shows towards his rivals, his honest acknowledgment and even his appreciation to understand that his unbreakable desire to win stems from somewhere else. He understands that winning is simply overcoming obstacles to conquer an objective. From there he perceives his rivals as people who cooperate with him to achieve it and competition is nothing more than a way of achieving it. The better his rivals, the more they help him. Thanks to them he can improve every day, go beyond his limits and become the best tennis player he could be. He knows that both need each other to grow. They cooperate and compete. They "coompete".

From this interesting perspective, Nadal is not afraid of winning and his hand does not tremble during the most heated moments of the match. He is not crushing anyone nor losing their respect. He knows that neither his worth nor his rivals are being questioned. Nobody is defeated under this powering belief. Both competitors profit from the effort needed to overcome the rival's endurance. The two of them grow stronger and each one partakes in the development and growth of the other. From that viewpoint, Nadal is doing them a favor by giving his best and forcing them to do the same. That is what he expects from his rivals, and that may be why he thanks them publicly in the great finals.

We compete to win, though the secret is not worrying about the final result (something out of your control that only generates anxiety) and focusing all your energy on every point and piece of play. Making the maximum effort to be present and fully conscious of every action. That is the true challenge: overcoming every obstacle, improving and growing in every piece of play, point and match until you become the player that deserves to win. Victory is this process's natural result.

Those who mistake their identity, their essential and true Self with their victories, results, achievements or their skills, ignore the incredible and immeasurable value of every human being. Those who compete only moved by this belief are possessed by an excessive eagerness to win that eclipses everything else. The tragedy is they will not find the plenitude, serenity, respect and love they desperately seek when they achieve the brief success of victory.

They chase after glory, but glory is not sought, it is found by walking a path without shortcuts. A path exclusive to the brave ones that dare connect with their authentic values and that inspire others with their example, leaving an indelible print in the memories and hearts of those who admire them for their courage and determination. This might be the best definition of greatness: giving your best without any expectations or guarantee of success, starting something valuable that does not end with you. Maybe leaving a true legacy is about that. That is perhaps what defines a leader.

Convers(a)ctions help athletes and managers to connect with the true meaning of competition and wake up their "coompetitor", so that never again winning or losing a match questions their priceless worth as people, because that simply is "Sacred Grounds"[8].

Values

Values, as I understand them, do not come from the outside to the inside, but vice versa. Ethical and moral principles, and beliefs –religious, cultural, social, sporting or any kind– may or may not match personal values. They are not what you should be or what your family, friends, managers, environment or press expects you to be, but who you really are. They are the best you can offer. What defines you as a human being that plays and trains is a father, a mother, a boss, a friend... Your values are your compass, and they are personal and non-transferable. They are your treasure, those that turn you into a valuable, special and different being, and they are precisely those that will allow you to shine connected to your best version. You are no more important than anyone, although you are not less either. Nobody other than you is willing to provide your family, team, company, community or the world what you only have and are. Your essence is what makes you be a unique, incomparable, exceptional and invaluable being.

The best human values have a place in the sports world at their finest. Everyone can play, coach, manage and lead while fully connected to true values that also are a part of the game's essence. This is the sports' greatness and this is why it constitutes a privileged scenario, so that we can both find out who we are and how we are allowed to be it.

---

8   Article published in the blog *Píldoras de energizol* on September 2013.

"Eau d' Pep" essence

I was enormously privileged of counting with Pep Guardiola to co-star an eight video informative collection titled "This is football" in 1998. The Barcelona FC captain already was a big star and it was not easy to contact him. Thanks to the help of a common friend, we met up at a gathering of the team in Valladolid. Being a planning and methodical man, he granted me fifteen minutes between lunchtime and naptime to inform him about the project.

I perfectly remember how carefully he listened to me and the feeling I had that he really cared about what I was telling him. When I finished my pitch, he proved his curiosity by asking some questions about me and my project. He finally said that he liked the idea as well as its purpose, shook my hand and confirmed his participation. He did not mention his salary and when I brought it up, he told me to pay him the same I would pay others. His decision was key to move the collection forward. After he agreed to, Julen Guerrero, Kiko, Alfonso Pérez Muñoz, Aitor Karanka and César Sánchez joined the project, all of them at their peak as footballers. This way I completed an extraordinary roster of stars that I thank from here due to the trust they put in me.

Four months later, after the first preproduction phase was completed, the previously chosen dates to record Guardiola were delicate moments for him. He suffered from a sinewy lesion in the femoral biceps that had been keeping him from training, and media pressure over the recovery issues was growing. From the distance, while reading the Catalan press, my concern about him backing out also grew daily. It would have been reasonable that he chose to give up because of his physical problems, or that he decided to delay the recording thus risking the project's viability. Fortunately, that did not happen and he did what he had promised he would do.

He was unable to come to Bilbao as was initially planned but, in exchange, he spent a whole day with us in a field of the Centro de Alto Rendimiento (High-Performance Centre) of Barcelona to record the technical gestures and the demonstrations and explanations that constitute one of the collection's most precious treasures.

I could feel his notable capacity for expression and communication that day. As we were aware of the difficulties most of us have to speak in front of a camera, we wrote down the texts on blackboards or sheets of paper so that every star learnt them or read them before recording. The result was generally not particularly good. They were correct, but they were not the best, except Guardiola's. We gave him the texts, and he asked us to wait a couple of minutes as he walked away a few yards to read them. Shortly after he adapted them to his language and style with such strength and conviction that he had a great effect on those who listened to him.

He gesticulated with his hands, he empathized with his voice, and he even asked the cameraman to follow him while he walked in the field proving with his whole body how essential it was to use both legs to execute an imaginary control and to continue the piece of play without missing a second. He was brave to dare add sentences that were not in the script, and was creative to express them in his way. His presence and connection levels to the experience were such that, while seeing him live during filming, I knew that our collection would achieve its purpose thanks to him. I felt that any kid that watched that part of the video would not be able to wait to get down the sofa and start kicking the ball with the "bad" leg.

Another great virtue of Guardiola for team leadership and management was already present there —his enormous talent to convince, persuade and seduce. I perceive that in everything he has said and he has felt before. His is not only a rational speech, he is not limited to saying what he has to. He does not feign nor pretend to be someone he is not. His message, his passionate way of transmitting and putting it into practice is deeply connected to what he is, to his "true self" and his true values.

I could also intensely feel the overwhelming passion and contagious enthusiasm that he shows when he talks about football, as well as a borderline obsessive search for perfection. There was an explanation during the first recordings that we all approved in the first take, except him. He politely asked us if he could repeat it, and did so several times until he was fully satisfied with the result. His high demand level and full attention to detail, distinctly visible characteristics of his training technique, were already part of his nature. The values he bases his leadership on and that have turned him into the most admired manager in the world were inside his "acorn" from the start. That is how I felt it on the spot, and I keep a nice memory of the gathering.

I perceive Guardiola to be a brave fellow who dares to live connected to his essence. That coherence between who he is and what he says and does, linked to his deep knowledge and love for the game, exercises a formidable impact on his followers, who perceive him as a transformative leader, emotionally intelligent, highly inspiring, a compromise generator, and above all, worthy of being trusted.

Some people attempt to mock him saying he "is splitting hairs" (or "pissing cologne", as it is said in Spanish). What I think is that he gives off a pleasant, fresh and new aroma of authenticity. Since we are in the Christmas holidays, you could perhaps gift yourself a perfume bottle of *Eau de Pep*, because it is said its fragrance helps you connect with your essence and the best part of yourself. That would undoubtedly be a great resolution for this new year[9].

____

9   Article published in the DEIA newspaper on January 5th, 2011.

Plenitude

The British golfer Brian Davis gave up victory in the Verizon Heritage tournament, awarded a million dollars, when he warned the referee that he had brushed past a reed when he hit the ball. Nobody had noticed. After living for five years in Florida in order to become a golf professional, this was his first great success in one of the most important US circuit tournaments. It was his time to go from a modest 98th place at a worldwide level, to the first places of the ranking. That was the finishing hole and it was his first big opportunity for achieving his dream, but Brian preferred being honest. Brutally honest

Finding out who you are and what is important to you, knowing what connects you to your essence is only the first step to living in plenitude. Knowing is not enough. What makes a difference between life in plenitude and life in conformity is being brave enough to align our acts with your true self. It is not easy. It is extremely difficult. If it was easy, why would we not honor our values all the time? It is because our fear is greater than our wish of plenitude.

When he decided to warn the referee, I can imagine Davis' "saboteur" judging him and telling him things like "you have gone mad", "you are stupid", "you are going to embarrass yourself", "you will never win another tournament", "everyone will laugh at you", "the others wouldn't do it", "your wife will leave you because of your foolishness", "it is our last chance to be a golf professional". Brian likely thought his "saboteur" was trying to protect him from danger, shame or failure, because often that voice is too cautious in key moments when we are asked to take brave decisions towards a fuller life. Brian chose not to pay attention to his saboteur and he jumped without a net daring to be who he is.

Plenitude is a radical act and is not the result of having everything I desire or achieving my goals, nor do I need all the circumstances that please me to feel complete. Instead, it appears every time I dare to be brave and I act aligned to what is really important to me before any situation or circumstance that life puts me through.

When I see someone like Brian doing something as drastic as letting go of a million dollars in exchange for living connected to his Essence, I feel deeply inspired by his integrity: doing what you must, even if nobody is looking. Brian Davis lost a tournament and plenty of money, but he bested himself and earned universal praise. How much is that worth?

...

"These are my principles; if you don't like them... well, I have others" said Groucho Marx. The sentence: "I transform myself on the field" is frequently heard in the sports world. Nobody is buying it. You, any one of us, share what we are in the field, or under pressure in life. Our best and darkest side.

Some cheekily defend that tricking referees, provoking and insulting rivals, feigning and faking fouls or acts of aggression, complaining about everything, forcing the rules and twisting it until it remains unrecognizable are all part of the game and spectacle. "Football is for the smart ones" they smugly claim. I do not know if they are a part of the spectacle, but I am sure they are not part of the game, and I admit I feel second-hand embarrassment when I witness such behaviors. They are cheating. They all know what they are and they have never been a part of the essence of any sport. On the contrary, cheating is betraying the game's essence by tainting competition and the sport that is claimed to be defended. Not everything is fair play. That is not the only truth, and defending this belief is not free.

Taking every chance or game situation to trick, provoke, fake, exaggerate or complain costs you dearly. Being in the field thinking about all that involves you being disconnected from the game and yourself. When a player is in such a state, he allows the creation of a space where the loss of attention and focus, huge mistakes, foul play, irritability, anger, lack of control, cards, quarrels, "saboteurs" and a lot of thoughts that do not help you play better can happen. The other way around, you stop being present, straying yourself in the opposite way of plenitude and maximum potential.

Questions and resonance

We open our ears, we are present and all our senses are focused on the person we have before us when we listen to the *convers(a)ctions*. We track the valuable and essential things for them and we know we have run into "something real" when we discover the resonance, the external reflection, the echo of something deeply true. We do not exactly know what it is, but we feel its importance and authenticity, which is born from the deepest part of the Self. When this happens, when we perceive that the person we have in front of us is resonant, there are many symptoms that we can observe: from the smile, the tone, the cadence and the rhythm, to the shining eyes, the tears, the body language, the lit-up face, the deep bliss or the silences that reflect genuine and intense happiness. We know "something real" is going on when someone is resonating.

As I have already mentioned, I see the leader as a treasure hunter that explores the depths of their "acorns" helping them to connect what matters to them, with what moves them and makes them resonate. One of the *convers(a)ctions* initial goals is to increase their awareness to discover the compass that will guide them in their fascinating transformative journey from what they are being to what they could be. When someone's commitment is the result of the connection with their true values, then their challenges, previously inaccessible and frustration, fear and distrust generators, become desirable and achievable and, the energy to achieve it (*energizol*), as inexhaustible. Identifying and naming values is beginning the way to the commitment with oneself and to the character's definition that will push us to become the person we want to and can be.

We accompany others in their *convers(a)ctions* in search for the treasure, and we use again the powerful questions to unveil what is there, hidden, helping the person we have in front of us to name and identify which are the emotions that move them and directly connect them to their deeper and truer Self. We seek to excite emotion with them, turning the volume up two points so that they can live it and feel it more intensely for as long as necessary to load up the *energizol* they will need to get into action, now fully connected to their "true self" that will get them closer to their best version.

Practice!

Shall we try with you? I am going to ask you some questions that will take you out of your current context full of doubts, worries, limitations (real or fictional), binds, responsibilities, fears, and expectations, so as to connect you to a removed scenario from the situation you are living and all the circumstances that define it, easing the access to your internal wisdom: deeper, more authentic and essential. These are questions to get you out of your mind and connect you to your emotion and intuition, to your intelligence's top speed.

Now it is time to reflect and find out what is important to you. Some of the questions will impact you and others will not. Ignore those that do not and focus on those that are thought-provoking, those that connect you to important and valuable things, and those that move you. Let the others go, there are more than enough questions! Since I do not have the pleasure of knowing you, nor do I know your age, sex, job or sport you practice, I will ask you various questions. Pick those that you like the most and, after the first answer to every question asked, keep pondering about what is important, where that reflection takes you, what it makes you think of, and keep looking! What scenario it shows you, what reveals you about yourself, about who you are, what surprises you about your own replies, and what value there is: try to give it a name. Explore in depth every question you choose.

With the intent of giving you a model for this intimate *convers(a)ction* with yourself and considering I will not keep re-asking you after your first answer to every question, I will offer you a real example of a conversation with a manager to discover values:

Coach.- *What would you do with ten million Euros?*

Manager.- I would travel nonstop.

That was his first answer. I keep asking until finding something "real" from that answer.

C.- *What for?*
M.- To discover other countries, cultures, traditions, people...

C.- *How would that be good for you?*

M.- It would help me understand better other realities, be more tolerant, appreciate more what I have, be more thankful, learn, be more humble, and know more... It would help me grow as a person.

C.- *What does growth mean to you?*

M.- Being more empathetic, and generous, connecting better with people, understanding them, being calmer, having more self-control, searching for a meaning and purpose for what I do, knowing myself better... Growing would help me be a better manager, which is something really important to me.

C.- *If you grew and were a better manager, what would you do differently?*

M.- I would communicate better and have a better connection with my players, talk much more frequently with them, ask and listen to them for real, get angry less often, not yell at them as much, respect them more, encourage and acknowledge them, hug them, be much closer to them, laugh with them, enjoy training sessions and parties more...

C.- *Who would you be?*

M.- Then I would be an open and available manager, less distant, more serene, cheerful, and present. I would feel useful, someone who provided them with real value/courage, much further than game matters, someone who believed in them and made them feel valued. All of them, not only the best or those who play. I would be a manager who transmitted enthusiasm and confidence, they would believe in me and trust me. I would be able to express how I feel and listen to how they felt, I would feel there is a point to what I do, and then I would be a leader... I would be bloody brilliant!

C.- *What value would you be living there? What would be important to you?*

M.- (Prolonged silence)... Helping... Serving.

Once we have found a golden nugget, something valuable for him, his own resonant and authentic value (serving), we keep digging. We keep asking him to become aware of how present that value is in his life, whether he is living it intensely or he is very disconnected from it:

C.- *What does "serving" mean to you? How do you feel when you are at the service of others? What is possible when you act like that? What are you capable of? What is the impact you have on your players when you do it? If you could choose an image, metaphor or symbol that reflected what that value means to you, what would it be? Is there anyone you admire a lot due to their serving value? What do they do?*

C.- *If you had to mark from 1 to 10 how you are living your serving value right now, what would it be for you?*

M.- A 5.

C.- *Describe what a 5 is to you. What do you miss? How does it help you? How does it limit you? How do you feel? What are you missing out on? In what situations do you miss not doing it? What does your "saboteur" tell you? How are you acting?*

These, and many others, are questions to make others land in their lives, to become aware of their reality, of how they are acting, what impact they are having and the price they are paying to live disconnected from what is important to them.

C.- *How would two points more feel? What are you doing? What is different now? How has the situation improved? How do you feel? How do you talk to your players?*

How is a leader at the service of others? How is it positively impacting your team? What makes it special? What is possible for them that is not for others?

We use those powerful questions we saw in the previous chapter to help him overcome his "saboteur", feeling how he *resounds* when he is connected with his serving value, filling up with the *energizol* he needs to define and execute an action plan that puts him in the path to transform into the *leader at the service* he really can and is wishing to be.

After every question, clinging to the "acorn belief" that illuminates this book and from the genuine curiosity the other person is creating, we keep digging in every answer. We accompany them with more questions until reaching places they had never got to on their own, searching and exploring until they find something resonant, surprising and true. A value, a small part of their treasure, of what is inside their "acorn", of what they are and what they have become aware of; feeling it and making it theirs to have it much more present in their life, decisions and actions.

I shall leave you with a series of questions. I know having the recipe is not the same as baking a cake, although I hope this inventory serves you as a guide to wake you up and connect, little by little, to your "true Self". Treat yourself by going more deeply and elaborating all you want in your answers, searching for what is hidden, important and valuable behind every one of them. Enjoy it!

Which athlete or coach do you admire? What do you like the most about them? In what historical period would have you liked to live? What film or TV character would you have liked to play? If you had a time machine, where would you travel to? If you could choose, who would you have lunch with? What do you like the most about your best friend and why? What five words define you? What is your hobby and what does it provide you? What is your favorite film/book/ song/videogame/song? What was one of your memorable experiences? What is your dream? What ten things would you like to do before dying? What is your childhood's best memory? What would you do with one billion Euros? Where would you like to live? What would you do if you only had one year left? Which were your best holidays? What words would you like to be written in your gravestone? What would you like others to say at your funeral? What makes you happy/cheery/sad? What would you do if you were the president of your team, company or country? If you were an animal/instrument/car/color, which one would you be? When was the last time you got mad or laughed out loud? What grinds your gears? If you could choose a lifelong advisor, who would it be? What would you do with a magic wand? If you could choose a superpower, which one would you like to have? What is success or failure for you? If you were not a manager or an athlete, what would you like to be?

Tuning values

At the start of this chapter, we have named nearly 50 values with a place in the game's essence, and there are many more not even mentioned (maybe one of those you have just discovered). However, classifying everything that is and means a value for everyone under a tag is complicated. Doing so offers you an essential but insufficient approach to feel that these values belong to you. The values' names end up turning into common places that lose meaning if they are not personalised and made your own. The word itself, any of them (generosity, respect, humility) may have, has!, different meanings for everyone. We need to personalise values, and "tune" them. Expressing what this value means to me, define it with my own words, in what situations I live it, what is it like and how I feel in the field, on the court and out of it, on the bench and at home, how it is reflected and how it impacts me and others. Going more deeply in its meaning, feeling it intensely, resonating with it until you make it all yours, all yours.

It is very likely that you can search for an image, symbol, metaphor, word, etc. that embodies everything that this value represents for you, in order to pin this concept to the deepest of your Self. The point is finding an "anchoring" or structure so that you can access this value without intermediaries, in an immediate fashion. Everything that this resounding value means to you will come by bringing this image to your mind, allowing you to access your own and inexhaustible *energizol* tank to keep doing what you must, wherever you are and whatever the situation is.

"Chocolate"

That is one of my wife's tuned values. She concluded that one of the values that lit up her life is enjoying life when she was reflecting on them. What she loves is enjoying intensely, relishing. By going deeply into what "relishing" means for her, she became aware of what fulfils her is sharing the little things with their loved ones and thus she found out that she likes creating "special moments of intense presence" for herself and others: a breakfast, a conversation, a walk, organising a dinner, a detail, many details...

When reflecting on an image that could embody what "relishing" meant for her, she came up with the idea of black chocolate. Tasting one chocolate nugget, slowly savoring it, intensely enjoying the taste and the moment, calmly. "Chocolate" is the image that represents one of her values, very present in her life, even more since she found out about its impact on her and others. In fact, "I am chocolate" is her introductory WhatsApp message and every week an alarm goes off on her phone to remind her of who she is.

When I make a sausage patty, I fill it with many slices, I even grab three at once and put them carelessly. I eat it furiously and wolf it down in four bites, without having enjoyed it in particular. When she makes it, even when she puts fewer slices, she does it with love; the sausage slices perfectly peek out from the sandwich edges, she places them one by one, she buys them and demands them to be cut thinly. She heats the bread a little, and it becomes crunchy, she makes it with love, and then it tastes different. It is just a patty. "Chocolate".

The "fruitful insight"

"We are all geniuses, but if you judge a fish based on its skill of climbing trees, it will spend its whole life thinking it's useless".
ALBERT EINSTEIN

When we work on Promoting in our coaching workshops, we set up a very simple but very powerful dynamics that offers the searchers a radical perspective change with astonishing results. When I experienced it for the first time, I was to such an extent surprised by its impact, that nowadays that discovery is one of the keys in my daily job.

We divide the participants into teams of two and sit them face to face. We only tell them: "the person before you is a problem for you". They have to make an effort and imagine that they are a problem to feel it. They look at each other in silence for a minute. When the time ends, we ask them what was the experience like, how they felt and what their attitude was. "Awkward, tense, looking forward to finishing the activity, uncomfortable, I couldn't even look at them, I am judging and tagging them, I want them off my back, there is no opening on my end" are the most common answers. Body language confirmed all those sensations: closed, crossed arms and legs, avoiding each other's gazes, sitting backwards. The general behaviour is "I don't want to listen to them, I am not available, totally disconnected, I am closed". That is our (physical) reaction when we see someone as a problem.

Next, we suggest a different second look. The new instructions are: "The person before you is not a problem for you, but they have issues". We ask them to notice the difference and give them another minute. When the time ends, we ask them what was different. They reply that they felt "better and more available, more empathetic, wanting to listen and understand them, more aware of them, not judging them, more connected and wanting to help them fix their problems". Body language once again confirms these new sensations: a more relaxed body, limp arms and legs, closer and more open.

Lastly, we offered them a third alternative of looking and seeing who is sitting before them. This time we told them "the person before you has a purpose in life, something very special they can offer. They don't know it, you don't know it, but they have it, as well as problems. But they have a purpose". After the following intense minute, we asked again what had happened. The answers and energy they gave off clearly express the transformation that had happened: "I felt a real curiosity to find out what they have, I was very eager to ask them, inspire them and encourage them to search for it, I was totally open, very connected, I believed in them, I wanted to listen to them, the change has been amazing". Their body language did not lie this time either: smiles, body slumped forward, total openness, honest looks, fool faces, admired and astonished before someone with a treasure to discover...

When we asked them what were they focused on, whether on their purpose or their issues, the answer was unanimous: on their purpose. When we questioned who it depended on seeing a person like a 1, a 2 or a 3, a revealing silence followed, as well as unanimity: on me. It only depends on me. It depends on me to see those I have the honor of leading as "acorns". The "fruitful insight" is not even an option, it is an obligation for all those who wish to transform into leaders at the service of others.

I need to believe that this person or team already have inside of them the resources they need to overcome their difficulties, blocks or limitations, besides addressing their improvement areas with strength and energy, achieving their goals, and believing they can change, transform and be better than they are at the moment (so can I). In order to have a "fruitful insight" I need to believe that everyone has a purpose (and search for mine), even if they have problems and their current behaviour and attitudes show otherwise. I need to believe they possess a treasure that makes them unique, special and different, waiting to be discovered. Valued. I need to believe in order to create a better and different future, a possible future, so as to be a reality's transformative leader. And I can do it.

The "Pygmalion effect"

> *"I will always be a florist for Professor Higgins because he always treats me as such. But I do know that I am a lady for you because you have always treated me like a lady".*
>
> Eliza Doolittle
> *in 'Pygmalion' by George Bernard Shaw*

The "Pygmalion effect" has inspired plays and musicals, books and films, and has been the subject of much research in many areas: from psychology or medicine to economy, the most famous being the one put in effect in the education field in 1968. Carried out by Rosenthal and Jacobson, a group of primary education teachers were informed of whose students had got the best marks on an evaluation test. They were also told that those students were expected to perform the best in the school year. And that was precisely what happened. Everything seemed normal so far: it was normal they got the best marks since they were the best. The interesting fact about this research is that the evaluation test was never put into effect and the 20% of students with the alleged best marks on the test were randomly chosen, without taking into account their real abilities.

Starting from Rosenthal and Jacobson's observations, it was noted that the teachers had created such high expectations about these students, that their behaviour favored their fulfillment, supporting, trusting, demanding and believing more in those students with better skills than the rest. The "Pygmalion effect" therefore questions one of the basic postulates that define scientific analysis, which is using the results of the research to make predictions. Under this new perspective, it may be the other way around and be the prediction itself that generates the event.

"Pygmalion" Bielsa

Legend has it that Pygmalion, king of Cyprus and sculptor, modelled in ivory Galatea, his ideal woman. That statue was so gorgeous and perfect that he fell in love with her. The king begged in the goddess Aphrodite's temple for his statue to come to life to be able to love her and for her feelings to be mutual. When he returned home, he kissed Galatea and his expectation, full of desire, finally became true.

What is known as the "Pygmalion effect" is a process through which, when someone truly believes in somebody else, their expectations affect the former's conduct to such a degree that the latter tends to confirm them with their behaviour. It is not a magical effect. It does not only happen due to the mere fact of *believing* but because of how my behaviour towards others changes when *I believe*. Thanks to my "fruitful insight" I transform my gestures, words, statements, conversations, judgments, and even non-verbal language. Everything is different when I believe.

I suspect that, like Pygmalion, something similar happens to Bielsa. After spending his whole life seeking excellence in the game, he now faces the challenge of breathing life into a half-made statue (perhaps a sleeping lion) that was waiting, anxious and unknowingly, for expert and passionate hands that gave it life and made it dream of another possible future, ambitious challenges, surprising upgrades, objectives so far unachievable, impossible victories, epic matches, dreaming of glory. Someone who truly believed in them and helped them get out their best version at the service of a team worthy of being in our memory and hearts.

Bielsa has come to lead a group of footballers who, for too long, have heard that they are limited; they must add and subtract; they have to be realistic with their goals; they cannot compete against the great ones; other teams have chosen other players; they have a limiting philosophy; they cannot fight the competitors' budgets, Lezama's vegetable garden works on streaks, players do not manage with the "other football"; the league is all that matters,it is better not to dream because the fall will be harder... It must be difficult to grow in that environment. All these limiting beliefs do not seem to have room in Bielsa's rucksack. On his first day, just as he arrived, he summed up his message with the following statement: "Athletic Bilbao will play like the great ones. We will always go into the field to win, either home or away, we will be the stars, we will own the ball and respect the rules and referees". I almost fell off my chair when I listened to him. "I know now why he is called 'the crazy one'".

He decides and he chooses to *believe* for real. I perceive in him an enigmatic, shy, perfectionist, very demanding, brilliant, obsessed person who is passionate about the sport, and who firmly defends the game's essence. This is how a possibility is created: declaring it and believing it is possible before having proof that it is real. A statement binds whoever makes it and it does not mean saying how you want things to be, but to make that things be that way. Bielsa daily makes them a reality, he talks about it, shares it, and integrates it in his conversations and public statements making us believe that it is possible. And he has the courage of doing it without any guaranteed results or proof that others will follow him in this little *reasonable* bet.

Generating a *transformative vision* is quite uncomfortable at first because no possible future seems realistic at the beginning. Its job, from that reality declared as possible, is to identify what is lacking and change it until achieving it. It also consists of leading the necessary growth and transformation of the team until making it worthy of achieving that possibility. That is creating a *possible future*, creating something that does not exist and has nothing to do with a *predictable future*.

Little by little, despite the initial poor results, he is managing to attract players, team fans, media and football fans towards that powerful vision. Vision is pure possibility and cannot be predicted. If it was predictable, it would not be a vision. Reasonable dreams do not inspire anyone. We start to believe we can do and achieve it again, we can enjoy a great team and be champions again. Why not?

His powerful transformative leadership's distinctive element is that he lives his vision daily, in every press conference, in every detail, in every match and every decision. Bielsa lives that vision at any moment. A powerful and inspiring vision that drags the club, the team and every member towards that new reality he wants to create. By making no excuses, giving no justifications, making no populist statements; by taking risky decisions, by respecting the referees, by not using cheap demagogy, and by admitting his mistakes, he exclusively focuses on believing in his players, making them grow every day and in every match, accomplishing in some cases unthinkable transformations and surprising performance improvements in others.

I am unaware of his integration level in the city or his involvement in the club, the quality of the relationships with the rest of the institution groups, not even if he intends to stay longer than the year he signed for, but I am not interested. He was not hired to design the club's future, nor being their spokesperson nor the Lezama technician's teacher. It will be other professionals' responsibility to pick up the learning of what is going on in order to consolidate what is worth, strengthening and spreading it like powder throughout the organization, so that what we are living now constitutes a legacy on which to keep building the Athletic Bilbao of the future.

Bielsa has come to do exactly what he has been asked to: a revolution. I cannot fathom the industrial doses of enthusiasm and energy he needs every day to face such a challenge. The extraordinary challenge he is facing consists of finding again a course and helping us reconnect with what we really are, allowing us to rediscover what we identify with in the field. After seeing what and how he does it, I feel confident that he will not give up on what is unnegotiable to him: leading this brave, ambitious, generous, caring, respectful and noble team like no other.

There still is a long way to complete the mutation but, like Pygmalion's Galatea statue, I now see this Athletic Bilbao waking up and becoming aware of its true nature and what it is capable of being. Now *I also believe*[10].

"You will score goals"

I had never scored strategy goals. I was dominating and skilled in the defensive airborne game, but I was harmless on offense, except when running into someone, although I did not score. I used to run up the field, jump and head some balls but I honestly did not do much. I did not play with the objective of scoring. Maybe shooting rebounds, yet I do not remember scoring goals with headers until that season. I was 25 years old and, from the start in preseason, I could see that the manager had blind faith in that I would be the model player in the team's offensive tactical moves. The manager Blas Ziarreta was quite experienced, his teams dominated the free-kick moves and they always performed well in that area.

The first thing that came to my mind, following my usual line of thought at that time, was: "oof, shit! I will be in trouble once he realizes I can't head on offense". I could have thought many good things about this situation, but my mind refused to, it aimed at eliminating real or imaginary risks, and protecting me from ridicule: "How embarrassing it will

---

10   Article published in the *DEIA* in October 2011. This article was published a few months after Bielsa's arrival in Bilbao, when the results were still mediocre, Athletic gameplay still generated many doubts and no one could even imagine the enormous wave of admiration that the team would unleash that same season in all the world of football for its indomitable spirit and its spectacular game. What happened later is another story.... maybe for another book. Anyone interested in understanding what could have happened in the manager's second season, they will find many and very clarifying clues in the book *The Resonant Leader Creates More* by Boyatzis, Goleman and McKee, (in leadership styles, pages 87 to 124).

be when everyone sees that you can't score headers!" What a lovely mind! Always trying to help.

Blas did not care about my internal dialogue. "You will score!" he told me. He knew me well, he was an expert and he knew my ailments and limitations in the airborne game. He knew that I was tough and unafraid of contact when running and head-on. He believed that if I was good at defense, I could also be good at attack, and he chose to believe in me. Every week we trained corner kicks and side fouls for me to head for hours. Little by little I felt better and more confident when heading, to the point I felt as a magnet, I knew that the ball would come to me and I headed with extreme determination. I really wanted to score.

I scored 12 strategy goals in those two seasons. I shot many times and missed most of them, but I enjoyed it like a kid. I felt powerful, valued and acknowledged. My confidence got a big boost, I dared to do more things, to be braver and to assume more responsibilities. Every time there was a chance of running to the other side to shoot, I believed I could score and I even thought it would be easy. My mentality changed radically in that regard and it was his belief in me that made it possible.

It is not enough for someone to believe in you, you also have to do your bit when you believe. Blas believed I could do it and he worked with me. He insisted on shots, corrected my area penetration, explained how I could be more effective, and gave me the freedom to make mistakes, he did not lose his patience and he kept believing I could do it. And I did it. I did it for me and I did it for him, to not disappoint him. When someone makes you the great gift of believing so much in you, how on Earth aren't you going to try your hardest to confirm that belief? Believing in your players is not an option, it is the only way of achieving their transformation into what they could be but they still are not.

The negative "Pygmalion effect"

> *"If you tame a horse by screaming at it, do not expect to follow you when you speak".*
> DAGOBERT D. RUNES

Unfortunately, as we saw in the previous chapter while discussing "tags", the "Pygmalion effect" also works the other way around. When you feel –because you can feel it– that those who should lead you do not trust you, you feel as if your wings were clipped, your confidence plummets and your transformation and learning possibilities disappear. That lack of confidence is perceived and transmitted in many ways, some of which unconsciously for those who apply them, although their impact is visible for those who suffer them. Simple gestures, looks, comments, lack of physical contact and communication can sometimes turn into sarcasm, irony, yelling and arguments. On top of that, if you do not become aware of their negative impact, those attitudes can derive into emotional abuse with humiliating punishments, loathing and unjustifiable offences.

Do not kid yourself, if you find yourself doing that at some point, generating tension and fear as dominating emotions among your players, be aware that you are light years away from your best version, and you are very close to becoming a despot or tyrant who deplorably uses the power granted by their rank. To make myself clear and erase any doubts about it, if such behaviour is unacceptable with adults, it becomes despicable and reportable when using it on athletes in training. From your manager's responsibility, you have a socially relevant role with which you can influence positively and profoundly impact your young athlete's lives and future. Do not waste it! Stop worrying so much about winning or losing, about being famous or acknowledged and focus on deserving to be remembered by your players as the one who helped them be better than they were by making them feel valued, capable and special.

That is possibly the ultimate goal of those who behave in such an authoritarian manner and they are convinced that treating youngsters that way (maybe as they were treated back then) is the best way of helping them. They can even justify that behaviour by claiming that they are doing it for their players and they will thank them one day. They won't! Such behaviour drags them away from the leadership at their service we suggest in these pages. Any untrained moron can behave like that and you, if you are reading this book, you are not anybody.

"If your players fear you they will obey you. But if they love you, they will die for you and you will achieve extraordinary results together", is an adapted quote by Sun Tzu. If you truly want to encourage your players, dare to apply the "fruitful insight" with them. Leading from there is very commendable. You need to be brave for that, to learn and develop new abilities and leadership competencies, work on your patience and self-control, believe in them and not tag them, boost them and acknowledge them, listen and ask them, be open, available and vulnerable, accompany, support and keep believing when you are about to give up, ask them for feedback regarding how they perceive you (you do need a lot of courage to ask that), rub off your energy and enthusiasm on them, enjoy your privilege and be thankful for it... to see "acorns". Brave people who dare to not be a nobody, shine connected to their best version and be models and light for their followers are needed for all this. Do you dare to?

Acknowledgment

"It may happen that once every century, a compliment may ruin a person or make them insufferable. But what is certain is that every minute, something worthy and generous dies because it was not acknowledged".

JOHN MASEFIELD

Listening to some of Simeone's press conferences in which he acknowledges the brutal effort his players make on the field, and the solidarity, intensity and devotion they show in every match is a pleasure. I love how he publicly congratulates them for their behaviour and spirit, for their involvement and compromise with the effort and demands he requires from them to be able to compete against his billionaire rivals. I enjoy listening to how he boosts those that play the least, how he makes everyone feel important, how he goes over what they do well, again and again, he compliments it tirelessly, he pays attention to details and focuses on their strengths.

He makes the most of every chance to passionately and sincerely acknowledge his players, he admires and is thankful for what they are being, what they are achieving and how they are doing it. I feel that he truly enjoys every chance he has to publicly declare that he loves his team, without worrying about that limiting belief about "compliments make you weak" and other truths of the sort: "they are only doing what they have to" or "they get paid a lot". I greatly admire the brave ones that dare to make powerful acknowledgments.

Too often gratuitous and easy praises or smarmy and manipulative compliments are mistaken for honest and authentic acknowledgment. The difference is that the first comes out of your mouth and the second one spurts from your heart. Acknowledgment directly focuses on someone's essence, it does not only refer to what they are doing, but who they are being when they do it, to the deepest and best part they have. It is not about cheering or congratulating someone due to a good piece of play or action, nor is it the feedback or information to improve upon a particular matter. The point is recognizing their *being* through their *doing*.

It is similar to discovering a gold nugget inside someone's "acorn" and itching it offering it. When you see it, when you perceive there is something valuable and special behind what someone does, you cannot help getting close to them, you feel the need to tell them without expecting anything in exchange and without anyone asking you to: "Oi! Look at what I've found, it's yours and it's fantastic. Take it!". You want them to become aware of the value that defines them, to make it theirs, to feel it and have it be more present in their game and life.

"Whoever keeps an acknowledgment, they are keeping something that is not theirs", said the genius Pablo Picasso once. Offering an authentic and honest acknowledgment is making a priceless gift we barely use since we are controlled by limiting beliefs of the sort: "it's their job", "they will get cocky", "they will think I am soft if I do it", "they will not respect me", "my task is correcting what they do wrong", "too vulnerable", "I am not paid to educate them", "my job isn't loving them". Recognizing someone is like lighting up someone's essence and making it visible. How valuable that is! It is gratifying for the one who does it and it can be radically transformative for who he receives it. Accepting an acknowledgment, in the way we are expressing it here, is as if you were punched directly in your heart. It leaves you breathless. Acknowledgment is brief and direct. It makes you believe.

There are many ways of expressing acknowledgment. I shall offer you some examples within the sports world in case they can help you: "I value a lot the bravery you show when you face your rival again and again, even if things aren't working out for you" (boom). "I know how difficult it is for you as a goalkeeper and I appreciate it a lot how you commit to our idea of playing every time you receive the ball without getting nervous and waiting for your mates to offer to keep playing" (boom). "I am moved by the optimism and happiness you are living in the process of recovering from your grave lesion. You inspire all of us" (boom) "I acknowledge your humility in how you train every day without ever giving up, even if you play little. You are a gift to this team. Thank you." (boom). "What I value a lot about you is the calmness and serenity you rub off on us when things go South" (boom) "Your limitless courage and commitment you show when facing every action, struggle and match is admirable. Your passion and nobility are a blessing for this team" (boom). "When you run to defend and help your winger when nobody is asking you to, I see in yourself the caring player we eagerly need. Keep it up!" (boom) "When I see you leading the warm-up at the start of the training every day, so cheery and connected, and with so much presence, I feel that your enthusiasm rubs off on me and I feel thankful for being able to count on you" (boom) "Every time I see you daring to kick it with your left leg, even if you fail, I greatly admire your desire to improve and learn, and your determination to not give up to become the player you can be. Stay on this path!" (boom). You probably have guessed what the "boom" means, it is the sound of an honest acknowledgment directly impacting the heart."

Now that you already know the "fruitful insight", aside from paying attention to, as you should, what is not working, what has to be improved, and what is not right and has to change, you can also apply your new talent to discover what every one of your players and helpers has inside their "acorn", what makes them special and unique. That has always been there but, even though you were aware of it, you had not paid much attention to it until now.

If you are a manager, I challenge you to think of that player or helper you dislike, the one you keep an eye on because they are usually bothering others, they help little and, on top of that, are not good. I want you to think of them as an "acorn" and, if you have come this far reading the book, I know you can do it. You can search for what they have until finding something valuable inside of them, something they excel at, no matter if it is on the field, locker room, or in the way they behave, play or interact with others. Think of a moment or situation in which they have performed adequately and have been worthy of being complimented. I am sure there is something! And now I ask you to give them a sincere and authentic acknowledgment. Feel it! Do it for real, from your heart, and let it echo in theirs. Make them visible, they may be the ones in more need of that.

We need to know how to shine to do it; what can we use to support ourselves, and what is the best thing we have inside our "acorn" that makes us valuable and different. We need help to discover it and make it visible, to make us visible, to connect with our true values, identify them and name them, to feel them more intensely and have them more present in every training session, every match and throughout our life.

We are generally not aware of it and we blindly stumble through it, as if covered by fog, without knowing the impact of our actions, nor how it is perceived. We need to be confident enough to know what we are good at to dare to face our improvement areas with energy, perseverance and determination to grow until we achieve our maximum potential.

There are five key messages linked with the deepest needs of any human being that a leader needs to keep in mind. They can be summed up in a few words:

1. You exist.
2. I see you.
3. You are valuable (and unique).
4. You have important things to share.
5. You belong to this group (you are welcome).

Some time ago, when I started my company path after I was done with football, someone who took the role of leader at my service and believed in me even more than I did at that point appeared in my life. He helped me find out and put into practice skills not even I was aware that I had. Seven or eight years ago took on different paths but we try to meet up and talk at least once a year. Every time we do it, he greets me like this: "Imanol, I am very glad to see you" and he tells me with intense presence, looking in my eyes, firmly shaking my hand with an honest smile. While reflecting on it, I have discovered that he is sending me three of the five key messages with that greeting alone: *you exist, I see you and you are valuable.* And, from that point onwards, visible and accepted, I feel acknowledged and capable of anything[11].

You, a manager, parent, teacher, boss, you have the great opportunity of making me visible, helping me find out who I am, and what is the best thing I have to offer, being part of a transcendental possibility, distinguishing and shaking what it is not yet but could be. I need you to love me, even if you do not like me, to dare to improve and grow until you become a leader that shines for me, and to believe in you and me so that we can transform together.

---

11   "*Sawabona*" is a Zulu greeting used by some Southafrican tribes that means: "*I see you, I respect you, I value you and you are important to me*". As a response, others say "*shikoba*", which means: "*then, I exist for you*".

Reinforcement

Some years ago, when one of my daughters showed me her really good quarter marks, my eyes instantly focused on the low mark in the "lunch room" section. I immediately asked her what was going on and what she was doing to have got a mark, I gave her a speech about respect and politeness in the lunch hall. I guess I got over-excited about it and I grew louder about it until how two tears of rage and helplessness rolled down her cheeks. I then realised what I had done (quickly noticing mistakes is one of the big benefits of increasing awareness in coaching because, as you can see, you can still mess up). Instead of taking the chance to reinforce and support her in that successful situation, so that she got a lesson out of it and to define new goals and improvement plans, instead of leading from her strengths, I did the opposite I preach and achieved the same or similar effect those who normally act like this achieve.

I could have sincerely acknowledged her work and behaviour during the last school quarter, her commitment and her special interest in a particular subject. I could have also valued positively her responsibility and desire to improve and, from there, we could have faced that bad mark of "lunch room behaviour" with confidence and serenity.

When she came back with her report card the next school quarter, I was ready and I kept in mind my previous blunder, so I was willing to apply my best stimulating skills. This time her polemic "lunch room behaviour" had notably improved. After seeing that, the least I could do was say "I am very proud of you" loud and clear as if she only had to get good marks for me, as if I only loved her when she got them. Once again I lost another chance of making the most of a successful situation to truly stimulate her, helping her become aware of who she had been that school quarter to achieve those marks, what had changed and what had been different. And, at the end of the conversation, I would have told her "you make me so proud". It should not have been the only and last thing to tell her.

I admit I deeply enjoy applying the strengthening ability to go deep into successful situations. When a manager is accomplishing results or a player has dominated the match, I make good use of that moment to generate an awareness conversation, to help them land and find out who they have been in that match and what they have learnt. As always I use questions: *what are you proud of? what have you done best during the match? what have you found out about yourself during the match? what have you learnt? what have you dared to do? what has changed? what have you done differently? what personal value have you lived intensely today? Who have you been today? How do you feel? What would you like to repeat in the next match? What are you struggling with still? What do you want to improve this week? How are you going to do that?* At their service, leading, accompanying them, helping them discover what they are capable of and that they can manage to do it, connecting to the best they have, to their resources and their brave nature so that they can face their improvement areas with determination, confidence, cheerfulness and energy.

If you are a manager you can do the same with your team after a good match, openly asking them, with presence, respecting every question, thanking all of them for the questions and without judging any of them. Asking them *what they have done differently, what they are proud of, what they have learnt, what they have liked the most, what they have proven, what values they have lived intensely and in what moments, pieces of play or situations they have felt them, what they have dared to do, what has been the best part, what they would like to change for the next match...*

Powerful questions to become aware of whom they are and their best sides so that they can do it more often and more intensely. That is strengthening.

Athletes' lives are very short, they need to make the most of every experience to extract teachings from them and shorten their growing-up process by squeezing every one of their experiences like a lemon to discover who they are being, what their challenge is, what is costing them, what they want, and who they want to be before every situation. Help them wake up, and create their own Identity to transform into the people and players they can be, need to be and want to be.

Promoting is making others' essence visible, it is looking and seeing, it is helping them discover their treasure, what is inside their "acorn", marveling and acting like a privileged witness at their surprising discovery. It is pushing them and inspiring them to dare be who they are. We only need a sort of behaviour to accomplish it: the "fruitful insight". Believing in the greatness of every human being and their immense potential, deeply respecting their "Sacred Ground".

The carpenter's workshop

It is told that there once was a strange meeting in the carpenter's workshop, a tools gathering to settle their differences. The hammer exercised the presidency, but the meeting notified its dismissal. The reason? It made too much noise! And, on top of that, it spent the time hammering things. The hammer took the blame, though asked for the screw to be kicked out as well since it went roundabout ways for it to be of value. The screw accepted as well, albeit it asked for the sandpaper tool to be struck off the rolls in exchange. The screw explained that the sandpaper was quite rough and it always rubbed off with others. The sandpaper tool agreed as long as the tape measure was thrown out as well because it always measured others according to tailored measures as if it was the only perfect one.

The carpenter came in while they were arguing, put on his apron and started working. He used the hammer, the sandpaper tool, the tape measure and the screw. Eventually, the starting rough wood became a beautiful piece of furniture. When the carpenter finally left his workshop, the meeting resumed the deliberation. It was then when the handsaw took the floor and said: "Ladies and gentlemen, it has been proven that we all have shortcomings, but the carpenter works with our strengths. That is what makes us valuable. So let's not think any more of our weaknesses and focus on the usefulness of our virtues".

The meeting then found out that the hammer was strong, the screw linked and gave consistency, the sandpaper tool was special to put the finishing touch to wood and file down the rough edges and they observed that the measuring tape was accurate and exact. They then felt that they were a team capable of producing high-quality furniture. Pride filled them as they thought of their skills and ability to work together.

The same thing happens with human beings. Observe them and you will confirm it. When someone in a group starts looking for shortcomings, the situation turns tense and negative. On the other hand, by trying to perceive and honestly recognize other peoples' strengths, the best human achievements bloom. Finding faults is easy, any idiot can do it. But finding talents is only possible for the superior spirits that are able of inspiring all human successes[12].

---

12   By an unknown author, presented in the book *Cuentos para ser humano (Tales to be human)* by Luis Benavides.

Promoting in 7 pills

1. Your values define you, not what you think you are, nor what you should be nor what others expect you to be. When you live connected to your true values, to your "true self" and act accordingly, you experience sublime plenitude moments that bring you closer to your best version.

2. *Plenitude* is not the result of having everything you want or achieving all your goals, nor is it the result of all circumstances that suit you happening for you to feel full, but plenitude appears every time you dare to act connected to what is important to you, in any challenge that life puts before you.

3. *Resonance* is the echo of something deeply true and born in the deepest part of our Self that reflects a genuine and intense emotion. We are treasure hunters and, when we see that someone is resonating, we know we have found something valuable and essential, something "real".

4. I choose to see human beings as complete, creative and full of resources ("acorns"), like all those people I have the honor of leading, opting to believe in them and accompany them in their transformation process from what *they are* to what *they could be*.

5. Sincere and genuine *acknowledgement* is directly focused on someone's essence. It is not about what they do, but who they are when they do it, to the deepest and best degree. Acknowledging someone is shining light on their inner "acorns" and making them visible so they become aware of the values that define them and therefore they can feel and own them.

6. The "Pygmallion effect" proves that —when you believe in someone else, your expectations and beliefs have such an effect in their own behaviour that they tend to confirm those expectations with their conduct. Unfortunately, it also works oppositely.

7. **P**romoting is *looking* and *seeing*, helping others discover and connect with the best they have inside their "acorn". It is pushing and inspiring them to be who they could. It is telling them that they exist, that you can see them, that they are valuable, that they have important things to provide and that they are welcome since they belong to that team. It is believing in every human being's greatness and immense potential, respecting their "Sacred Ground".

em**P**athizing

> *"If we truly managed to be able to understand, we could no longer judge".*
> André Malraux

In 2013 I was invited to participate as a speaker in the first International ASESCO (*Asociación Española de Coaching* [Spanish Coaching Association]) Congress. My lecture's title was: *From manager to leader. What would you do if you were not afraid?* I spent a week preparing a two-hour long presentation with 40 slides, 3 or 4 surprising videos and a bunch of stunning quotes. The result was amazing, or at least that is what I thought. I arrived in the morning at the hotel's hall where the congress was held, confident that my lecture would be a success, and I attended the excellent lectures that were developed from 9:00 am throughout the day. My lecture was scheduled at 18:30, but because of the accumulated delays and after the last break, the 200 congress-attending coaches returned to the hall at around 19:30. Temperatures were high, it was late, and people were tired and unfocused. I started to worry... On the one hand, I thought "you worked hard on a very cool presentation, you just give your lecture, and done. Them being tired or delays happening are not my responsibility. I am positive some will make the most of it, and the rest... tough luck. It's not my problem". This is what my "saboteur" told me. On the other hand, my intuition told me I should not give my lecture proving how good I was and how much I knew... I felt those people needed something else at that moment. I did not know what to do.

When they all sat down I expressed my doubts out loud and I asked them: "How are you doing? Please raise your hand all of you who are tired, who is already a bit saturated? Bored? Full? Who is already thinking of what they are up to next? Of toilets, dinners and tales? Who exercises regularly? Who is passionate about sports? Who has been looking forward to this lecture all day? Please raise your hand..." That is how I did it. I gathered all the information that confirmed all my suspicions, and I decided it was time for something else. Something more dynamic and participative. Something that made them be present and connected despite their tiredness and the time it was. Yes, I know I could have thought of it when I was preparing my lecture, I already knew it was the last one and the like, but I did not do it then. A lack of experience, foresight, who knows. But there I was, everything in the air and nothing prepared.

I chose to change it almost completely, showing more of what I am and less of what I do, daring to offer something from the bottom of my heart. At that moment I chose to put myself at their service and accept that it was not about me, but of them. Those two hours' objective was not to satisfy my acknowledgment needs, nor to prove my alleged competence and skills, but to answer the "hunger" within the room. It was time to reply to their curiosity and take something useful and practical out of the lecture. Strengthening their belief in the coaching's transformative power regarding leadership. Sharing the excitement to keep exploring a vast land to conquer, and feeding the hope that every one of those 200 Congress participants had great development opportunities in the sports world.

I ignored the presentation and slides I had prepared and we shared the experience of feeling the presence's impact, of connecting, if briefly, with everyone's essence, of thanking and honoring those that at some point in our lives saw us as "acorns", we experienced the power of the "fruitful insight" and we discovered the impact of *believing* to *create*. We laughed a lot, at ourselves and at our cowardly "saboteurs", and we managed to generate a hopeful, energetic and exciting space for all the attendees. When we finished (the two hours went by in a flash), I felt I had been brave, I had had enough courage and confidence to empathize for real, to really put myself at their service, to be humble and place their needs before mine, and replying to them consciously and properly. I felt full and thankful.

Leadership and humbleness

After these last years in which I have studied, educated myself and professionally practised coaching and leadership, I have concluded that one of the essential values that set the greatest humanity leaders apart is humility and, when having reached this point, reviewing this concept. Until not so long ago, I mistook *humbleness* for *simplicity, modesty, obedience, discretion*, for not *drawing attention to myself* until I discovered a much more inspiring and powerful interpretation. I do not claim that the previously mentioned attributes are not admirable and typical of humble people, although I believe they do not define it.

I understand that humbleness is not about underselling oneself, but instead how you can think less about yourself or *think about others before thinking about yourself.* Putting my team, players or mates first. That is big talk.

Although I know many simple, discrete and sensible individuals, I know considerably fewer people with the necessary confidence and trust levels to be brave enough to put themselves at the service of others. One needs to be quite brave to dare to be really humble, to lead, which may explain why there are so many managers and so few leaders.

"Emotional hijacking"

We were playing a playoff match to be promoted to the Second Division. Whoever won the match would almost certainly win the first prize to escape from the Second Division B hole to return to professional football. We urgently needed that. After last season's demotion, the Club had made the effort of keeping the contracts to being promoted in a year, and we all felt it like an obligation. We played at home, where we had only scored a goal during the whole season... things seemed fine. We had lost 1-0 in the previous match and we had to score two goals to achieve the objective. We had scored two goals by the first half 40th minute and we were performing extremely well, but then they scored two in the fateful last five minutes. We returned to the restroom in shock.

At that moment a hurricane unleashed. Our manager, prey to an unstoppable wrath and fury attack, spent the following fifteen minutes venting on us with insults, threats, humiliation and disparagement. There was no escape from the storm whose damage became apparent in a shameful second half in which the team had left their heart in the restroom while trying to recover from the impact. We played soullessly. We lost 2-3, we were not promoted and, aside from punishing us with extreme training sessions during the last two competition weeks, the manager did not talk to us again during that season.

I do not know whether the result could have been different or not. However, what is clear to me is that those unforgettable fifteen minutes did not help at all to motivate us to go out on the field with the best emotional and mental willingness to achieve our goal. It is likely the manager was right in his error analysis, in how we should have defended, in the lack of focus and everything else. Nevertheless, it was not time for that. It was not about being right (an ego thing), but about accomplishing our objective: winning the match.

Self-control is probably one of the most important competencies a leader has to master. Being a victim of an "emotional hijacking", like the one from the previous story, leaves you helpless and without access to all your resources. It makes you react uncontrollably instead of searching for the most suitable answer in every situation. It prevents you from exercising the role of *leader at your players' service* that, at great tension and responsibility moments like the aforementioned one, is essential. Leadership is precisely required in the middle of the storm. There is no need for a captain when the sea is calm.

We sometimes mistake being at the service of the needs of the people we have to lead with being a slave to their wishes or being at their mercy. Big mistake. Being a slave is doing what others *want*, while serving is doing what others *need*. There is an abysmal difference between satisfying *wishes* and *needs*. They seldom match. During that unforgettable 15 minute break, my team did not need that uncontrolled and brutal scream and discrediting discharge from our manager. Our manager's behaviour would have possibly suffered a radical transformation in case he had taken a minute to empathize with us if he had asked himself a simple question: *what do my players need from me now? How do they feel now? How do I feel? What is happening to me? Who do I need to be for them? What is my challenge here?* Thinking of others before thinking of me. Humbleness. A leader at their service[13].

Humbleness and empathy

I used to think that one was born humble, either you were or were not. I know now that *empathy* is the skill that connects you with *humility*. Although it may be one of the most challenging skills one may learn, it can also be improved and developed. We sometimes are so entangled in our beliefs that our way of seeing and understanding reality, from our perspective, that we do not give ourselves a chance to visit others' realities.

Through empathy we become aware of the great possibilities that open when we dare to walk in someone else's shoes and take ours off first. Without clinging to our "truth",

---

13   Published in the blog *Píldoras de energizol* on April 2010.

without defending it with tooth and nail and without giving it up, we only suspend it at times to deeply explore other "truths" and perspectives, free from our absolute judgments, opinions and certainties. When we allow ourselves to empathize in this way, we increase our understanding of ourselves and others, thus overcoming the layers that hide their true essence. Empathy increases our connection because we show our authentic curiosity and worry for them and their life with it. It allows us to offer more suitable answers for every situation and open new *convers(a)ctions*.

The revealing and transformative point of this process is that the way we see others is not the same after daring to explore someone else's world and wearing our shoes again. That way has changed. We have changed. We then find ourselves wishing to have done something we previously did not think about to support and help them, putting ourselves at their service.

Fancy a little cup of coffee?

There were only four matches left and we had to win all to achieve the promotion to First Division. That way we would make sure of the Club's viability, as it was going through grave economic problems. Not winning all of them would possibly mean the Club's disappearance, something that did not leave our minds. We were playing on another field against a team in the last place of the classification, and, despite being May, it was a winter day. It rained cats and dogs and a freezing wind blew. They scored the first goal right after the start, and we felt the goal in our hearts. We were extremely tense and all sorts of ghosts and negative thoughts that took us out of the match started to fill our heads. These thoughts lead to continuous mistakes and loss of focus, ingredients that anticipated the disaster.

The thrashing we received was spectacular and we were losing 2-0 when the break arrived. When we entered the dugout some argued, others yelled and most of us looked absently at the floor, anticipating the imminent disaster that would inevitably happen. Anguish, helplessness and a lot of fear were the dense emotions that filled the room. Anguish made our minds work like crazy and made us see ourselves sunk, failing and with an uncertain future ahead of us. A wave of fatalism flooded everything. The atmosphere was heavy. Silence fell.

Five minutes later, our manager entered the restroom. We were all expecting him to join the emotional chaos in some way. At the same time as he fixed his coat's collar, he calmly said with a smile: "Darn, is it cold or is it cold? Does anyone want a cup of coffee?" And he started serving us cups of coffee. The unexpected answer's effect on the team's mood was surprising. The resources he proved having to control his impulses and stay calm, despite the pressure we all felt, meant an instant release for all of us. His capacity to connect with the team, feel our emotions, self-control and empathize with our stress had a profoundly transformative impact. With a few words and a warm smile, the dark clouds that forebode the catastrophe started to vanish, leaving room for a fresh gush of wind of renewed excitement, hope and optimism. We began to look each other in the eye, raise our heads, utter some shy but encouraging words, and smile a little. We could still make it!

His resources to stay calm and not unleash his anger and frustration on his team due to a shameful first half that risked everyone's future helped him to think clearly. It also helped him to make some changes and tactical modifications that turned the gush of wind of confidence into a hurricane of playing and goals that allowed us to overcome our anguish and win the match. He chose to put himself at our service and, during the five minutes he took to enter the restroom, he may have asked himself: *what do my players need of me now? How can I help them? Who do I need to be for them? How am I feeling? What is happening to me? What is my current challenge? What do I need to do or say?*

His decision to be a leader, to connect with the group's needs and to put it first, changed the match and our fate that season. We were finally promoted. But now I know we managed it during that break, thanks to a *leader at the service* who dared ask: *fancy a cup of coffee?*[14]

Empathy and "sublime listening"

I understand it is easier to empathise with people you feel an affinity with, but if you are a manager (teacher, CEO, boss…), you need to be at everyone's service, even those you do not like. At least until the season is over.

"The secret of sublime listening is knowing how to attend to the right thing". That is what Moisés Cordovero, a Jewish mystic, stated in the 16th century. Rafael Echevarría discovered this sentence while researching for his book, which he reflected on with great lucidity in his book *Actos del lenguaje (Language's acts)*. "Sublime listening" is a concept that may help us lead for everyone.

If now I asked you if you sometimes voluntarily hurt the people you love or care for, what would you reply? When I ask that question in the training workshops barely anyone raises their hand. I understand they may feel guilty and they may not want to admit to something like that in public. If anything, a couple of them per group will shyly confess they hurt others willingly. The rest will explain that they might do that too in certain situations.

---

14   Published in the blog *Píldoras de energizol* on April 2010

When asked about those situations, they sum them up in two: when they feel threatened or scared or when they have felt hurt, harmed or unfairly treated. Paraphrasing doctor Echeverría, "when we feel vulnerable or insulted we allow ourselves to hurt those we mark as responsible for the situation". If that happens to us, we can acknowledge that may happen to others as well.

When I feel attacked, they may do that because they may have been offended by my behaviour in exchange, purposefully or not. I may be responsible for their actions.

This new perspective, this "sublime listening", means a radical change in my way of looking and seeing others. It also changes the way I perceive the situation that immediately modifies the observer I am, my interpretation, the emotions and reactions that their behaviors generate. From the "listening of the right thing", I do not feel attacked or harmed anymore, but instead questioned by someone who feels hurt, threatened or abused and who wants to attract my attention. By applying this superior listening level, I now feel curious and compassionate. I appreciate their vulnerability, I am looking forward to understanding them. I am almost ashamed of my first instinctive and aggressive reaction. I feel the need to help them and put myself at their service, notably increasing my compassion (not pity) for them.

Compassion: empathy in action

Similarly to how I mistook the concept of *humility*, so did I with *compassion*. I believed *feeling compassionate* and *sympathising* were synonymous. I did not see any difference. Now I do; it is a huge one. Sympathising does not mean pitying someone. When we pity somebody we are not seeing them as an "acorn", as a complete being, creative and full of resources, but as a victim. We are underestimating them and we do not consider them capable of overcoming the situation they are facing. Only when they are going through an enormous loss can they use our pity.

Compassion is a value based on *empathy,* wishing to connect with others and deeply understand their reality, putting ourselves at their service and answering their legitimate needs. The coach Herminia Gomá defines compassion as "empathy in action", and implies an honest and genuine consideration for others by whom you take action. The point is not to influence others for your benefit but to steadily help them in their change and improvement process. You can do this by supporting and inspiring them to achieve their goals, desires and ambitions, for which leaders must put others first. When leaders are humble and compassionate, they are more open and in direct contact with their people. They are available and do not isolate themselves. Leaders evolve and help their players and collaborators evolve by stopping to feel they are sacrificing themselves for others. They enjoy doing it and they feel they are accomplishing their true purpose, which is much more than managing players. They lead people and help them grow and improve. Compassion is undoubtedly a value that makes us wiser, more aware, humbler and better leaders.

Leading is loving

> *"I do not have to be keen on my players, but I do have to love them".*
> VINCE LOMBARDI

Lombardi refers to love as a behaviour, not as a feeling. You do not need to be keen on your players to behave generously, kindly, humbly, lovingly and respectfully. They are your players and require you to love them to win, not because they won.

When one of your players is being rebellious, lazy, unruly, selfish, unmotivated, absent, behaving inadequately, even harmful to the team, you may feel attacked, and your authority threatened. You may feel he does not respect you and he is hurting you and your team. Faced with a situation like this you can react and take drastic measures, remark on his bad behaviour, put him in evidence before all his mates, punish, threaten and throw him out from the training or even the team. All these actions would be justified and you would have numerous and strong reasons to take them. Nobody could accuse you of being unfair. However, you could also apply the "sublime listening" or "listening to the right thing". You could think that this player does not want to hurt anybody even if he is doing so Perhaps, like you sometimes, he may feel vulnerable or offended.

What would it be like to apply the "sublime listening" to any of these situations? What would it be like to not see your player as a problem or as someone harmful, but as a master that life offers you and as a challenge to your leadership? In situations like this, and before taking radical decisions, you could ask yourself some powerful questions: *what is the challenge here? What does this situation want from me? What does this player need from me? How can I help him? What is he asking for? What am I not seeing? What is needed to do or say and I am not doing? Who do I need to be for him? What things am I not daring to do? Who must I choose to be now?*

After reflecting on these matters, your behaviour will likely change radically regarding that person or situation (whichever it may be). You may not feel attacked anymore, or need to defend yourself or sense that he is threatening your authority. You may feel compassion for them ("empathy in action") and real curiosity to understand them more deeply. You have to understand and ask them, recognize, promote and be available for them, and help them discover and become aware of their resources.

It is easy being a leader with those well-behaving and uncomplicated players who obey, play well and we like. The true challenge, the merit, is being at the service of others, inspiring and believing in them, and applying the "fruitful insight" with them in particular. This is where the "sublime listening" acquires its authentic dimension. Tell me how you talk to and treat your worst player, the one who plays less, the one you dislike, and I will tell you about your leadership quality.

"Lucas' Land"

When my Club's technical director (let's say he is called Miguel) opened the morning paper and saw his manager's statements on the first page, he almost fell off his chair. "I didn't choose this playing staff. It's not my responsibility," the manager said. After reading the full interview, Miguel called me and said: "All right, know-all, tell me how the h*ll I can apply that 'sublime listening' we discussed in class". He was hurt and mad. Miguel felt betrayed by a manager he had hired barely two months ago to replace the first manager who had started the season. This second manager he knew him well because they had worked together with other teams in the past. Even though the results were not good, Miguel trusted the manager's skills.

"He will hear about it. I'm going to throw him out today! Better still, I am going to summon him to my office and call him every name in the book. Who does he think he is! What an ungrateful guy! What a coward! He is publicly accusing me of not knowing how to do my job. He is throwing me to the wolves. What a son of a gun! What a traitor!" After spending 20 minutes venting non-stop, I asked him who he wanted to be at that moment and whether he was willing to do an easy exercise to apply the "sublime listening" in this situation since it was perfect doing it.

Despite having more than enough reasons to feel unfairly and directly attacked by his manager (let's say he is called Lucas), I asked him if he considered it worth exploring his technician's reality with curiosity to understand him better before meeting up with him. From there, Miguel would feel in better shape to generate a *convers(a)ction* with Lucas, much better than a sermon, a ticking off or offending him in exchange. I was asking Miguel, by applying the "sublime listening", to take responsibility (partly) for his manager's inflammatory statements and become aware of the fact that Lucas may have felt vulnerable or offended because of all he was going through, reason why Lucas was instead asking and demanding Miguel's help. I was asking Miguel to be compassionate to have the possibility of choosing to put himself at Lucas' service and be the leader that the situation required.

As the brave student he was, Miguel accepted. I then asked him to close his eyes and invited him to walk in his manager's shoes, after having taken off his first. I also asked him to briefly suspend all his opinions, judgments, sentences and certainties that he had just spewed. It was not about giving them up nor defending them, just about suspending them to explore "Lucas' Land" with a new and clean look for a while. Miguel would be Lucas for some time and he would answer my questions from "Lucas' Land". Then Miguel would freely access the information he had about Lucas which he had not allowed himself to feel until that moment. The reason? All his own "truths" limited him. I gave him a few seconds to journey to "Lucas' Land" and, when he said he was already there, we began exploring the new territory. I asked him:

"Lucas, what is your daily life like in this city? What is the best part about it? How is your family adapting? How are your kids doing at school? How is your wife dealing with it? What do you feel passionate about in your job? What matters to you? What would you like to achieve here? What is your dream? What worries you? What is the worst part? How do you feel here? What is your greatest fear? What is the best thing you can provide this team? And the Club? What would you like to tell Miguel? What do you miss about him? What would you like to ask him? How would you like him to treat you? What would you like your relationship to be? What doesn't Miguel know about you? What do you need about him? Lucas, do you want to add anything else?"

Miguel spent the following 30 minutes answering my questions as if he was Lucas. When we finished, only silence remained. Miguel was Miguel again, he had put his shoes on and everything had changed. After exploring "Lucas Land" so honestly, his situation's interpretation and the manager's understanding changed. He did not feel harmed anymore. On the contrary, Miguel was almost embarrassed because he had not noticed so many clear things about Lucas' reality. Now he only wanted to call Lucas, meet him and help him. He thanked me and hung up.

The next time we saw each other, Miguel hugged me. He explained they had enjoyed a profoundly transformative conversation (a true *convers(a)ction*) in which he apologized because of his distance and Lucas apologized due to his clumsiness. Miguel said, since then, both the communication level between them and the relationship's quality had improved by two points. Miguel was enormously thankful and touched by his surprising discovery.

Miguel had more than enough reasons to act very differently and nobody could have blamed him for it. Lucas's statements were out of line and they questioned Miguel's professional competencies. He could have chosen to feel threatened and impulsively react by defending himself from the attack, but he chose something different. He chose to apply the "sublime listening", "listening to the right thing", calming his mind, being compassionate, humble and showing himself as a true leader at his manager's service. Wise choice.

Practice!

You may not be in such a conflictive situation as Miguel's, or you may be. Nonetheless, there is likely someone important in your life with which you would like to improve your relationship's quality. They may be a collaborator, a player, a parent, a CEO, a friend, or one of your children. Someone you care about. We shall do this simply; I invite you to walk in their shoes and visit "their Land". You will not do this from your Land's distance and judgments, but by travelling to theirs, entering it and accessing all the information you have about that person and their reality, which you do not allow yourself to access due to your opinions and certainties.

Have you chosen now the shoes you are going to walk in? Yes? Good. You can take yours off, leave some room and clean the path. Empty yourself and let yourself be surprised by everything you know of them that you were not even aware of. Now, from the "Land" you are exploring, go to the previous page to choose, adapt and answer some of the questions that I asked Miguel to recognize "Lucas Land". I hope you enjoy it!

Our "Land"

While taking into account that differences are an inevitable aspect of any group or collective, respect represents much more than tolerating or accepting differences. It means recognising and valuing them as well as those who are different. Exercising empathy with their players or collaborators may be one of the basic skills that a manager (or a boss) needs to develop to exercise efficient leadership, applying one of emotional intelligence's fundamental pillars.

If we translate this to football, we hear specific complaints often. For instance, the forward does not defend or move, the centre forward does not dare to or hides, the defense kicks the ball without aiming, the winger does not lap, the goalkeeper does not leave the goal, this player does what they want, the manager is so and so, etc. Everyone lives in "their Land", with different rules and expectations and, sometimes, opposite priorities. Every spot on a team, every person, every "Land" is an individual territory, independent and different, with its own beliefs, needs, fears and challenges.

When the system (team) learns to appreciate every "Earth's" creativity, diversity can become a powerful ally in the team's cohesion instead of being a threat to it. That way we can create a new "Shared Earth" that picks the best of everyone. Offering your players the possibility of discovering the happiness of having differences and developing respect and appreciation for the richness that exists in diversity is an unskippable step to achieving the magical transformation of a group into a team.

Other "Lands"

"Working as a team is not a virtue, it is a conscious and voluntary choice that appears when creating trust bonds based on human vulnerability that the team members show before their mistakes, fears and challenges".
PATRICK LENCIONI

At times I have worked with athletes groups that share a restroom and a t-shirt yet they are still far away from being and behaving like a team. In these situations, one of the dynamic activities I suggest to them is visiting "other Lands" to understand their mates' realities slightly better. To do that, I invite them to walk in the shoes of the position of the player they want to explore.

For example, if I am on a football field, I will ask the players to get in the goal. All the playing staff will get in it. Then, I will ask them to close their eyes and feel that all of them are, now and for a few seconds, the team's goalkeeper. Then, they will reply to my questions aloud. Any time we want to empathize we need to suspend all our judgments regarding that "Land" and allow ourselves to go in with a curious gaze to discover what is valuable inside and which we had not noticed.

Now, when everyone is walking in the goalkeeper's shoes, they are the goalkeeper and they start answering aloud from this "Land", without order but one at a time: *what is it like being here? What do you love about this Land? What is your greatest difficulty here? Who is your "saboteur"? What is the worst thing that can happen to you? What is good in this Land? What are the emotions here? How do you feel? If you were an animal, who would you be? What do you need from your teammates? What would you like to ask of them? What don't they know about you? What would you like them to know? What do you need from your manager? What would you like to ask him? What else is there in this Land?*

After answering and listening to all the answers, a deeper understanding of the goalkeeper happens. We understand his difficulties, fears, needs, and desires and his teammates' compassion toward him increases. They worry about him, they are more willing to help him, and they are more available. Next time the goalkeeper makes a mistake their answer will be very different.

We can visit all the positions we want, do it by lines, spots or by making use of any situation during the match or training to do this exercise, to walk in someone else's shoes. For instance, a regular reserve player. I shall share with you the answers that I heard while working on this dynamic with a team exploring the "team bench Land":

−What emotion is here?
−Envy, anguish, blame, disillusion, disappointment, despondency, annoyance, anger, excitement, hope, concern, fear, resentment, rebellion.

−What is the worst part of this "Land"?
−Not feeling the same when we win as when we lose, not helping, feeling like a failure, giving up and deserting you, feeling like a victim, useless, being unrecognized and unimportant.

−What do you fear here?
−I am afraid of going out on the field and not being up to the task, wasting my opportunity, feeling judged for some minutes, feeling asphyxiated just as I go out, not having the team the following season, not showing what I am, giving up and losing motivation, my family suffering, them thinking I am not good enough, playing and disappointing everyone, being affected personally.

−What motivates you? What does life offer you here?
−My passion for football, the challenge of overturning the situation, improving until I deserve to play, proving what I am capable of, having the discipline to not give up, the re-

spect for myself, helping the team in any situation, overcoming adversity and getting the best I have out.

—What do you need from your manager?
—Him talking to me, being honest and clear, telling me what I have to improve, asking and listening to me, making me feel I matter, acknowledging me some time, not only telling me what I do wrong, feeling him closer to me, giving me a chance and not punishing me if I don't do it well, treating me like a regular player...

—What do you ask from your players?
—Them making an effort, respecting me, walking in my shoes, not pulling faces when they are swapped and I have to go out, them being happy for me then, cheering and trusting me, them valuing their place in the team, making me feel useful and valuable.

By listening and understanding what they need, what they fear, what they have to offer or how my teammates and players feel, compassion increases and new acting possibilities open. These possibilities strengthen relationships, create shared visions, identify common values, illustrate the authentic compromise and design group action plans.

* * *

Sometime after finishing the "7**Ps**", one of my pupils, a businessman, came to me. He shared that right after finishing the workshop, he decided to put these dynamics into practice in his own company. He gathered the thirty people who were part of the company and he invited them to visit all the corporation's different departments.

Thus, he asked them to physically take off their shoes (having told them what this gesture meant) before walking in someone else's shoes. They began by sitting down near the entrance, where the receptionist was. She was the company's first face and voice, the woman responsible for picking up the phone, receiving and seeing the visitors, and listening to complaints and claims. They started asking questions to one another like the ones we have previously seen.

Every week, for two months, they explored a distinct "Land". They visited sales, marketing, production, design, finances, the legal department, the board of directors, clients, property, etc. They kept taking their shoes off before going deep into every one of these "Lands", with curiosity and respect, accomplishing until the unknown level of mutual understanding with results as revealing as they were surprising.

Both personal relations and communication notably improved and the conflict and criticism levels drastically decreased, which directly impacted the improvement of the working atmosphere, the productivity level and the company's income statement. The businessman excitedly told me how solidarity, respect, humility, kindness, service value and compassion had increased.

For the first time, they felt like a team. From that point onwards, the staff members were able to create a "shared Land" for everyone, in which every one of them felt listened to, understood, valued, acknowledged and important. Everybody committed to overcoming the difficulties they were going through together until achieving extraordinary results that, before the process, seemed impossible.

"Ubuntu"

An anthropologist suggested a game to the kids in an African tribe. He placed a basket full of fruits near a tree and he told them that whoever got there first would win all the fruits. When he gave the starting signal, all children took each other's hands, run together and then sat together to enjoy the prize. When the anthropologist asked them why they had done such a thing if only one of them could win, they replied: "How would one of us be happy then if all the others were sad?" That is "*Ubuntu*".

It is a South African ethical concept based on the most profound human values, focused on people's loyalty and relationships. Archbishop Desmond Tutu, Nobel Peace Prize winner, was the one who pushed the "*Ubuntu*" philosophy during his country's reconciliation process and spread it throughout the world. It has become so widespread nowadays that it has won many followers in many activity fields as well as in the sports world. It is an expanded concept of noble ideals which, when applied to a high-performance team, we could sum it up in this sentence: "I am because we are, otherwise I would be nothing". I cannot think of a better definition of a team.

During the 07-08 season, the Boston Celtics team, the most victorious and traditional franchise of the NBA, changed its historical yell of "*one, two, three... Celtics*" for "*one, two, three, 'Ubuntu'* ". This change happened because of this term's incorporation into the team's mysticism, recognized in the basketball world due to their great work as a team. When the manager, Doc Rivers, was informed of the signing of the two superstars Kevin Garnett and Ray Allen, he knew he had to establish special chemistry and disposition in the staff. He managed to do this through the "*Ubuntu*" ideology, leading the Celtics to their 17th Championship.

I talked with Unai Basurko, a prestigious Basque seafarer and "7Ps" pupil, and I asked him what *team* meant to him. He explained that he knew that his technically experienced and competent sailors had become his *crew (team)* when he observed simple details on the high seas. For instance, when a sailor went below deck for the water canteen to give it to those working on deck without being asked to. When he covered a mate with a blanket while on a stakeout during the night, prepared coffee for the one swapping shifts in the next shift, closed his book or switched off the light if he was asleep, etc. By appreciating these and other small details, Unai knew he had a crew to face the risky crossings they had to endure to achieve their demanding challenges.

That is "*Ubuntu*". They are small gestures and behaviour that every team member makes without needing anyone to ask them and not expecting anything in return. They are generous and humble behaviour a leader has to highlight, promote and recognize to help become aware that we are on the road to accomplishing the surprising transformation that goes from *group to team.*

My "Ubuntu" experience

The instant the team's captain started reading during the press conference the note in which we declared that day started our sit-in in the sports installations as a radical protest and condemnation measure because of our unstable situation after ten months without being paid and fed up with trickery, lies and fake promises, our manager and his staff, save someone who was by our side until the end, left the stadium. We were alone.

It was May, and despite our bleak economic situation and the dark omens regarding the Club's future, we had classified for the playoff to promotion to Second Division A. Uncertainty was huge, and we felt abandoned to fate. The only possibility of being promoted, being Córdoba and Castellón fearsome group rivals, and Mensajero as the season's revelation team. Our staff was made of a small team of veterans who earned three or four promissory notes every year (out of funds), and a troop of younger players who had their monthly salaries and had an easier time. They all rallied behind us and joined the initiative, assuming the risk of possible reprisals that sunk their blooming careers. Regardless, they still did it and their brave decision changed our destiny.

From that moment on, we started trusting each other while locked up in the restroom. We shared how the situation was every day in the gathering; suggestions, initiatives and ideas were proposed, and we were handed responsibilities and chores. All of us, regular and reserve players, veterans and rookies, started to feel listened to, understood, respected and valued. Little by little, happiness, good humor and laughter returned to a restroom that had forgotten them. We started to feel there might be hope for us and felt proud of belonging to this new team.

We fearlessly debuted in the playoff, full of faith and firmly convinced that we could do it during the first sit-in week. We won. That evening we celebrated it together, in the middle of the field, in the dark, under a myriad of stars. We sang, laughed and drank beer, with the pleasant sensation we were sharing a memorable experience to remember. We competed for the whole playoff feeling intensely wrapped up, supported and acknowledged by the people of Sestao. Sestao is a village located upon the left river bank of Bizcaya, hard-working, humble and caring people, proud and committed to our cause. Thanks to different initiatives and steps we managed to generate momentum and solution possibilities that kept us cheery and hopeful. We were more united and felt more confident, outside and inside the field.

Four regular players were missing when we had to play in the fourth playoff match and we had to replace them with reserve players. Their performance was extraordinary and we drew the match while visiting which brought us to the doors of promotion when there were still two matches left. (Today I know they performed that well because they felt their teammates' total trust during the sit-in).

Drawing the match was good enough for us when playing in Castellón. There could only be one. The public felt amazement and expectation due to our little miracle, and Castalia stadium was packed. Promotion and salvation or ruin and extinction. When the referee marked the end of the match with a 1-1 score, I felt profound, intimate and genuine satisfaction for having devoted myself to my teammates and team. I became aware that I had emptied myself and offered the best of myself during those six weeks. I found resources, skills and competencies I did not even know I had. At that moment, I was overwhelmed by a tremendous sensation of plenitude and immense gratitude toward all of them for having given me their trust, helping me be more aware, responsible and brave, and growing and improving.

During those special moments, we created a powerful bond that kept us closely united. We were "*Ubuntu*", we worried about each other, we cared, we swapped the *I* for *us* and we dared to behave with true humility, without feeling it like an obligation or sacrifice, but as a privilege. By doing this, we gave meaning to the word *team* ("I am because we are otherwise I would be nothing").

In this absolute devotion context, we were brave to share our doubts and fears, we were open, available and vulnerable. We stopped judging each other and we started listening, accepting and understanding the others. We were at the service of everyone. *We all were at the team's service.* Thus, everyone's authentic compromise appeared with uncontrollable force from this unbreakable union adversity's face. This compromise is the great hidden gift we all have inside and we look forward to offering it when suitable conditions appear.

Together we found out what we were capable of and we transformed into a team that deserved to accomplish extraordinary deeds.

In my opinion, the unforgettable memory we all share was not the promotion (the cherry on top). It was finding out how we were capable of breaking our limits, achieving impossible goals, facing difficulties with courage and firmness, bringing out everyone's best, overcoming our "saboteurs", and being surprisingly courageous. This is how we managed it, holding hands, "*Ubuntu*". (I shall use these lines to thank and acknowledge Aitor, Juanlu, Maixi, Karmo, Basti, Ramón, Alvaro, Gorka S., Javi, Gotzon, Alvaro, Joseba, Gaizko, Jon S., Jon N., "Kali", Danielo, Gorka G., Jorge and Luis for that unforgettable experience).

Twenty years after that promotion, a "7Ps" pupil, currently a manager and with whom I had the pleasure of sharing that sublime moment, gifted me this acknowledgment. He did it publicly, so I shall share it with you:

"Twenty years ago, you led a group of players and together we managed for "real" things to happen. Generosity, courage and humility were the values we shared, which supported us in overcoming all those adversities until we achieved such a remarkable result. Thank you, I know I did not thank you then, but your attitude changed my life".

emPathizing in 7 pills

1. If you have to serve to lead, *humility* may be the essential leadership value. Acting with humility does not involve behaving like you are less than you are, but thinking first about others and not yourself. You have to be very brave to admit you are humble.

2. We connect with humility through *empathy*, that increases our understanding of others and their reality. This way, we show authentic curiosity and worry for them and their lives, overcoming the layers below which their true essence hides, allowing us to offer more suitable answers together with generating new *convers(a)ctions*.

3. To em**P**athise, I need to take off my shoes and suspend all my "truths" for a while. I will not cling to my truths nor reject them. I will free myself from my judgments, opinions and certainties before walking in someone's shoes to explore "their Land" with fresh eyes. We have changed and are willing to put ourselves at their service when we put our shoes back on.

4. Applying "sublime listening" helps me not feel attacked by comments or actions of people who may have felt offended or vulnerable because of my attitude. From this superior listening level ("listening to the right thing") compassion appears. *Empathy in action* is the value which makes us wiser, more conscious, humbler and better leaders.

5. The leaders' challenge is being at the rebels' service, of those the leader dislikes, who are annoying, and also applying the "fruitful insight" on them. Then "sublime listening" acquires its actual dimension.

6. *Respect* is much more than tolerance or acceptance. It means recognizing differences and valuing them along with those who are different. Working on your empathy with your players or collaborators and your team offers the possibility of finding happiness and appreciation for the richness that exists in *diversity* as a previous and essential step to achieving the magical transformation from *group* to *team*.

7. When a group's members worry about each other, take care of one another, change the I for us and dare to behave with genuine humbleness, thinking about the team before themselves, then they transform into "*Ubuntu*". This inspiring team definition ("I am because we are. Otherwise I would be nothing") will allow them to achieve unbelievable results.

PROCESSING

"What you resist, persists, and what you accept, you can transform".

SUFI PROVERB

Emotions, feelings and moods

Emotion is the automatic and involuntary organism's chemical answer to a certain stimulus or event. On the other hand, *feeling* means connecting that emotion with reason, giving it awareness, which can lead to a mood with enough time. *Emotions* are related to how we react to events, and we cannot avoid nor choose them, whereas moods determine the behaviours we show. Regardless of being aware or not, we are always in a particular *mood* that we cannot choose nor control, which defines our behaviour, opening or closing action possibilities.

"We can say we have emotions, although moods really have us and become our own moods. By the time we observe them, we already are sunk in them". This sentence is what Rafael Echevarría states in his treatise *Ontología del lenguaje (Language's Ontology)*. We are not responsible for feeling emotions nor being in moods, but we are for the time we decide to remain in them. We need to realize that the mood we are for competition determines our performance.

It is said that sports are a mood. If this is true, what is the value of those leaders able to create transformative mood conversations, both individually and collectively? And what are the skills needed to develop the ability to redesign new possibilities generating moods? In this chapter, we will try to offer some tips that help us find adequate answers to these questions.

Emotional alphabets

The consulting room of a psychologist I know is full of papers with emoticons on the wall. Those faces represent all sorts of emotions and we use them to complete our messages, WhatsApp texts, emails, etc. When I asked him why he had that curious décor, he answered that the younglings had trouble recognising their own emotions. He was using images as a resource to help children learn to identify, name and express them. They are not the only ones who suffer this lack, however.

The first time I ask how are they doing, to all the athletes I work with or to our workshop students, be it due to shyness, lack of habit or vocabulary scarcity, I receive similar answers, "good" or "bad" ("fu**ed" when we are in a colloquial situation). Few bits of information, though I guess it is something. When I ask the same thing to my teenage daughters, they give me even fewer clues and reply with a brief "meh".

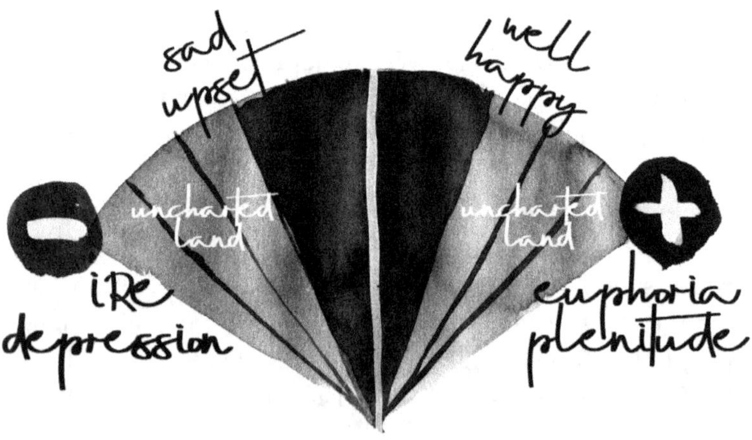

If we had an open emotional range in which we could identify and gather all existing emotions, we would place "meh" in the center. From there to the right side of the range and from a lesser to a greater impact, we could name the *positive emotions* (a mistaken classification since emotions are neither good nor bad, but this division is helpful to establish the idea). To the left side, we would name the negative ones with the same criteria. From the center of the range, going a bit to the right side to reach *good/happy* and going a bit to the left side with *bad/sad*, we would find the narrow emotional range in which we move through easily and we can feel with a certain ease. Like all other emotions, as we get closer to the extremes, the difficulty increases until it becomes uncharted, hostile and dangerous territory.

This is how things are; we become emotional illiterates. Due to our upbringing and culture, we refuse to discover and connect with our inside world, and we hide it as if we were ashamed of it, of having emotions and feelings. Some beliefs that determine our erratic behaviour still matter. "Truths" of the sort "crying is for the weak", "men don't cry", "showing your feelings makes you vulnerable", "decisions are made with your head", etc. They reinforce this limiting belief and turn us into "emotionally constipated people". We are unable to recognize and deeply know ourselves, adequately express ourselves and listen to our informative bodies.

Identifying emotions

There are hundreds of emotions. It is said there are more emotions and their variations than words to express them. Experts do not seem to agree to define the primary emotions from which all others generate, nor how to classify them. This is why we will use Daniel Goleman's work, a model at a worldwide level in this area and the author of the bestseller *Emotional Intelligence*) to present a valid classification that helps us achieve our goal: learning to process emotions and transform moods.

Goleman defines eight primary emotions from which others come. These families of emotions derive from the first ones, as he believes it is useful to think of emotions as groups of especially relevant cases of the infinite shades of our emotional life. Every family groups together around a fundamental nucleus from which the rest derive. A possible classification:

- ANGER: rage, annoyance, rebelliousness, jealousy, irritability, hostility, aggressiveness, resentment, rancor, wrath, fury, exasperation, indignation, indifference, frustration, obstinacy, bloody-mindedness, animosity, hate, violence, etc.

- SADNESS: affliction, sadness, distress, apathy, disappointment, disillusion, pessimism, melancholy, boredom, desolation, helplessness, reluctance, dejection, nostalgia, dissatisfaction, loneliness, pain, mourning, suffering, weariness, dismay, laziness, despair, bitterness, coldness, emptiness, depression, etc.

- FEAR: worry, doubt, anxiety, apprehension, uncertainty, dismay, distress, concern, confusion, distrust, insecurity, impotence, resentment, uneasiness, nervousness, anguish, scare, phobia, panic, terror, etc.

- HAPPINESS: joy, delight, fun, dignity, relaxation, pleasure, motivation, pride, satisfaction, optimism, enthusiasm, ecstasy, euphoria, passion, plenitude, feeling alive, awake, etc.

- LOVE: acceptance, affection, trust, security, attachment, closeness, connection, harmony, calm, kindness, tenderness, serenity, compassion, feeling valuable, important, recognized, grateful, forgiven, patient, empathic, brave, quiet, adored, at peace, liberated, in love, complete, hopeful, wanted, loved, etc.

- SURPRISE: startle, wonder, curiosity, interest, intrigue, perplexity, bewilderment, admiration, stupor, terror, etc.

- AVERSION: contempt, indifference, pettiness, disgust, antipathy, disgust, repudiation, rejection, repugnance, etc.

- EMBARRASSMENT: discomfort, remorse, humiliation, regret, ridicule, feeling persecuted, accused, observed, singled out, criticized, rejected, prosecuted, etc

In this catalogue, we have identified more than 180 emotions (I have dared to include a few that were not in Goleman's classification). It is nothing more than a list, but as we said in the previous chapter, language creates reality and every emotion takes us to a different place with a different impact and intensity. Every emotion needs to be identified and named to recognize it and take care of its existence. This way, we will express it properly, and accept and transform it if necessary.

This is one of the aspects I spend more time on in my *convers(a)ctions* with athletes, and that is linked directly to their emotional intelligence development. This is a section from our upbringing/education that is not trained adequately, which causes us to behave like "emotionally incompetent people" with terrible consequences in our lives and relationships. If you believe this is not your case, I shall share another seven noteworthy features of the "emotionally incompetent person" so that you can auto-evaluate yourself:

1. They always want to be right.
2. They search for a culprit for everything that happens.
3. They always play the victim.
4. They are an expert in excuses and justifications.

5. They are a professional pessimist and they behave like a critic and realist.
6. They are very susceptible and get angry with ease.
7. They live deep in distrust.

How many of these features do you relate to? That many? Congratulations! As we said in this chapter's subtitle, "what you accept you can transform". You are not hopeless.

While in a *convers(a)ction*, I encourage others to tune to their emotional dial, helping them identify and name which emotions they feel, what their mood is and what their body is telling them. This way we create an instant of stillness and presence so that they can become aware of how they are feeling before moving on to other matters, or lingering for a while if they need more room and time. It seems clear that feeling concern is not the same as feeling anguish, fear, panic, or being scared to death. It is not the same feeling sorrowful as feeling melancholic, sad, depressed or desperate. Being happy, enthusiastic, euphoric or *"on fire"* do not match either.

Once, when I asked a player I knew he was going to be up to the task of the process we were in how he was doing, instead of replying "well" or "happy", he thought about it and replied: "I feel on fire". I was quite curious about his answer, so I kept asking him how that felt, where he felt it, and what that sensation reminded him of. I ended up asking him: *what is possible for you from there?* "Nothing is impossible!" What are you capable of while on fire? "I am capable of anything". Then he proceeded to excitedly and confidently tell me the series of actions he planned on doing in the following weeks. Being "well/happy" is not the same as being "on fire". Nor is the same as expressing, feeling and becoming aware of what new horizon of possibilities this mood creates.

Sometimes, when people ask me what coaches do, I like answering that I consider myself a "positive mood catalyzer" for the people and teams I work with. An interpretation rebuilder. A story cocreator. By transforming moods, I become a generator of new spaces from which I can act, spaces previously inaccessible to me. I love this part of my job.

Feeling emotions

We generally have little contact with our emotional world, which is why it sometimes is blocked. Nobody has taught us to manage emotions properly so we are afraid of feeling. It seems like a dangerous and sinister world to us. We keep thinking that some emotions are "bad" or "negative" and we repress them. We do not allow ourselves to feel them because we believe they will hurt us. We have a hard time accepting that we constantly feel emotions; most of them have little impact on our bodies and attitude. Some are positive and connect us with enthusiasm, joy and confidence, pushing us to action and opening new possibilities. Others are awkward, even if necessary, and we cannot ignore them because they exist. They are there and have a lot of information and learning to offer.

The effect of repressing and refusing to acknowledge or feel these negative emotions is that we tend to avoid those situations, people, decisions and relationships that cause them. We pay no attention to the messages our body keeps sending us because we try to hide the pain we erroneously think they will generate. Thus, our world of possibilities grows smaller. Every time we dare to expose ourselves less, we are afraid of being vulnerable. Little by little, we keep distancing ourselves from life creating a shell based on alcohol, drugs, medicine, and passing pleasure so as not to feel.

As doctor Jeanne Segal, an expert in emotional intelligence claims: "All emotions provide us with important information. We must learn to avoid the fear of feeling. When someone feels comfortable while being emotionally uncomfortable, they can remember the emotionally painful facts without being beaten. It is possible to endure the current emotions until the pain is gone and the message is delivered. This way, we are not only able of enduring the emotional experience but of leaving it with more energy, deeply relaxed and with a greater sensation of achievement and self-control". We have a hard time accepting emotions are part of the natural human functioning. It is not a sickness symptom. On the contrary, someone complete, creative and full of resources (an "acorn") has full access to their emotions. Our feelings provide us with a way to express ourselves. Although this process can be very liberating, if we do not allow our bodies to release and discover what they are keeping inside, we will not grow.

Processing emotions

When speaking of processing emotions, I am not referring to controlling or handcuffing them. Instead, I refer to letting them and observing them (like we did with our thoughts in the first chapter) without mistaking them. We know they are not us, but they are a part of ourselves. They need room to express themselves. We shall let emotions flow freely through our bodies without repressing, avoiding, judging and not being ashamed of feeling them. Processing emotions means becoming aware that hurtful things will keep happening in my life, even though I will not add the additional suffering of resisting what is happening.

Two days after Barcelona FC lost the final of the 2014 Copa del Rey, I heard Andrés Iniesta state this: "If it hasn't gone well, you feel bad and cry. Then you get up and keep going". Emotions may hurt. However, our interpretation that generates additional and unnecessary suffering is what harms us.

On top of the performance impact and decrease, emotional instability also increases the possibility of getting injured. As Dr Nelson Torres claimed, "our bodies yell what the mouth does not say". Processing means listening to our bodies and paying attention to our emotions in all their dimension, identifying and recognizing them. Being able to express them and stop fighting or denying them. When I finally learn to accept my emotions, my body is freed and starts leaving room to transform them.

Accepting them is feeling how they come and go through my body without resisting. This prevents them from getting stuck there and blocked, limiting, belittling me and making me feel afraid of feeling. I will hardly be able to help my players and teams process and transform their emotions if I cannot handle mine.

I have slowly learned to feel comfortable with others' hard, negative or awkward emotions. I do not get anxious anymore when someone expresses their feelings, nor do I blame myself for not knowing how they feel or calming or stopping their emotions. On the contrary, I now feel privileged for helping them by creating a safe space that allows me to feel what they feel without having to justify or rationalize it. Now I do not feel attacked when someone expresses an emotion, even if sometimes they do it aggressively or improperly. Nor do I get defensive, and I do not tell them how they should feel. I have learnt to bear emotions without evaluating, approving or discrediting them. Now I know how to help them feel more deeply, to express and transform their moods. It will depend on the occasion, but when I do this, I get closer to the compassionate and obliging leader I want to be.

Maintaining emotions

> *"The most beautiful people I have met are those that have known defeat, struggle, suffering, and loss and have managed to find the way to get out of the depths. These people have an appreciation, sensibility and understanding of life that fills them with compassion, humility and profound loving interest. Beautiful people do not come from nowhere".*
> ELISABETH KÜBLER-ROSS

We can use the rappelling from the depths of a well metaphor for those situations in which we feel difficult or negative emotions. We can imagine ourselves being trapped down there, at the bottom of the hole, struggling to get out, resisting staying down there in pain. We climb its walls losing our nails without making progress. We are frustrated, uncomfortable and ashamed because we cannot get out. We do not understand that is what we must do, stay there for a while and learn something before getting out and going our way.

When we are trapped down the well, we feel pain and hard and awkward emotions we must process by decoding the message they have for us. These emotions reflect our inner world and inform us through our body of how we interpret what is happening around us. Our body can only relax and calm itself down with its objective achieved when it comprehends that we have understood the emotion's implicit message.

If we want to leave the well we need to lighten the load by getting rid of the emotions that are weighing us down by expressing them, freeing our body and leaving room for other experiences and situations that will help us transform and generate new emotions. Sometimes we need help to leave the pit and keep going. We need someone who tosses a rope at us from the top of the well to support us, establishing a trust bond that generates a safe space where we can feel listened to and understood.

Pulling the rope

We can use the rappelling from the depths of a well metaphor for those situations in which we feel difficult or negative emotions. We can imagine ourselves being trapped down there, at the bottom of the hole, struggling to get out, resisting staying down there in pain. We climb its walls losing our nails without making progress. We are frustrated, uncomfortable and ashamed because we cannot get out. We do not understand that is what we must do, stay there for a while and learn something before getting out and going our way.

When we are trapped down the well, we feel pain and hard and awkward emotions we must process by decoding the message they have for us. These emotions reflect our inner world and inform us through our body of how we interpret what is happening around us. Our body can only relax and calm itself down with its objective achieved when it comprehends that we have understood the emotion's implicit message.

If we want to leave the well we need to lighten the load by getting rid of the emotions that are weighing us down by expressing them, freeing our body and leaving room for other experiences and situations that will help us transform and generate new emotions. Sometimes we need help to leave the pit and keep going. We need someone who tosses a rope at us from the top of the well to support us, establishing a trust bond that generates a safe space where we can feel listened to and understood.

When are down there suffering and someone tosses a rope, we can then dare to express how we feel. However, whoever is grabbing it from above feels as uncomfortable with our intense emotion as we are. Their natural reaction is pulling us to get us out of there as quickly as possible. Those helping us do not understand that is not their role; they just have to hold the rope so that we can slowly climb out of there with their help until we reach the exit. We can only do this when we have processed our emotions properly.

A Mexican manager, a "7Ps" pupil, wrote to tell me that one of his players, an 18-year-old football player with huge international relevance, had burst his knee and was suffering a very grave injury. After undergoing a complicated surgery, the manager visited him in the hospital. The young man came from a numerous and humble family and his future as a professional football player was their hope to change their future. The manager told me his player was alone when he got to his room. The boy's depression, anguish, sadness and fear of not playing again were such that, when he asked the boy how he was doing, the young man started talking but he could not continue because he began crying inconsolably. This is what the manager wrote to me:

> *"I got so nervous because of his sorrow that my reaction was to keep speaking for the whole 45 minutes I spent with him. I tried to cheer him up, telling him to calm down and to stop crying. I assured him he would play again soon, everything would be the same or better and the situation would make him stronger. He looked at me in silence, forcing himself to smile politely from time to time, until another visitor came at last and I could say goodbye. I admit I felt relieved.*
>
> *I am writing to you because some days ago after this event, I did the "P" of Processing workshop with you and I felt like banging my head against the wall. In that workshop, I became aware that it was not him who was awkward when crying and genuinely expressing how he felt. It was me. It was I who could not deal with those*

tough emotions. Instead of supporting him, creating a privileged space so that he could vent and express what was happening to him, I started pulling the rope with all my strength. Instead of letting him unload his body intensely feeling his emotions, I made him ashamed of feeling like that. I forced him to repress himself. I took his space from him. I was unable to put myself at his service.

I returned to the hospital two days later. I apologised because of my previous behaviour, I tossed him the rope and held it like a champion. It was an incredibly transformative conversation, even for me. I felt great and I wanted to thank you and share it with you."

Thanks to you.

Going down the well

Other times, the reaction of those who toss the rope at us when they start listening to us is letting go of it. They show solidarity with us and go down the well to comfort and hug us. They also feel uncomfortable with our emotions: "I understand you perfectly, I also feel the same, you have all the right to feel that way, I am going to tell you what happened to me". They share similar comments that value and evaluate my emotions (approving them in this case), but they want me to stop, they do not want me feeling this way. I do not need that either. I need them to empathise with me and understand my emotion. They should not feel it like it was theirs, just to connect with it without submerging in it. Now having no rope, how are we going to exit the well?

Letting the rope go

Lastly, it can also happen that someone who initially tossed the rope at us decides to let go and leave because they do not consider our emotions valid. They judge and reject them. They leave us there, feeling worse than we were at the start, ashamed of having shown vulnerability and guilty because we felt that emotion. They say things like: *"you deserve it, it can't be that bad, it's your fault, you shouldn't feel this way, you never listen to me, I told you so"* It is necessary to highlight that awkward and negative emotions are not the only ones that need their room to be expressed and supported. The exaggeratedly positive ones also need that room, and we do not feel particularly comfortable with them either. How often does someone tell us about a remarkable achievement or something they are proud of and we immediately drag them down when we feel too much emotion in them. Some of the things we tell them are: "do not get cocky, these things turn quickly, don't get cocky because sports have no memory, don't be too proud because there's a lot of envy around". This way we keep deflating the balloon until their euphoria level decreases and they get closer to a more restrained emotion, like "good" or "happy", we can live with easily. Once again, when we act like this, awkward and unable to maintain an emotion, we stop others from intensely living their own experience and we take their emotional learning and discovery. We almost make them feel guilty for feeling that well and invite them to repress their excessive happiness. At the same time, we so wisely (ironic mode ON) remind them not to get too excited because the fall will be even worse. We behave in this way on too many occasions. We are emotionally incompetent. You only need to hold the rope, not pull, go down or let go of the rope through which the emotions we want to help them process have to flow.

Emotions and Metaphors

It is not easy discussing emotions, not only because of our difficulty in allowing us to feel but also because feelings are indescribable. We cannot talk about them with absolute accuracy, we cannot describe what they are like, although it does not mean we cannot identify and name them, nor it is not possible going deep into them.

Poetry is an art that deals with exploring and expressing emotions and feelings by using it in a lofty way with metaphors, among other figures. Metaphors, like tales, fables, stories or legends, help us take distance from these emotions and observe them from the outside as if they were not ours. They allow us to play with images instead of words and get us closer to the subconscious where the unspeakable emotions dwell and those we do not allow ourselves to feel and keep locked under lock and key.

Sometimes, when we want to help someone who has difficulty expressing how they feel, we can use metaphors as a powerful resource to ease the experience. They will help us feel emotions more intensely and deeply in our bodies so that they flow and we can transform them. From a high presence level, connection and respect for those we have before us, we ask them to help them take emotions from the mind toward the body, which is what feels them. We stop talking about our emotions and begin feeling them. This is the only way our body can deliver us the message and learn all that the emotion-generating experience has for us.

After identifying, recognizing and naming the emotion, we ask them: *how it is, where they are feeling it, how strong it is, what their shape/color/size is, what that emotion looks like, if they could choose a metaphor that embodied that emotion, which one would it be?*

"Where are you now?"

Some years ago, during a training workshop I attended as a pupil under Sir John Withmore, I looked to my right when he proposed the dynamic in which we had to work in pairs and I recognised a famous writer I had just read his last work. I wanted to duck out because drawing is not one of the 1000 things I do best, and I did not want someone I admire checking my uselessness in such matters.

Regardless, he raised his eyebrows and invited me with a smile, so we sat together to complete the exercise. It was about replying with drawings to three simple questions –*Where do you come from? Where are you now? Where are you going?* A mere trifle. Aside from remembering my colleague was gifted in that regard, I can only remember the doodles with which we replied to the second question: where are you? His was an imperial eagle who had taken refuge in a mountain's crest; it was experimenting a profound renovation process, tearing the remains of its eroded claws to leave room for others to grow that allowed to keep it connected to its eagle essence. His drawing and the emotion that filled him when he shared it captivated me. Allowing himself to deeply experience the emotion and his courage to express it before a stranger also impacted me.

We were so absorbed by his metaphor that he had taken up nearly all the available time. When my turn came and I showed him my drawing, I discovered I had doodled a desert. I could not believe it myself. I started explaining my representation and began feeling that intense emotion inspired by my colleague's example. Then the facilitator announced time had run out and we were moving on. I clung to that drawing for a while. I felt awkward and uneasy, but the need to be present in that privileged workshop made me shelve the issue for the time being.

Back home, while driving to my office in the morning, with my wife, she asked what had been the best thing about Withmore's workshop. I started telling her about that dynamic and mentioned with laughter my drawing of the desert. I discussed it without going too deep when she asked me: *How do you feel in the desert?*

I felt as if she had unclogged a long-ago disabled tap. Suddenly and fiercely, I shed tears down my face with a feeling of sorrow I did not even know where it was coming from. I had to pull up on the verge because I was crying rivers. I had connected with the deep anguish of that change and transformation moment. I felt alone and lost. I did not know where I was, where I was going and I did not know what to do. Thirsty, hungry, burnt-out and about to give up, I became aware that I was down a well and she had tossed me a rope to support me. She was calm and present, very connected to me. She took her time and did not pull nor let go of the rope, supporting all emotions and creating a haven so that I could feel, recognize, identify, name and express what was happening. Not feeling awkward with my emotions, she did not make me explain them, nor did she judge them or make me feel guilty. She just listened and helped me experience my emotions more deeply, asking with curiosity and calm about the desert's metaphor.

What is the sand like? How intense is the light? And the desert's colors? What are the days like? And the nights? What are you doing there? What is your daily life like? How do you feel? Where do you feel it? What is the worst part? What did that sensation remind you of? What is the sky like? And the stars? Can you hear anything? What is it like listening in silence? Is there anyone else with you? Who are they? What are they doing? What are they saying? What would a nomad do in that situation? Is there any oasis, a break?

What scares you about that desert? What is good for you in that desert? What are you discovering about yourself? What have you learnt? What are you bringing back from that desert? What is different now? And now, what is that sensation like?

For half an hour and with my eyes closed, I enjoyed a deeply transformative conversation. I observed myself from afar, accepting myself and allowing my body to shake off emotions I had resisted for a long time and had me completely blocked. It was a very liberating process, as if I had grown an inch after that experience that changed my mood, enhanced my eyesight and generated new possibilities of change to face the process of profound transformation I was dealing with by then. Thanks to my wife, who knew how to hold an invaluable gift.

Moods

What starts like an *emotion* linked to a particular event (be it a fact or a crucial situation, after giving it awareness and sifting it through reason) can become a feeling. This feeling may become a mood if it remains with us long enough and goes to the background from which we act. Everyone is always in a specific disposition, even though we do not even realise it on too many occasions, and resign because we do not see a way of changing it. All athletes know that mood determines performance and, were they able to transform it, so would be their expectations and results.

In this chapter, I would like you to become aware of the power of *convers(a)ctions* as tools to modify moods, as well as the range of possibilities associated, of what is and is not possible in every moment. Depending on the spirits we find ourselves we may turn into one or another reality observer.

The way we tell our story to ourselves is not what generates a certain mood. Instead, our interpretation of reality arises from the emotional state we find ourselves in. If I change my mood, my world and its possibilities change along it. Therefore, if we wish to modify our mood, we need to change the observer we are, permanently going over our reality judgments and interpretations.

The Chilean biologist Humberto Maturana claims: "conversations are not just a linguist phenomenon, but a combination of two basic factors: language and emotions". Leaders know the power of language to modify emotions and, thus, redefine what is possible. What was possible at the start of a conversation is not necessarily the same when ending it. They can transform, design and rub off on their teams a new possibility and action horizon-generating mood from this new emotional watchtower.

Winning duet

In May 2012, the Europe League final against Atlético de Madrid football club was held in Bucharest. Thirty-six years had passed since the only European final had been played and lost by Athletic Club against Juventus.

After a spectacular and unforgettable season, and thanks to Marcelo Bielsa, Athletic Club was about to play the first of two finals in fifteen days. The big red-and-white family had been waiting for so long and the team had generated such expectation throughout Europe that the huge emotional pressure was too much for the players and overtook them to the point of transforming them into a blocked, unrecognizable team incapable of facing "Cholo" Simeone's powerful group. Inevitably this translated into a defeat and terrible disappointment. That black Wednesday the tears shed by the

Athletic players also flooded Bizcaya. We all shared the pain and distress of our broken dream.

The second the match ended, the team's fans threw themselves onto it. They sent thousands of support messages, hoping the playing staff would quickly recover to play the second and imminent final. It all happened too soon. A million people pulled the rope together to take players out of the well where they needed to be at that moment. They needed to adequately **P**rocess the emotional tsunami they were experiencing. After that cruel defeat, it was likely that doubts, insecurity, distrust, the fear of losing again and not being up to the task, not to mention sorrow, disappointment, frustration, rage, guilt, distress, and physical, mental and emotional exhaustion would be present in that changing room. There probably was a lot of pain, as it happens every time we suffer an irreparable defeat. That long-awaited title would not be back. That hurt a lot. Turning over a new leaf was not possible.

"How do you expect to cheer up your players after such a defeat?" a reporter asked the Argentinean manager in the press conference after the defeat. *"Having another final in fifteen days is reason enough to recover. Whoever is not able to do it cannot call themselves athletes"*, replied Bielsa. But it was not enough. They kept training at a very quick pace the two weeks before the second final. Maybe it was time for something else.

Perhaps it was time to elect a leader at the team's service to recognize, share and express how everyone felt, to express what was happening to them and how that loss was affecting them. They needed a private moment to process emotions; not a moment to reflect and analyze the match, fix their mistakes or know the players' opinions and explanations on why they had lost. All those essential matters would have their place and time.

Perhaps they should have generated a privileged and safe haven for everyone, coach staff and players alike. An area without judgments or criticism, where nobody had to rationalize or justify their feelings. A space where they just allowed themselves to connect, observe, feel and accept those painful emotions until they could unload and free their bodies before refueling to be in the best shape to play a new final.

Maybe what the leader had to do was to facilitate a new *convers(a)ction* with their team, being present and at their players' service, listening, em**P**athizing with them and walking in their shoes. Understanding them without judgment, asking them to express and feel more deeply, **P**rocessing and sustaining emotions, **P**romoting to connect them again with the essential values that identified that team and **P**ositivising in order to discover new reality interpretations that generate enthusiasm and excitement. In short, using the power of *convers(a)ctions* to change a suffering and resignation mood into another one of ambition –a creator of new possibilities and previously inaccessible actions.

I suspect this task was not in the competencies arsenal of the unforgettable and incomparable Marcelo Bielsa. The emotional skills needed to develop this activity were not the highlight of his leadership style. Fifteen days later, the team's soul was still clinging to Bucharest. The players that went out onto the Vicente Calderón football field did not compete against Guardiola's legendary Barcelona FC. Missing in action from minute one, Athletic Club gave up the match and title without offering resistance.

Nowadays, and not only in the sports world, we need emotionally wise and competent leaders.

Vulnerability

In the leadership world, in any activity area, people still assume that showing one's vulnerability is a sign of weakness a respectable leader cannot afford without understanding that one needs great bravery and courage to do so. Many beliefs and "saboteurs" confirm this "truth". Aside from some that we have shown at the beginning of this chapter, we could add: "life is tough", "there is no room for weakness", "eat or be eaten", "do not show mercy", "if they see you weak they will go after you", "this is the jungle", "if you show them how you are, they will not accept you", "they will see you are not good enough".

All these "truths" awake our shame, our fear of being unable to connect, not being accepted or worthy of love and belonging. This is a universal epidemic. Connections with others give meaning to our lives. If leadership is based on a powerful bond with our followers, we must show ourselves. That superior connection level is an honor reserved for the genuine people who allow themselves to be who they are, those who accept themselves as imperfect human beings who also appear close, open, available and without hiding their fears, doubts and feelings.

Shining and accepting our light does not mean hiding our darkness. We all are in a permanent struggle, we suffer and feel pain, even though only the authentic ones dare to express it. They know that everything that makes them vulnerable is what transforms them into beautiful, unique and valuable human beings. They are brave to commit themselves without any guarantees because they know that is where all their strength to connect deeply with their followers lies, achieving amazing leadership impact that way. The big paradox is when we see someone being vulnerable and overcoming shame, all we perceive is strength, bravery and inspiring courage instead of weakness.

Those who lead from the limiting belief that identifies *vulnerability* with *weakness* will have notable difficulties expressing their emotions and will be unable to support others and transform their moods. It will be quite hard for them to em**P**athise (shame's best vaccine), acknowledge others honestly, generate enthusiasm, create inspiring and shared visions with their teams, be curious to ask and listen, be grateful, admit their mistakes and generate compromise with their teams. Besides, others' perception of them will be of a distant boss, distrusting, uninterested in others, unwilling to listen, authoritarian, intolerant and inflexible, someone who causes antipathy and rejection in their surroundings, which will remind them of a despot or tyrant.

True *leaders at others' service* need to have the courage (from Latin core = heart) to, instead of always saying what they think, express what they feel more often. They need to dare to speak from the bottom of their hearts and say: "I don't know", "I need your help", "I can't do this alone", "thank you", "I admire what you're doing", "I'm afraid of...", "I feel...", "I'm worried about...", "I am sorry, forgive me", "I recognize my mistake", etc. They need to show themselves for real otherwise, they will not be connected to their team.

Connecting with our vulnerability does not involve going head-on constantly and everywhere, nor does it involve permanently whining or playing the victim. Not at all. It just means recognizing we are imperfect human beings with weak points who commit mistakes, feel uncomfortable emotions, suffer the embarrassment and fear of showing ourselves, and think that others consider us not good enough. Regardless, we should feel grateful that all this is part of our nature. It is what we are and makes us feel alive and powerful and we do not need to hide it to be worthy of the love we deserve.

Transforming Moods

We have reached the end of the chapter, the decisive moment of putting into practice all the skills seen until this moment to generate a privileged space to transform spirits. When you perceive a dense, awkward and hard emotional atmosphere blocking your team's performance that, before being transformed, it needs to be expressed, you will have to dare expose yourself and be courageous enough to be open and vulnerable and allow yourself to share "something real" with them. Something that does not grow from your head but your heart.

I shall offer you a real example of a mood-transforming experience carried out by a manager and his team. He was a "7**P**s" former pupil, and he had to face a situation full of emotions that they had to express and a very limiting mood in the changing room. To develop this experience and ease this *convers(a)ction*, he applied the skills and competencies of the first six "**P**s" we have seen. For context, his team was a professional team that had not been paid adequately for five months and was at their limit. Before the *convers(a)ction*, they did not see another way out save stopping the training and playing during the season. The changing room's emotional tension was about to overflow with unpredictable consequences.

"They feel rather worried and anxious. Some players have difficulties paying rent and their children's schools. They are doubtful about the club's future and the signed contracts. The club is likely to disappear and leave them without any money. Some players are asking their parents for money to survive. They feel extremely distrustful and angry. Too many unfulfilled promises and expectations generate resentment, bitterness and suffering. They feel fear. This is the situation".

I ask you to imagine YOU are the story's manager. Remember that life and sports are "things that happen" and that is where one of the leader's main responsibilities lies: being able to search for other interpretations of reality and design a different mood in a critical situation like this one. This mood should generate new possibilities and actions that did not exist before nor were possible before the conversation (they could only think of quitting until then). Remember that your objective is not fixing the collection problem –that is above you and out of your control–. Your goal is to ease a *convers(a)ction* to stop the general mood from blocking other decisions (other than stopping playing and training), helping them discover a new reality observer that strengthens the group during adversity and opens new action possibilities.

The key to success in this conversation is in you. You will be the one who defines this dynamic's authenticity level and impact. If you dare to connect with your emotions and express them, if you allow yourself to do it honestly and sincerely, if you show your vulnerability and put yourself at their service suspending all your judgments, truths and absolute certainties for a while, I am sure all will be fine.

We shall define the following sentences that will be your reference to face this conversation with guarantees of success. You do not have to improvise it since you can prepare it beforehand:

1. ***Presence* and connection**
   The first essential requisite is having total **Presence**. Before saying anything, you have to sit down, *look* and *see* everyone's faces and check they can all *look* and *see* one another. Look at everyone in the eye, slowly and silently make them visible, generating a strong connection and intense **Presence**. If anyone interrupts this or breaks the silence, you politely ask them to wait a minute, explain you want to tell them something and, before speaking, finish your *looking* and *seeing* round.

2. ***EmPathy* and vulnerability**

Next, you have to explain how you feel. It is not expressing how you are living your difficulties, fears and anguish in this situation (since you are not getting paid either). Instead, it is em**P**athizing with them, walking in their shoes, understanding deeply how they are feeling, how everything that is going on is affecting them and how they are feeling. When you finish *looking* and *seeing* every player, you put your shoes back on, and then express *how you are doing* in your situation. Your players know already you are not getting paid and going through difficulties, as many or even more than them. However, it is not the time for you to tell them your issues and tell them you are also having a hard time. That is fine, but it is not enough. They need a *leader* at their service to help them overcome the difficult situation, aside from seeing you are on the same boat during the storm. That is your challenge.

Giving a rant of the sort: "I know how you are feeling and how hard all this is but now more than ever, we must keep going and overcome all hardships. Together, we need to give it all on the field and prove what we are made of" is not the point either. You do not know how they are feeling because you have not even asked them yet. Because they do not feel listened to or understood. Because they have accumulated too many uncomfortable emotions that they have not expressed and are about to burst. It is not time for that. It does not work and it may have the opposite effect you want. They may turn against you, accuse you of being with the other side and distrust you. It is impossible to transform a resentment, anguish and fear mood with some motivating sentences, no matter how good they are. First, you must clean and disinfect the wound (*express*) and then suture (*transform*).

You need to connect to "something real", personal and meaningful by searching in your heart for answers to questions like: *from your leader's position, how are you living this situation? How is it affecting you? How do you feel about their collection problems? What are you proud of and grateful for? How do you feel about their work and commitment despite the issues? Where do you find the strength to keep going? What is something that makes you renew your enthusiasm daily to come to work? What would you like to acknowledge about them? What are you discovering this season? What is your biggest challenge? What are you learning about yourself and them?* The point is looking inwards, taking off the "superman's" armour and speaking to them with your heart in hand. If you allow yourself to feel and show your vulnerability, you allow them to follow your lead. If you are brave, so will they. If you dare do it this way, you will feel a profound connection with all your players and then you will be in shape to generate a truly transformative conversation with them, a *convers(a)ction.*

3. **Expressing and maintaining emotions**

    We seek to create a space where their bodies can offload all the toxic and limiting emotions they keep, making them suffer needlessly. The point is letting them feel, helping them name and express their feelings without judgments before transforming them into other, more edifying and promoting ones. It is similar to letting others out before going in. That is the task and you must follow it that way. To **P**rocess emotions, first you must express and then transform.

    Once you are connected and present, have taken your time to process your emotions and put yourself at their service, you need to ask your players how they are doing. Remember that if you only ask: "how are you doing?", they will reply they "are very f*cked", followed by a stream of complaints that will not help you reach the conversation's goal. We want them to dare to go deep into their emotions, allow themselves to feel them and have the courage to express them like you just did.

Instead of "how are you doing?" you can ask about different emotions. You will then name them out loud and one by one. *Who's stressed? Who's feeling blocked? Who wants to quit? Who's feeling furious? Betrayed? Who's feeling mad? Who's desperate?* For every question you make, you can raise your hand and cause whoever identifies with it to recognise it immediately and also raise their hand. From then on for example, for anyone who has raised their hand with the question, *who's rather stressed?* You keep asking them to help them feel it in its entire dimension: *how is it affecting you? What's the worst thing about it? How is it at home? During training sessions? What is your energy level? What is taking away from you? What is it costing you?* You must be curious, present, supporting and at their service.

Santiago Ramón y Cajal once said, "what is going on with us is that we do not know what is going on with us". You do not have to fix anything in this dynamic because nothing is broken. You do not need to provide solutions or evaluate emotions. You just need to create a special moment of intense **Presence** so that everyone may observe what is going on with them, putting it into words and expressing how they are feeling, connecting with their vulnerability and letting them be seen, feeling listened to and understood by everyone.

In this phase, we will avoid debates, arguments, attacks, etc., because we are in a unique judgment-free space where we will seek for everyone to feel safe and dare to express themselves. We will seek for everyone to talk and be listened to. It is a venting phase of releasing and freeing their bodies from the complex and shared emotions so that they return to being calm. When a player has finished expressing their feelings, we will thank them for their courage and will continue with someone else who has raised their hand. Or, we can ask another question (*who's mad?*) until all of them have had a chance, a moment and room to share their emotions with the rest.

If someone says, "I can't keep going", you can ask them: *how does being unable to keep going feel? How is it to train and play like this?* If someone tells you: "I am scared", you ask them more about that emotion, how it affects them, where they feel it, what it looks like, how it limits them and who it turns them into. *Who's feeling weak, powerless?* You accept all the sprouting emotions, the more the better. You help them observe them, without judgment or criticism, until you feel how they stop being awkward while their bodies begin to free themselves and relax. The point is about going deep into it, of creating a sharing space, to feel your and their emotions, and we should not hide. On the contrary, we need to observe, pay attention, listen and express them since they are a wonderful opportunity to know ourselves better and show our authentic selves before others. Your job until now has been holding on to the rope and emotions. It has not been going down into the well with your players, pulling them out with the rope or letting it go. You have just held on to it. What a gift! Take it easy. Everything is fine. Before leaving the well, we all need to lighten the load we have been doing until now.

4. **Transforming emotions**

Once every team member has had the opportunity of expressing and sharing their difficult and awkward emotions, your next objective will be to transform that resentment or resignation mood into one that allows them to create a new reality for the team. This new mood will let them accept what they cannot change and will focus all their attention, effort and energy on what does depend on them.

In order to do that, we will keep asking them. Asking is and will be our essential tool. We will ask questions that connect them with what matters, their essence, personal and group values and who they are when they are not emotionally hijacked. Questions that make them resonate, plug into their *energizol* tank and open new spaces of possibilities and previously impossible-to-discover actions from the spirits where they were before. We shall do it this way because we consider that team, as a system, is also an "acorn" that already has all the resources inside it needs to face and overcome that delicate situation. Once again, it is not about putting in but getting out what is already there, latent, waiting to be revealed.

While keeping an intense presence, we will keep asking: *what are we proud of? What matters for this team? How do you want to remember this situation ten years from now? How would you like to tell your kids? Who are we going to be in this situation? What is life challenging us to do? What is our challenge now? What is important for the team? What is the best thing everyone has to offer to the team now? What do you need to discover about yourself now? How would it be to overcome it together? What kind of team would we become? What would we lose by giving up? What would we win by quitting now? What is the worst thing that could happen to us (apart from not getting paid)? What would we be capable of if we were not scared? What would we dare to do? What do you truly want right now? What are we committing to if we dare to keep going despite all this? What would we be agreeing to? What would we say no to? What do you need from me? How may I help you? What do you need from your teammates? What would you like to ask/tell them?*

Answers will follow questions and this profoundly transforming conversation will help the team to change the reality observer they were until now. It will renew the changing room's emotions by transforming the team's mood, enhance cohesion and communication, increase compassion and empathy levels and will cause, after listening to each other, every one of them to forget about themselves a little and care more for their teammates, putting themselves at their service and discovering new possible actions hidden before the conversation.

This conversation's purpose is for your team to grow, take fate into their own hands, strengthen their commitment to adversity, increase their awareness and responsibility, and choose who they want to be in this difficult situation and who they want to become, choose what they want to do and how they want to do. To do all this you need to accomplish a mood from which you create a new reality and generate new possibilities. The current example is a grave situation of non-collection although we can apply this methodology to any other situation that causes dense and awkward emotions without the need for them to be dramatic. We know that emotions influence directly and negatively people's and teams' performances; a negative result strike, a final, a match for demotion, a playoff, a loss or passing, cycle changes, etc.

We need to become mood observers and assume our responsibility as leaders to intervene in the design and trans-formation of the spirits of our teams and ours. We can do it. We just need the courage to be open, available and vulner-able. You may be thinking: "Ooof, that's complicated!", "too risky", "too exposed for me", "what if I don't know how to do it?", "what if the players don't dare to follow me?", "what if I don't do it properly?", "what if I am not good enough and someone laughs at me?", "what if they think I am a softie and weak?". My friend, being vulnerable is dealing with those thoughts. You must overcome your embarrassment and do it without any guarantees of success, blindly believing that others will see bravery and inspiring fortitude where you can only see your weakness.

Internal Operative System (IOS)

To top off this chapter, I shall introduce you to a simple but valuable idea for you to reflect on how our "Internal Oper-ative System". Like any other operative system, the IOS is a complex set of internal processes that define what is seen from the outside, on the screen, on a computer, or my actions, in the case of human beings.

To explain the IOS, what I am, or someone's identity, we can use the picture of an iceberg. Our attitudes and behaviour, our results, and what others see of us would be the iceberg point, what sticks out of the water and you can see on the surface. Everything else, both in the iceberg and the others, is hidden. As we have already mentioned, essence and values are a part of the deepest side of the Self. It is what constitutes and makes us unique, memorable and different. It is like a promise, a possibility about to be revealed, deep inside everyone's Self, in the iceberg.

The ideal thing would be that what anyone can see is the exact reflection of what is deep down, our behaviors being coherent with what we are, with the best we have to offer. Unfortunately, we know this is not usually the case. Normally there are interferences between the depth and tip, between the invisible essence and the visible acts that distort the formidable and desired alignment between who I am, what I say and what I do, preventing our performance or results reflect our true potential. There, in that complex group of internal processes, is where negative thoughts or "saboteurs" dwell, those limiting beliefs and emotions that become toxic when we cannot express them adequately. We will call these three elements "distortions".

We can set out a formula to study athletes' performances:

$$\text{Performance = Potential - Distortions}$$

How often have we seen players with huge potential, unable to steadily take performance to their skills, and limited by their inability to manage their distortions. Nine in potential, four in average performance. An insufficient, disappointing, infuriating result finally leads them to give up and quit. We all rest easy and avoid responsibility by saying "their mind is not in the right place" after the fact. This also works the opposite way. How many athletes there are (not only in the sports world) that do not stand out due to their potential or special talent, but they do manage to perform notably and steadily through time. They improve every season until they become value and behaviour models for everyone. Athletes with an initial potential of 7 and a steady seven performance and upwards throughout time, thanks to outstanding distortion management. Increasing our performance by maximising our potential and decreasing our distortions is what we seek in our *convers(a)ctions*.

The 6 "**P**s" we have seen until now have been useful to work on and improve the three elements in the equations (R=P-I). You need Presence to ease those *convers(a)ctions* in which we can talk about "things that matter" and emPathise to exercise humble leadership at the service of those under your responsibility. You need to Promote and apply the "fruitful insight" to help them, discover and connect with the best of them, with their talents, strengths, resources, values, and true potential. Using the skills we learned in Posing questions, we eliminate negative thoughts and overcome "saboteurs". By Positivising, you know that you can be the creator of your thoughts and can break down your limiting beliefs and choose what sort of reality observer you are. From there, you can control your attitude. And, of course, you can Process by practising your new skill to create privileged spaces, maintaining emotions and transforming moods.

After these six first "Ps", we are about to polish the iceberg's tip. We only need to apply the last "**P**", making a Pact to become competent in action plan design we need to set in motion to begin the transformation that brings us closer to our best version.

Processing in 7 pills

1. *Emotions* reflect how we react before events. We cannot avoid nor choose them. *Moods* determine the behaviours from which we act, opening or closing action possibilities. We are not responsible for our spirits, although we are of the time we decide to dwell in them.

2. Feeling emotions is not an illness symptom. On the contrary, an "acorn" (complete, creative and full of resources) has full access to its emotions. Our *feelings* provide us with a way to express ourselves. The process can be very

liberating as long as we allow our bodies to unload and find what they are keeping to themselves.

3. Processing means listening to my body and paying attention to my emotions, identifying, recognising, naming and expressing them, and stopping to fight and deny them. When I learn to accept them, my body frees itself and starts leaving room to transform them.

4. Emotionally intelligent leaders can support someone's emotions without pulling or letting go of the rope and going down the well. They do not get defensive or feel awkward or attacked. They facilitate others feeling and expressing what they feel without justifying or rationalising it, without feeling judged or guilty for feeling.

5. *Metaphors* help us feel and express emotions more intensely and deeply so that they can flow and we can transform them. We shall stop saying *speaking of emotions* and we shall start feeling emotions. It is the only way our body can deliver the message and learning that generating experience has for us.

6. My mood transforms me into one or another reality observer. My interpretation of reality appears from the emotional state I find myself. If I change my spirit, my world and possibilities change with it.

7. Connecting with my vulnerability means recognising I am imperfect. I make mistakes, feel awkward emotions, and I suffer embarrassment and fear to show myself. Despite all this, I am thankful and accept that all this is part of my nature, a part of what makes me feel alive and powerful, and that I do not need to hide it to be worthy of the love I deserve.

MAKING **P**ACTS

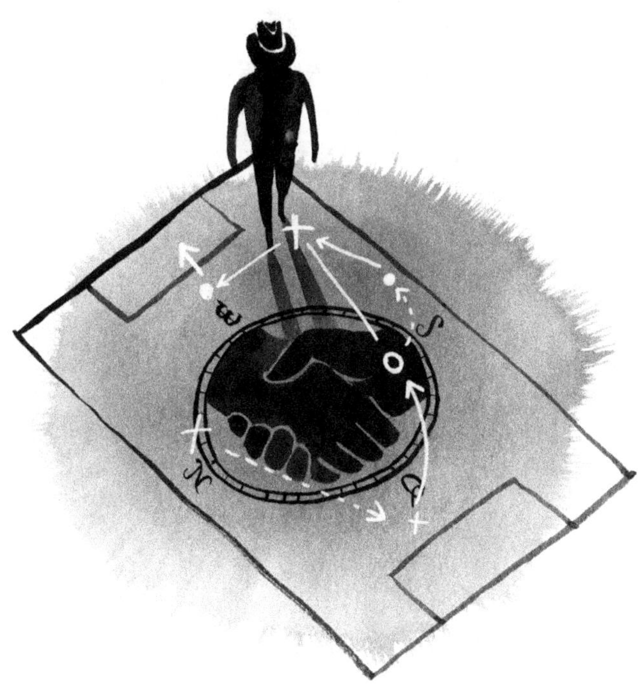

Every week I have *convers(a)ctions* with managers and learn a lot from them. They share how they feel, what they think about, and their greatest desires, fears and worries with me. I know their difficulties and the complexity of their task and I am well aware of the enormous challenge of facing their responsibility daily below the Damocles sword of results. They know better than anyone that the "I order and command" is no longer enough not only in the sports world but also in companies, the education system, and even their homes. The new generations do not accept (which is good) that sort of authority and rebel against those worn-out demagogues and despot sergeants who still understand power and relations that way. They may manage to achieve briefly the troops' obedience that stems from the fear of consequences, but it is not enough to accomplish what they desire most: their genuine commitment.

Learning how to make Pacts will help us cross the bridge from obedience to commitment, a personal decision required, discovered and strengthened in adversity. When the fun is over, when the situation starts to go South (which it always does) we need for that commitment to appear and prove itself. Managers/bosses need to understand that forcing a player —or anybody— to commit is impossible. Although I hear how they usually and eagerly demand it, they have to realize that you cannot require commitment because it is the best gift a follower has to offer their boss, provided their boss earns it by being trustworthy.

There are four immutable and eternal leadership principles. For centuries, their validity as trust-generating elements in people, relationships and organizations has remained in force. They are so simple that not applying them is unbelievable.

We need to listen actively to understand deeply.

We need to be kind and considerate, worry about others (be empathetic and compassionate) and be mindful of details.

It is essential to follow through with what we say (fulfill your promises!)

We must speak the truth.

You may think these are rather obvious and you would be correct. When I undergo a small internal audit to know my compliance degree with such easy recommendations, I cannot help but realize and be shocked at the enormous improvement margin I still have before me. On too many occasions, I find myself listening with the intent of speaking instead of understanding and I know others are not feeling listened to, understood, or valued. Other times, my gestures, snorts or wry faces disgust me since I know they upset those I love. Impatient, fast and unkind answers and my little or null attention to details I know are vital though I do not value or recognize them properly are some of my other issues. It seems common sense, though it is clear that sense is not so common.

The "broken windows" theory

"In 1969, at Stanford University (USA), Professor Philip Zimbardo carried out a social psychology experiment. He left two identical cars on the street, of the same brand, model and even colour. He left one in the Bronx, already a poor and conflictive New York area. He left the second in Palo Alto, a rich and peaceful neighbourhood in California. Predictably, the car left in the Bronx was vandalised a few hours later. It lost the rims, the engine, the rear-view mirrors, the radio, etc. Everything useful was gone, and the rest was destroyed. Conversely, the car left in Palo Alto was intact. It is easy to blame poverty because of what happened to the vehicle, but the experiment did not finish there. When the abandoned car in the Bronx was picked apart and the one in Palo Alto was untouched for a week, the researchers decided to break one of the latter's windows. The result was the same as what happened to the former car. How could a broken window trigger that crime wave in an allegedly safe neighbourhood? It is not about poverty. A broken window in an abandoned car conveys an idea. This idea is one of deterioration, disinterest, and indifference that breaks cohabitation codes, such as the absence of law and rules, telling people that everything goes. Every new attack the car suffers reasserts and multiplies that idea until the escalation becomes uncontrollable, leading to irrational violence"[15]. They concluded the experiment there.

I read about this theory a while ago and the Bilbao Metro system came to mind. After twenty years into operation, the metro has remained as impeccable as the first day, winning international awards and being something the locals are proud of. How did they manage to pick up all discarded pieces of paper, clean up all graffiti on the subway wagons or quickly fix any perceivable damage on the platforms and seats? I reckon those in charge have not allowed the appearance of "broken windows" and they repaired the broken windows diligently once they appeared. But the deep reflection on this theory and its impact occurred when I applied it to my life. Sometimes I notice something similar going on to me like those half-abandoned factory walls made of rectangular broken glass windows. I suppose someone began breaking one, like in the abandoned car's case, allowing a wave of attacks that left no glass untouched.

Sometimes I tell someone I will do something simple like make a phone call, meet up to have a cup of coffee, send an email, offer feedback, etc. Nonetheless, I do not do it because I think I have other priorities or do not have enough

---

15   Read in Eduardo Martí's blog (http://www.lideryliderazgo.com).

time, or I will do it another time. I tell myself that "they won't remember", "it isn't important", and "nobody will notice". From then on, I justify myself to decide what promises and commitments with others are relevant. When I realize my mistake, I have already caused a broken glass mess. Being trustworthy, an important value to me comes down in flames. The incoherence between what I do and what I say hurts me. Other times I remain passive, I do not say or remind someone of something to avoid conflict ("don't get in trouble", "they are going get mad", "let it be") and I open the door wide so that they keep repeating that behaviour until I react at the worst time and in the least timely way. All this happened because I did not fix the first broken window in time. Expressing what I feel, and being honest, another value I am proud of goes down the drain.

Some days, out of pure laziness, I do not go to the gym as I should have ("you'll go tomorrow", "you aren't in such bad shape", "you have more important things to do"). Even though I justify myself because of lack of time (broken glass), weeks later I notice another glass window is shattered. My health, being available and in good shape for my family and keeping developing my profession have suffered. At times I delay difficult business because I fear they will not turn out like I expect them to. By the time I realize, they have stacked on top of each other and mistrust, worrying and paralysis trap me. By acting like this I question my genuine commitment to the purpose that gives meaning to everything I do. All this hurts me.

Suddenly and without realizing, freezing gusts of wind come through all the broken window panes and finding a solution becomes much more complicated. Every time I break a window and do not repair it, I get farther from who I want to be, the father I want to become or the professional I aspire to be. Every one of us knows what their broken windows are. It is about becoming aware of them and getting down to business immediately to fix the broken windows in their family, in sports, with their partner, in their job, with their friends, with themselves, with their vision and personal development. Breaking windows and not fixing them is giving up on being someone trustworthy.

Regarding hens and pigs

In the summer of 2012, seconds before starting the seventh and last "7Ps" workshop with managers and staff of the Mexican football national team, I got a message from Spain informing me of the passing of our dear Manolo Preciado due to a heart attack, just a day before his presentation as the Villareal FC manager. The news filled me with sorrow and sadness, although thinking of him during those four hours, precisely at the commitment workshop, helped us create a space with such energy and warm emotions that I keep an unforgettable memory of that experience. The image of Manolo Preciado always comes to mind if we speak of leadership as the essential attitude to generate *genuine Commitment* (with a capital "C").

Sometimes the example of a dish of eggs with bacon is given to picturing the difference between obligation and commitment. Who is more committed to cooking this dish, the pig or the hen? The hen lays eggs, does what it must, and fulfills her obligation. The hen is involved. The pig goes further than it needs to and loses its life trying. The pig is truly committed. Manolo Preciado was undoubtedly the model of commitment, being able to deserve and win over his player's trust. He believed the impossible was possible and he decreed the state of enthusiasm, faith and determination in his teams. I do not remember him winning many titles or medals or being acknowledged as a top manager. He needed nothing of this sort to leave a great legacy that speaks volumes of the best leaders at the service of their teams that I have known.

During the 1980s, when times were tough, Manolo was already a model in the conquest of footballers' labor rights. Those who, like him, stuck up for their coworkers risked their contracts and careers. They assumed great risks for others. Later, from afar, I admired his way of facing extreme personal situations. I appreciated him a lot as a manager but above all, I took my hat off to him as a person. Life hit him extremely hard, although he recovered every time with unmatched courage and firmness. He chose to rub off his incredible capacity to enjoy life and football on others without malice or resentment.

Some values that defined such a captivating personality were: hard-working, sensitive, close, brave, cheery and fun-loving. "If your players fear you, they will fight for you. If they love you, they will die for you", said Sun Tzu (adapted) in his work *The Art of War*. Manolo gave his all to his players so they died for him. His exemplary leadership has left a mark on all the football players who worked with him. Hens disappeared from the changing room if Manolo was there.

Two months before he died, I had a long talk with him in a taxi during a monumental traffic jam in Madrid. I asked him how long he intended to keep working as we discussed how stressful his job was. He looked me in the eye, smiled, and said in a snide tone: "until the day I die". As always, he kept his word.

Committing is choosing

Victor Valdés made a terrible mistake twenty seconds into the match, which led to a 1-0 against his team. It was an easy pass for him though he gave it to a rival who just had to push the ball into the net. At that moment, while his team was risking the Liga in the Bernabeu stadium, Valdés could have thought the rival team had already scored nine goals. He could have imagined the title getting out of their reach, his team getting scored, it being the start of the end of the cycle, thought "what a day", and a lot more negative and useless thoughts that would have not helped him at all. Nonetheless, Valdés decided to do something else. During that moment of maximum tension and as another player passed him the ball, he assumed the risk again of playing the ball as though nothing had happened, repeating and insisting during the ninety minutes. Valdés made more mistakes. It was not his best day, though by respecting his *commitment* with the respectable idea of playing that has made this team eternal in the memory of football fans, he grew another inch in his impeccable career to become a legendary goalkeeper.

Listening to the statements given by Xavi Hernández and Puyol while still on the field after the match praising their teammate's courage, or even Guardiola during a press conference informing them that he had publicly recognized Valdés' bravery for daring and insisting on what he had to do, reinforces, even more, the value of that commitment. It would have been very justifiable and easy to understand that, from his terrible mistake, Valdés would have chosen not to make his life hard and play safely, but that would have meant giving up for him. One needs a lot of courage to remain firm and persevere, facing one's fears and "saboteurs" and persisting in what you must do, what needs to be done. That tremendous determination to not surrender can only come from authentic *commitment*.

If I asked you now: *do you feel committed?* you would probably think about it for a while and answered that you were. This always happens when I ask the question of who feels committed in our workshops. Everyone raises their hand and I am sure they are. Everyone is committed to something different. Key in a team is that all players be committed and share values and principles, because that is what committing means. We say YES with our commitment to becoming aware and declaring which values, behaviors and actions bring us closer to the team we want to be. Those that we know take us away from where we want to be, we say NO. Committing is deciding who you want to be, choosing what you agree to and what you do not, and acting in consequence.

I get mad every time I listen to statements such as: "the team is very committed", "I am very committed", and "the club is very committed". Commitment is undoubtedly a great value, although it has no meaning when used that way. It becomes a circular word that is used for everything but explains nothing. If commitment is not specified and proven daily with actions, decisions and visible behaviors, it loses all meaning. That is why every time I hear that kind of statement about commitment, I ask the same questions: *what are you committed to? What is your team committed to? And your club? What are you choosing? What values are you agreeing/disagreeing with that commitment? What do they mean? How do you define them? And your team? What are the concrete decisions and behaviors that reflect that compromise?*

When, after his grave mistake, Valdés insisted on keep offering himself to his teammates, on temporizing until they got clear and offered him a pass-line, on assuming that they may put pressure on him and make his life difficult, on not giving the ball away, he may have been saying YES to being humble and thinking of his team first. He may have said YES to be at his teammates' service, YES to accepting the mistake as part of his learning. By behaving in this way, he may have chosen to say NO to his "saboteurs", NO to being cowardly and selfish, NO to giving up, NO to failing his teammates and NO to betraying a great game idea. It is possible that such strength, determination and bravery to persevere and not surrender during maximum difficult moments, comes from his commitment to unnegotiable values shared by his team.

The Athlete's Wheel of Life (AWL)

The Wheel of Life (WL) is a widely spread resource in the coaching world and self-knowledge techniques so that anyone can land in their own life recognising how they are, what is working and what is not. The WL provides the individual with an exceptional, graphic and individual vision of themselves, reflecting their life's balance or the lack of fluidity and power of their vital rhythm. It also serves as an excellent tool for making Pacts and creating compromising *convers(a)ctions*.

We can complete the WL with the values of those we are going to work with or their lives more important aspects if what we seek is going deep with a more holistic or integral view of the athletes. On this occasion, we will use the WL to give you an example of how it can be applied to an athlete, adapting it to the more related competencies to their performance, being able to customize it for every sport and specific spot. We shall call it "Athlete's Wheel of Life" (AWL).

I shall use this moment to make a recommendation to you. When you want to generate a *convers(a)ction* with someone, you do not need to say what it is about, just do it! Apply what you are finding out and what you think can be useful. Experiment with it to check if it works and can be helpful, but do not explain it. An expert teacher I had at the start of my workshop and with whom I happened to meet a couple of years later, made an interesting observation. I was talking about the coaching I was writing at the time when she smiled and told me: "coaching is like sex, you can talk a lot about it, but the real good thing about is doing it". Therefore, my advice is you not to take it too seriously, do not make it too formal, and do not pressure him or book an appointment in any office. Just do it naturally and simply, do not make it seem like a performance review (which it is not) or an exam that gets them defensive. Seek a calm space and moment to generate this conversation. You will need a pen and paper, you may only need a napkin to start.

I suggest you sit with them on the ground, on the bench or lean against a wall. We shall divide the exercise into three differentiated phases we call: *landing, resonating* and *taking off*. You will need to be present, connected and at their service to generate a *convers(a)ction*.

1. **Landing**

   In this first phase, we will ask them to draw a big circle on the piece of paper and start naming what they think the essential aspects to improve their performance are and consider they can work on it. Or, if it is a team sport, the key competencies or skills of their specific spot. We can discuss technical, tactical, physical, psychological, and emotional matters, whichever they may improve. They will name those they believe are more relevant until we have divided the wheel into eight neat named wedges.

   I shall offer you a real example of the practical application of this dynamic. It is about a central defender football player's AWL who stood out in the mastery of these essential eight-game sections to achieve high performance in his spot: *aggressiveness, long pass kick, airborne game, anticipation, marking, ball clearing, understanding the game and focus.* As he named them and explained why they were important to him, he wrote them down on a piece of paper, each one in every wedge until he filled the eight spots. There probably are other key game aspects that he did not name, though those were the ones that he considered most relevant.

Remember that this exercize's goal is not imposing my point of view on the areas I think the player has to work on and improve. Instead, I just have to listen and ask, helping them land in their reality. The time will come to provide and "drop" my observations and suggestions. What we seek now is for them to realise and assume responsibility for what is important for their personal and sports growth. You are only allowed to co-create his AWL with them depending on their age and maturity. However, nothing the athlete does not approve of can appear on the piece of paper. Do not cheat or it will not work.

Once the AWL is complete, it is time to help them land in it and help them feel how they are in every aspect they have considered key to their development. For that purpose, we shall ask them to mark, from one to ten, their current satisfaction level in every wheel wedge. We shall consider the exact centre as zero and the outside of the circumference as a ten. The score they have given themselves in a section may not match the manager's score. This tends to be awkward for the manager who thinks it is necessary to make the player see they are wrong. Do not focus or waste energy on it. It does not matter now. Remember that the AWL is not an evaluation tool. What we seek is the player connecting with their internal self-motivation source (*energizol*) so that they go into action by committing to their improvement and development plan. We do not aim to be correct but to achieve the goal. The opposite case may also happen; the player may score themselves lower than we think is their actual value. We do not intend to convince them here either (although we may take notes to strengthen them and recognise that aspect when it's convenient and necessary). Still, we accompany them so that they get in motion being responsible for their action plan.

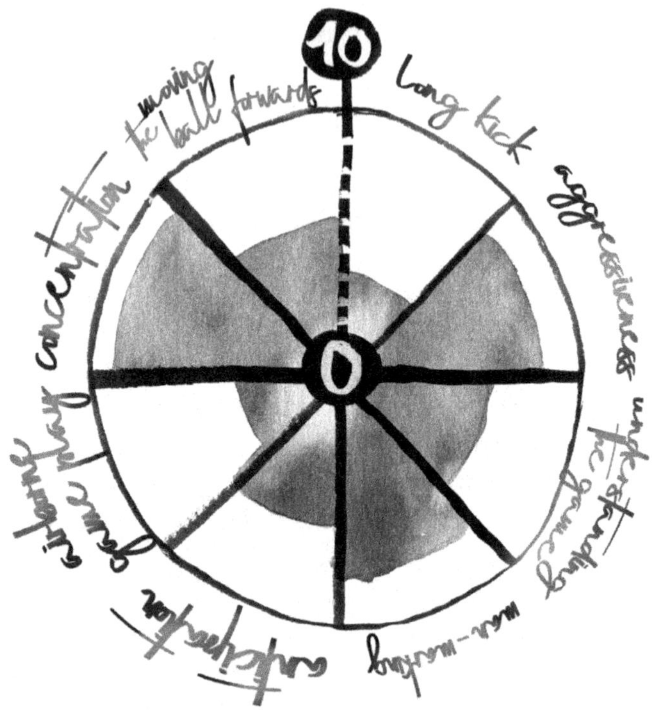

Once the player has finished scoring himself, we ask them to make a general reflection of their AWL. *How are they seeing it, what do they think about it, what would they highlight, what's drawing their attention, what worries them, what are they proud of, and how do they feel about it.* Immediately after, we ask them to choose one aspect of their AWL that is important to them and would like to improve. It does not have to be the one with the worst score, but one they feel they want to develop. Once chosen, we focus on this concrete aspect and start the first phase we have called landing so that they realise how they are and what is going on with them. As always, we do that with "powerful questions", curious, without judgment, open, and suspending opinions, beliefs and absolute "truths" for a while. These questions should help them land in their own sports life.

In this example, after carefully thinking about it and assessing the risks of daring to expose himself that much, the footballer decided he wanted to improve his airborne game, in which he had scored a 4. I had seen him play and had my criteria (in this case, he was not as mediocre as he thought). However, as we have mentioned before, my opinion was not relevant at that moment. The only thing that matters in this phase is him realising what is going on with that four, its effect on his confidence and possibilities, how it limits him and how he feels about that four. We use questions to land:

What's a four like? Describe it to me! What is going on with you a four? How do you feel there? How do you feel defending a corner or side foul? How do you feel when you fight for an airborne ball? What worries you? What does your "saboteur" tell you in these situations? What is the worst thing about this four? What's the worst part of losing the ball? How does it affect you? How does it affect the team? What are you missing out on? What is your emotion like? What's your mood? How is it limiting you? Who are you there? What sort of player does it turn you into? Is there something good? What is it? In this case, I keep him down the "well" with my questions in his four. I want him to remain there for a while. I want him to explore it, become aware and feel it profoundly. What we do here is hold the rope without pulling or letting go.

2. **Resonating**

In this second phase, we seek to connect him with the internal energy source (*energizol*) he needs to jump over his "saboteurs". Thus, he will find the courage, bravery and determination he needs to start and get into action. We keep asking:

What would you like your score to be in one/three/ six months? How would two or three more points feel? What is the goal/objective? What would a seven feel like? Describe it to me! What's different in a seven? What has improved? How do you feel defending a corner or foul in a seven? How does it feel to win many more airborne struggles? What is it like to clear the ball with your head with strength? What is the seven's impact on the rest of your game play? And that improvement's impact on your team? What personal value are you living intensely by doing it? Who do you become? How does that seven connect you with the player view we have worked on? How would it be to dare to improve that game play side? What would your players think about you if you did? And your manager? What would they tell you? And you, what would you tell yourself? Who would you become? What would be possible from now on for you? What are you capable of now? What are you committing to? What are you choosing? What do you agree to do? What are you saying no to with this commitment? How may I help you? What do you need from me to set about?

After this phase, if we have done a good job it is likely the player is full of *energizol* and looking forward to taking off in the direction his answers tell him. Now we only need to design a plan of action with which he can and wants to commit to 100%.

3. **Taking off**

We keep asking him:

What could you do these weeks to improve your airborne game play? (We write down all possibilities, exercises and dynamics that come up without judgment or evaluation). Out of all those options, what do you want to do? What are you going to do? How are you going to do it? (Which actions and how many times a week, at what time and for how long every day). How will you do this exactly? (Now we design the plan of action we pointed out in the second chapter). What do you need to do it? Who can help you? From one to ten, right now, how confident do you feel doing it? What do you need to turn it into a ten? What the difficulties to carry it out may be? What do you need to overcome them? Who could you rely on? How will you know you have accomplished your objective? How does this action plan bring you closer to the player you want to be? In what way does this connect you to your values? How do you feel now about your plan? What are you thinking of now? How do you feel? What is your energy level? What impact do you think setting off will have on your team? How may I help you to do it? The manager accompanies the player in this exercise of landing-resonating-taking off, providing the player with the light he needs so that he can discover what matters to him and what he wants. The manager is not the protagonist but a leader at the player's service that invites him to take the reins of his improvement and development process.

Making Pacts is cocreating the relationship you want to have with your followers. It is designing a space for *convers(a)ctions* that generate new possibilities. It is going from the exhausting and ineffective responsibility of having to exercise as an external motivator to helping them connect to their *energizol* source, the strength they need to identify and strengthen their commitment. Making Pacts means encouraging your players to take responsibility for the solutions and results. It is ceasing to impose you and start applying the "fruitful insight", helping them along their transformation path and inviting them to discover what they would be capable of if they dared to. It is daring to take the step from manager/boss to leader, from "do this!" to "what could you do?". Making Pacts is being complicit in a transcendental possibility, of what it is not yet, and what it could be with your help.

CSMATA plan

After completing the entire AWL exercise, the player dared to define an ambitious and resonating plan. He first drew it up negatively, "I do not want to be worried every time I have to fight for an airborne ball". Later he stated, "I want to improve my airborne game play". Finally, he managed to say it in a way that did not sound like an obligation, "I want to enjoy the airborne game play". This looked much better. We now had a challenging objective since it forced him to become the player he needed to turn into to deserve "enjoying the airborne game play". To accomplish this *(A)chievable* purpose we define landmarks along the way, with concrete tasks and actions we include in his CSMATA (Challenging, Specific, Measurable, Achievable, Temporal and Attractive) action plan.

His first task was to inform/ask for permission from his manager to start this specific exercise. The player also had to expose himself before all his mates showing himself to be vulnerable by publicly recognizing his lacks in that part of the game. That task was already highly *(C)hallenging* for him, as well as proving to what point he was committed to his objective and if he would be capable of putting it into practice.

His action plan started with something as *(S)pecific* and simple as realizing if he closed or opened his eyes when he hit the ball with his head. He designed an exercise sequence that went from the most basic and elemental to the most complex. This sequence ranged from individual dynamics in short distances while still to airborne struggles in long passes and attacking the ball at its peak, always with his eyes open. He defined particular goals for each task that facilitated that his progress evolution was *(M)easurable*. For example, he counted how many hits with his forehead (hard and with his eyes opened) he accurately returned (out of ten) to the chest of the teammate who passed him the ball as if it was a throw-in three meters away. Another exercise was counting (out of ten) how many frontal long passes he could hit at their peak while being alone and coordinating jumps, trajectories and distances.

For three months (the agreed *(T)emporal* frame to value how far he had come), he worked on an exercise battery. It sequentially increased their difficulty while learning to deal with mistakes as an essential part of his learning, without blaming himself or being ashamed of being imperfect. His progress was so clear that his confidence and enthusiasm to keep training increased daily. His initiative's effect on the team was equally surprising since, a few weeks after setting his plan in motion, nearly half of the playing staff chose to prolong their training sessions so that everyone improved their matters.

Every time we had a *convers(a)ction*, we revisited his sensations, progress and difficulties. I did not demand him to fulfill his promise nor felt upset or angry because he did not do it or judged him for not doing it the first two weeks he could not overcome his embarrassment to set his action plan in motion. On the contrary, I reacted by guiding him in his process, reflecting on his experience and extracting the needed learning from inaction so that he could keep going forward. I asked him: *what is it costing you? What is difficult for you? What is your "saboteur" telling you? What is a challenge for you? How do you feel? What do you need to set about? What can you do? What do you need to change in your plan? Who can you talk to? Who may help you?*

Opposition, fear and insecurity appear abruptly in those challenging and doubtful moments. They block us and prevent us from leaving our "comfort zone". Thus, we reconnected with the vision of the player he wanted to become, with his values, strengths and skills during those uncertain moments. I used feedback and support and admired his bravery for not being happy with who he was and daring to transform into who he could be.

Three months later, this player shared an exciting experience with me. While in a center and header exercise he had never stood out in, he connected two splendid headers that went into the goal like missiles. They must have been so good and spectacular that all his teammates started clapping and shouting in admiration. His most extraordinary discovery after that sublime moment and those months of intense work focused on a specific objective was that he was not afraid to defend a corner or foul or lose a struggle. He felt strong, freed and looking forward to keeping working and improving that and other aspects of the game. He had achieved his purpose and felt he could transform into the player he wanted and could be. He did not want to stop there. He was on fire! His plan also included the last letter, maybe the most important one, (A)ttractive, because its protagonist was looking forward to doing it, the only way for any plan to serve its purpose.

> *"Birds don't sing because they are happy, they are happy because they sing".*
> WILLIAM JAMES

Many athletes and managers have stopped singing while waiting to want to sing. As Alfonso Alcántara (@Yoriento) reminds us, it is very agreeable and easy to say "change your attitude", but it does not work. Our attitude is part of us and what we have lived through. The only way to change it is by changing the way we live little by little, modifying and planning our life with simple daily behaviours. These behaviours will bring us closer to obtaining our objectives and goals to make us think and feel differently. Any habit change requires organisation, time, effort and repetition. What we are, what we do and how we do depend on how we set up our CSMATA action plan to advance. Everyone shall go at their pace, in the direction our dreams tell us to go.

Natural learning

One of the tasks our player example included in his plan was imitating the model of great defence players who were strong in the airborne game play. Roberto Fabián Ayala, the Argentinian centre player of the Milan and Valencia teams, short but a master in the airborne game play, was one of the players he chose. Another centre player he selected was the Mexican Rafa Márquez, of similar characteristics. To achieve it, our player example searched and downloaded game play, matches and images from the internet and observed them closely many times because, for his body, which is the one that learns, knows and executes moves, a picture is worth a thousand words. Our body learns by observing what others do and imitating them. It focuses on emotions without thinking, absorbing all the intangible information to put it into practice, without the mind intervening or having to make an effort.

Our body does not need instructions or long and technical explanations to improve a movement or technical action. It does not understand them. It is as if you tried to explain how to walk to a toddler. Our body's language to develop its natural learning is not words but images and experience. It learns by practicing and internalizing visual and sensory pictures. It can fix its mistakes to the point of mastering and automating any movement with the help of adequate feedback. Our body is a miraculous machine deserving a lot more trust and respect and fewer interferences from a controlling mind that believes it knows much more than it does.

When I was a football player, I had such a hard time sleeping after the matches that I watched Argentinean League matches. I recorded summaries and matches to focus on some players who featured certain game play features I admired. For example, I was in love with Ronal Koeman's kicks. I especially observed his kicking technique with his full instep and inside instep, his diagonal shifts with the flying ball without spinning (I could almost see the stitches) at high speed and high enough to give all advantage to the forward player. It was such a show. I repeated the kicks in the video in slow motion until I dissected every movement. I remember a kick I analyses many times, a foul goal in the Camp Nou stadium. It was a tremendous kick with his instep to the goalkeeper's post, with such enormous power and precision that the goalkeeper could not stop it.

In every training session, I spent some time practicing the kicks my unconscious mind had dissected, gathering all the relevant information. My body would later attempt to execute the movement, correcting my technique little by little until I achieved a notable excellence level in this particular action. When we provide our body with a clear visual image of what we want to achieve, we only need to tell it, as Tim Gallway said, "do whatever you have to do to achieve this image". If we let it do it, the body can do it.

When our protagonist from the AWL dynamic practiced his exercises to improve his airborne game play, he only had one instruction: not to judge or blame himself for his mistakes. He had to trust his body, feel it, be very present, not think about it and let it happen. He had to trust that his body would calibrate and coordinate better the trajectories, contacts and struggles while applying his plan little by little. He had to have faith that his body would learn how to do it and he should simply let it happen. And that is what he did. And it happened.

"Playing for the sake of playing"

I joined the Lezama (the Athletic Club's lower categories) when I was ten years old and they immediately placed me as a right winger. I had scored hundreds of goals at school, on the street and everywhere. I played in any spot, I always wanted to have the ball and be the protagonist. I bored to death as a right winger (who on Earth wants to play as a right winger as a ten-year-old!). We competed in "Footboy-11", we won easily and I had the ball around ten times per match. It was an absurd competition system that forced the youngest to adapt to the demands of adult football instead of adapting football to children's needs.

Past football stars state that they learnt how to play on the street. At that time playing football was the most important and only thing. Football, a complex game, was not based on the repetition of analytical exercises with the only goal of improving technical aspects. Instead, through playing, they improved perception, decision making and execution of the most appropriate technique. *By playing, we learnt how to play and understand the game.* We respected natural learning, the sort of learning that makes our bodies, as the perfect and incomparable machine it is, shape unconsciously and learn quickly without needing an instruction manual to never forget what we learnt.

We created our games and rules. If there were few players we played without goalkeepers and small goals. If more players came, we moved the jumpers that acted as goals backwards or made the goals larger. If there was little room or it was not big enough to play with two goals, we played with one as "goal-goalkeeper" or "centers and shots". Unknowingly, we forced ourselves to adapt constantly, looking for new solutions to express our creativity and spontaneity in playful surroundings, totally unaware of the stressful demands of football's official competitions and its code of adult rules. We played as anything and in every spot. We risked it doing things we had not mastered without fear of committing mistakes and losing the ball. We had a lot of fun because only those who enjoy playing can be creative. Matches were endless and there was no referee since he was not necessary or manager. By playing, we learnt how to play, win and lose.

Excessive vigilance, constant instructions, rigorous control and permanent correction make us switch off and generate a feeling of lack of freedom and oppression that limits and bores us. We only had football back then, whereas today there are many ways of having fun for the younger ones. If they do not enjoy training and playing, sooner or later, they will quit football and any other sport. What we unknowingly did was enjoy autotelic experiences, as defined by Mihály Csikszentmihalyi in his book *Flow*. The famous author refers to activities that have a purpose in themselves and are not accomplished to obtain a future benefit, but instead because merely doing them is rewarding enough. During that "fluidity" moment, we only paid attention to the activity and enjoyed special moments in which time acquired another dimension until it almost vanished. We could play for hours nonstop, let the day dawn on us, and forget to have lunch. That did not matter. We only cared about playing while connected to the game without thinking. We immediately stop flowing when we focus on the game's possible consequences and results. Fun and magic end there.

Andrés Iniesta, after being lauded as the 2012 European Championship MVP, was asked if he aspired to win the Golden Ball after being chosen MVP. His answer was concluding: "I play to be happy, not to win 'golden balls'". Playing for the sake of playing. That is how things were in children's football, and that's how they should be[16].

Intelligent practice

> *"My goal is improving daily every time I practice.*
> *I need to feel I am a better player at something I have*
> *trained on that day, but I need to feel I am better to go back*
> *home in a good mood".*
> RAFA NADAL

"Intelligent practice" is a concept Daniel Goleman reflects on in his book *Focus*. He dismantles the myth of ten thousand practice hours someone needs to become an expert in any activity, be it playing chess, the violin or practising any sport. Goleman claims it is not practising but "intelligent practice" that brings its protagonist closer to excellency. Mechanically repeating the same incorrect gestures or movements is not very useful if we do not modify our execution. In order to develop a skill, we need to focus our attention on the specific

---

16   Article published in *El Correo* journal on January 2007.

action we want to improve. Repeated practice allows us to transfer a task's control that is made primarily with deliberate effort to execute it without effort and naturally. That is what sets amateurs apart from experts.

An amateur only needs to learn to hit some golf balls or return the ball over the net or simply have the necessary technique to ski down a medium-difficulty ski run. They may need around thirty practice hours to acquire the minimal skill to enjoy the activity. From then on, they feel satisfied with their skills and stop focusing on the task, doing it effortlessly. Whoever wants to achieve an expert ranking in any discipline or sport, including the leading art, never stops paying full attention to their training. They are very present and actively focus on the task and details they have to perfect daily, fixing and adjusting them continually. Experts like having someone experienced close by (manager/coach) that provides them with feedback about their execution and things to improve to review, modify and complete their action plan permanently.

Sports, due to their nature and unlike other activities, have the great advantage of using video resources. These are sensational tools that offer athletes neutral and objective information without judgment or opinion. If used correctly, videos are excellent *convers(a)ction* generators that open transformation possibilities. What matters is how we use the tool: we should never utilize it to evaluate or judge our behaviour, but to become aware and discover new possibilities and improvement areas to work on.

I remember the day one of our students, now part of the technical corps of a prestigious football manager sadly shared with the group what he considered to be a grave mistake with terrible consequences for his team. He was in charge of the video and edited the cuts of the opposite teams before every match. He spent many hours editing every piece because he loved his job. He also dissected many matches to select the best actions and game play of every one of the football players of the rival team. That day he recognized he was the cause of his team's delicate qualifying situation since he had realized how impactful those video edits he prepared were on the team. It was deeply demoralizing because he made it seem like every rival was the best of the world in his spot, which generated mistrust, insecurity and impotence in his players. The tool was excellent, though its use was inadequate.

When we consider the video to provide feedback to a player, for instance, a goalkeeper who is having trouble with airborne game play, we have to avoid them feeling ridiculous or ashamed due to their mistake. On the contrary, we will encourage them to acknowledge, befriend and accept it, decrease its weight and transcendence, because they can only access true learning that making mistakes provides. For that, the only thing we will do is offer them images that picture those that we want them to realize without any judgment. Once again, we will ask them:

How do you see yourself in this game play? How do you feel there? What is your "saboteur" telling you then? What does that game play need from you? What do you think your teammates need from you here? How could you help them more? What do you need from them? What would you like to say to them? What would it be like to go out on the field without fear to miss? What would a brave goalkeeper in exits be like? What would you be capable of? Who would you become? What would it be like to dominate the airborne game play? What would be different for you? And for your team? What would your teammates' trust be? And yours? What's your task here? Tell me about a goalkeeper you admire greatly in the airborne game play; what would he say? How do you think he does it? What do you reckon he thinks about? Would you like to work on this topic? What do you think we could do this week regarding this matter? Is there anything else? How could we do it? What do you need from me? How may I help you? How will we know you are improving? Would you like to say anything else?

Experts who manage to unleash their maximum potential also enjoy intensely practicing their activity. They seek to face a new challenge daily that forces them to apply and improve their skills, which means keep going and growing. We should distinguish between feeling pleasure and enjoyment. The former is evanescent and requires no concentration or effort, but you can only feel enjoyment when you face a challenging situation or activity that demands you to be better. The good ones know well that those who do not improve get worse. They also enjoy what they do, so much that they never stop learning or growing.

My *commitment* to the personal vision of the athlete or manager I want to be facilitates my Presence in every training session. It generates the enthusiasm and will I need to advance my action plan. These could be the three keys to intelligent practice in any discipline, even in leadership: commitment, Presence and planning.

Leadership and commitment

History tells us that Alexander the Great faced one of his greatest battles when he arrived on the coast of Phoenicia in the year 335 B.C. Upon disembarking, he realised that the enemy soldiers outmanned them five to one. His men were scared and unmotivated to fight their enemies. They had lost their faith and thought to be defeated already. Fear had destroyed these invincible warriors. Alexander the Great ordered all his men to burn down their ships. While they were going down in flames and sunk in the ocean, he gathered his men and told them: "Look how our ships burn. That is the only reason we must win because if we do not, we won't return to our homes. None of us will see our families again or leave this land. We must emerge victorious in this battle since the only way back is by sea. Gentlemen, when we return home we will do so the only way possible, in our enemy's ships". Alexander's army won that battle and returned home sailing the ships taken from their enemies.

A reality transformer leader is someone who commits, makes a promise to themselves and declares it publicly, creating a new reality where there was a possibility without probability. For someone to transform into this kind of leader, they need to identify with what they are committing to, what they cannot give up, what gives meaning to what they do, what new future they want to create and why they want to create it. Only this way will they feel, live, transmit and rub it off through all their skin pores, with every look and gesture, in every *convers(a)ction* and everywhere and at any time. This commitment is very freeing and sets you about to become someone you know you can and want to be, regardless of the current conditions, because you are aware your commitment does not depend on circumstances but your decisions.

The best leaders are not those who wait for opportunities. They are those who create their possibilities and can maintain their commitment, especially in the face of adversity. The firm commitment to our vision, purpose and values is the thing that drives us away from conformity, mediocrity, fear, excuses and justifications that close action possibilities and prevent us from advancing before the challenges and misfortunes life places before us. Commitment to who we want to be provides us with the strength to persevere, take difficult decisions and overcome adversity. By connecting with the *energizol* we need to keep going, we overcome "saboteurs", difficulties and challenges, growing, shining and lighting the path for others until we reach our best version, over and over.

Collective commitment

"I am not committed to any player. I am committed to the values we share, we have chosen and define us".
Cholo Simeone

Collective commitment is a gathering place every team staff member is invited. It transcends every one and makes them better. As we have previously mentioned, committing is a personal decision, an individual phenomenon. Team commitment is built on adding the commitment of every teammate, which has an exponential effect on collective performance. Commitment can and has to be worked on. It is not about waiting to see if we get lucky and the results are positive so that our group becomes a team. It is about being proactive and generating individual and collective *convers(a)ctions* to cocreate the identity of the team we want defined by values that identify us, by their associated behaviours and a stimulating and shared vision of the team we want to become. These are strategic decisions that you cannot impose. They require the support and agreement of those who want to carry them out, which is why it is convenient for everyone to participate in the decision-making process that will directly affect them and influence their level of commitment and the quality of the challenges the team can aspire to.

At the start of the chapter, we said that commitment is proven and strengthened in adversity. The decisive moment arrives in the sports world (and life) in every season. It sometimes comes unexpectedly, things get complicated, and pressure and difficulty increase. It is the moment of truth (what a curious thing to call them), where teams risk titles, playoffs, personal records, qualifications, promotions and demotions, etc. It is there when one demands and discovers the committed athletes and teams. Although victory may not be exclusive to them, they receive glory, greatness and extraordinary results.

Sometimes we practice an exercise in the classroom to work on the relation between the different styles in the leader's decision-making and the level of commitment everyone generates. To do that, we propose to agree on two values that should be very present in a high-performance team as the dynamic's goal. For that, we ask every participant to think about two of the individual values they consider essential in that group. Next, in small groups, everyone has to share their values and we give them a limited time to reach an agreement by choosing two values per group. Then, we put them together in bigger groups with the same objective, sharing and agreeing, until they finally return to the full group to reach a definitive agreement.

After twenty minutes of a heated argument in which everyone tries to convince others about the perks of the values chosen by their group, they choose to vote on every value and select the two "winners" when we tell them they have a minute left. Although it is a legitimate decision-making system in a team, not everyone accepts the result. It also does not necessarily generate the commitment with those who have "lost".

We get clear proof during the "process tasting" at the end of the exercise. We write six questions down on the blackboard and give each participant a sticker so that they score from one to five on their satisfaction level in every question: *I have felt listened to (0, not listened to at all; 5, totally listened to), I feel everyone has felt listened to, I have felt understood, I feel everyone has felt understood, I feel committed to the decision, I feel everyone is committed to the decision. The* image that is generally reflected on the blackboard is rather eloquent. It shows there are too many members in the group who have not felt listened to or understood, let alone felt committed to the result. By accepting the decision approved by the majority, we left them out of the ship, which is a mistake. When the storm breaks (because it always breaks), you will need everyone on board.

Consensus

Those who ease a *convers(a)ction* to reach a consensus need to pay attention to the process as well as the result. This means leaders need to create a space where everyone feels safe to participate and be understood and listened to. When people express an opinion or defend a value, you should not move on to the next one without paying attention to the former one. Instead, you must show true curiosity and keep asking or going deep into what they are telling you. Let them have room to express themselves without judgment or criticism. Let them be visible and feel they can truly influence the decision.

Once you have debated and everyone has given their opinion and defended their choices or criteria, you can ask them to raise their hands. Unlike voting, this is not definitive but merely informative of how things are. From then on, you need to focus on the minority, the ones "who" lost. You know those who "won" are already committed to the option they chose. What you need now is for the rest to commit to it. For that matter, you can ask every one of those: "what do you need to commit to this decision? How may we help you? What do you miss? What do you need to make it yours?" Once more, we want them to feel valued, acknowledged and significant... because they are! Although the majority did not pick their option, we want them to feel it is present in the team because, after expressing and defending it, the rest already knows this small group represents it, and also adds value to the bigger group.

Making Pacts also means learning to take some decisions by consensus that will make us trustworthy and deserving of the commitment of our players, without seeking unanimity because everyone does not need to agree. Instead, minorities have to be able to reply with an empathetic "yes" to the question, "can you live with this decision?" after having felt listened to, understood and participated in the *convers(a)ction*. Leaders need to work to integrate them and give them voice, because leaders know they need to align the individual commitment of the members at the service of an inspiring and shared vision in order to achieve the great challenges and extraordinary results leaders aspire to.

Purpose and vision

> *"May everything you do as if you could make a difference".*
> Wɪʟʟɪᴀᴍ Jᴀᴍᴇs

We cannot close this chapter about commitment or this book without referring to the personal vision and purpose everyone needs to discover in order to live a purposeful life. It is very complicated to involve yourself in a transformative process without knowing what you want to achieve, why you want to do it, what sort of future you want to create for yourself and your team, and who you need to become to accomplish it.

Purpose is like the compass that guides me and provides me with a direction to follow, accompanying me at every moment in this life adventure, answering the reasons why we are here and giving purpose to our lives. "Why am I doing this job? Why am I a manager? Why do I get up every day? What is my contribution?". It is not about having something to aspire to, a place to get to or a goal out of reach. One's purpose, as well as our deepest values and vision, is already inside of us waiting to be unveiled. We only need to make it aware, give it words and declare it.

Vision, on the other hand, is like the lighthouse that illuminates my path. I need it to be huge and powerful to never lose sight of it even if I am off course during the journey. It is the deepest expression of my desired future, which must contain, not only the objectives and goals I aspire to in the sports world, (job, family or any other field as well), but also who I commit to achieving my future from now on. An inspiring vision involves a deep and personal commitment to creating a new possible future for my followers and me. It then becomes my life's *raison d'être*.

In order to design a burning vision that strongly pushes me, aside from clarifying and identifying my values (see "Promoting" chapter), we need to define and declare our purpose.

Working on my purpose

"There are three types of happy lives. The most routine one, the one most people identify happiness with, is "pleasant life", in which they seek what they like, what gives them pleasure and they cultivate positive emotions. The second type is Aristotle's "good life", where what matters is enjoying what you do, in your job, in love or during your free time, until you allow yourself to be absorbed and you become one with what you are doing (flow state). The third one is a "purposeful life", in which you put your talent at others' service. It is a way of contributing, where you are part of something much bigger than yourself. That is the most authentic and profound sort of happiness".
MARTIN SELIGMAN

This thought-provoking image by Andrés Zuzunaga helps us represent graphically where everyone's purpose hides and why it is not easy to decipher. It is there, inaccessible, in a complex intersection of paths and requires a fascinating process of self-discovery for you to reveal it. Working on purpose and vision requires the necessary space and time to deeply reflect on these matters and the accompaniment of someone competent who helps you walk the way, a partner, a coach. If you do not have one, I offer myself voluntary to share with you this part of the way. You will need to grab a pen and paper again.

Once more, I pose powerful questions that search inside your "acorn" focused on every one of the four big circles on the drawing (what you love, what you do well, what you are getting paid for and what the world needs). The purpose that will give meaning to everything you do and will bring you closer to someone you are in essence, regardless of the activity or field in which you are at every moment, is hiding there, in the center that links your *mission*, your *job*, your *vocation* and your *passion*. Some questions:

What you love doing

What was your childhood dream? What touched you about that dream? And the one you had ten years ago? What is your dream now? What do they have in common? What thought makes you get up in a good mood every morning? What makes you wake up early and jump from your bed? What was the last time you felt happy? What did you do? Who were you with? What do you love doing? What is your biggest hobby? What do you love about this hobby? Who do you admire? What do you like the most and recognise from those you admire? What are the values that define them? What do they have in common? Who inspires you to do things (authors, mentors, friends, family members)? If you had to study for a degree again, what would you study? What do you like learning? What do you like reading? What sort of films do you enjoy more? If you could choose another job, which would it be and why? If you had a 6000€ life salary, what would you do? What would you do even if you were not paid? What is truly important to you? What do you want?

What you do well

What is the unique and only thing you can do? What three things do you think you are good at? What three things do your friends or relatives say you stand out in? What do they have in common? What things do you enjoy doing a lot? What sort of activities makes time fly? When they ask you for help, what is it usually for? What is the best thing you can offer? What do you do to help those you care about? What impact do you have on them? What kind of impact would you want to have? What skills do you have that have helped you develop in previous jobs or activities? What five situations have you lived in the past that you are very proud of? What did you do then? How did you do it? What did they share? Who were you in such special moments of your life? What is success for you? What has been your most outstanding success in that regard? When you are ninety years old and look back, profoundly grateful and happy with your life, what would be the achievement that makes you the proudest?

What the world needs

What worries you about your surroundings? What is the sort of environmental surrounding you want for your kind? What is the social surrounding you would like for your family? What economic level is enough for you? From the three previous things, what would you wish for those surrounding you? And for your town? Your country? The rest of the world? What does the world need from you? What would you like to change in the world? And in your world? How could you contribute to improving it? In what context? In what way? For whom could you be their light? What would you do? What is the best thing you can offer others? How could you provide value? And happiness? What kind of legacy would you like to leave? How do you want to be remembered? If you could do one thing to improve the world, what would you do? How satisfied would you be the next day? And next month? And next year? What would you like to tell your grandchildren? If your family's life depended on this decision (improving the world), what else could you do? What would your limit be? What is your contribution to sports, team, family, company or community? What could it be?

What you are paid for

What do you love the most about your job? Where do you make a difference? Where do you stand out? What is your impact, inwards and outwards, in your work environment? How do they perceive you? What do they say about you? Where do they say you stand out? What are your improvement areas? Where do you provide more value? What is the thing you do best? What is the thing you love doing the most? Do you prefer to work alone, be an employee or an entrepreneur? How is it working in a team for you? What do you like about your workmates? What is difficult about it? What do you learn from them? And about them? What is it like to help or integrate the new members? How do you feel about your workmates' successes? And yours? What would you need to enjoy your job more? What could you do? What would it be like to achieve it? What would be different? What would be better? What is your current contribution through your job to build a better world? What could it be? What would you work in even if you were not paid? How would you make a difference in that job? In what area would you be particularly good? What skills would you apply?

One night Nasrudin found himself going round and round a streetlamp looking at the ground when a neighbor came by. The latter asked him:

–What are you doing?

—I am looking for my key —replied Nasrudin. The neighbor stayed with him to help him search for it. After a while, another neighbor came by:

—What are you doing? —she asked them.

—We are looking for Nasrudin's key.

She also wanted to help them and she joined the search. A bit later, a third neighbor joined them. They searched and searched. After a long time of searching, they eventually gave up. A neighbor asked then:

—Nasrudin, we have searched for your key for a long time. Are you sure you have lost it here?

—No —replied Nasrudin.

—Where did you lose it, then?

—Over there, in my house."

—Why are we searching here?

Because there's more light here and my home is very dark —replied Nasrudin.

I know the previous answers are not easy and you will probably think you have no response for many. Do not worry. It is normal. Take it easy. I also keep searching, asking myself questions and I am alert to discover and interpret the clues I find along the way. I do not aspire for you to find your purpose hastily replying to some of the matters I have written down. What I expect is they will help you understand that you will have more chances of getting close to revealing it if, unlike Nasrudin, you decide to search in the proper spot. Inside your house, inside your "acorn", inside of you.

Statement of purpose

You should be taking notes of some words, images, symbols or sentences that shed light on the brought-up matters as you look inwards in search for answers while being supported by the previous questions. When you finish, check your notes and identify elements and patterns that repeat themselves. Observe which might be the common denominator –the skills, values and capacities that constantly pop up in your reflections. Start playing with words, until you can synthesise everything into a few sentences.

We need your statement of "purpose" to be powerful, full of meaning and sense, personalized and customized. A sentence you can anchor to your heart with strength that is always present and lights your decisions. A sentence that provides you serenity, happiness and clarity. A sentence that connects you to your deepest identity and to your necessity of belonging, adding value to something much bigger and transcendent than yourself.

A significant way I offer you to formulate your purpose is through a protocol that divides this declarative sentence into two distinct parts. The first one alludes to who I am in essence, to my best version, to the best I have and to my values. It is so immense and complicated to sum up in a few words that we will resort to metaphors again. These images or symbols help us connect more profoundly with complex meanings like the one we seek here and cannot express easily. By doing it this way, we will manage to gather all that internal wisdom about who we are in a couple of echoing and meaningful words for us.

The second part of the statement refers to what I can offer from my unique and valuable nature, replying to "why" I am here and what my contribution is to make a better world. The whole statement of purpose could be like this:

"I am a (metaphor) that (contribution)"

With the approval of their legitimate owners, pupils and clients, I shall share with you some highly inspiring statements of purpose for them, which I had the privilege of participating in their formulation and discovery process. I know they may sound somewhat frivolous without context, more similar to an ad slogan than a life purpose. However, I ask you not to judge them. You should understand they appeared after a lot of individual introspection work and you should know they are full of content and sense for their authors:

"I am the smile that makes you believe", "I am the sea that provides calm and bravery", "I am the cocktail that provides joy and freedom", "I am the dolphin who comes along in your journey", "I am the engine that feeds strength and energy", "I am the rock that leads from silence", "I am the lighthouse that is never put out", "I am the friend who believes in you", "I am the chocolate bar that provides moments of intense presence", "I am the curious apprentice who invites you to discover", "I am the gust of wind that leads you to calmness", "I am the smile that hugs you", "I am the pillar on which you can lean on", "I am the light that helps you shine", "I am the walker who accompanies you on the path", "I am the river that floods you with life", "I am the gaze that makes you visible", "I am the perseverance that captivates you and pushes you toward your dreams", "I am the wave that helps you grow", "I am the valley you return to", "I am the calm sea that reflects your essence in freedom", "I am the thunder that helps you believe". I shall use this moment to share with you the purpose that has guided, accompanied and pushed me in this book's creation and publication:

"I am a shooting star that sheds light on purposes"

Discovering, identifying, declaring and aligning with your purpose puts you on the path to living a meaningful life.

Working on "my vision"

If you want your team to be brave, dare to be brave. If you want them to be cheery, show your enthusiasm. If you want them to be intense, rub your energy off on them. If you want them to be respectful, show them respect. If you want them to be noble, be their model. If you want them listening to you, listen to them first. If you want them to trust you, believe in them first. If you want them to improve, improve yourself! Become what you want your team to be!

An adapted legend tells us that, while building the old stadium of Saint Mamés, recognized as the football cathedral in Spain, three construction workers were at work there. They asked the first one about what he was doing. He gave them a surly and tired answer saying he was bricklaying. The second one, bored and unmotivated, said he was building a wall. The last one looked upwards and proudly stated that he was creating a cathedral in an enthusiastic and grateful voice. The three men were doing the same! Nonetheless, while a task without a vision is nothing more than heavy labor, a vision with a task is a realized dream.

My "personal vision" represents my best version. It is me in the future but fully connected to my essential values, what I want and what is important to me in every key aspect of my life. My vision pushes me forward to the person, father, manager, athlete, husband, and friend I know I can be, and who I want to become from today on! For that, you can use the Wheel of Life exercise again and fill it with the different life sections important to you and in which you desire to live connected to your best version.

Grab a pen and paper again. Draw a circle and divide it into six or eight wedges. Write an aspect of your life for which you want to design a vision in each of them. For instance, sports, job, love, health, free time, money, personal development, family, friends, religion, etc. For the time being, I shall ask you to focus on one only, the one you feel is more urgent, or the one you fancy working on at this moment. Later you can complete the remaining wedges in the same way. Eventually synthesize it writing down and declaring your vision, gathering the most relevant sentences of each of your life aspects.

Before jotting down "your vision", I shall offer you an example that might inspire you to write your text. It is the professional vision that Xesco Espar shared in his book *Jugar con el corazón (Playing with The Heart)* that he defined before starting to coach the first handball team of Barcelona FC. He said: "I lead the team toward an extraordinary season with unlimited energy. The hyper-galvanized state is my base state! I instantly increase my players' performance by fueling their motivation to the maximum. I am an example of high aspirations, even impossible aspirations. I trust my players and they trust me. I am committed to constantly giving them positive models to make them self-confident and personally powerful. I face every challenge with astounding attitude and conviction levels to accomplish my final goal: inspiring people". His vision encompasses his purpose, his essential values and the values he wants to transmit to his team. It is written with passion, optimism and faith, reflecting the manager or leader he wants to be and the impact he wants on his players or followers in a handful of resonant sentences. The club won the Champion League that season after some years without any titles.

"If you want to build a ship, do not start by searching for wood, sawing planks or handing tasks. First, evoke such longing for the free and wide sea in men and women".
Antoine De Saint Exupéry
The Citadel

If shaping and sharing a passionate and inspiring vision is indispensable to leading and moving others, it is even more important to define, firstly, your vision to lead yourself. This vision will strengthen your commitment before the difficulties and adversity that will undoubtedly appear when you decide to leave the safety of the coast to search for new horizons and find out what you are capable of.

A finely worked-on vision must encourage you to grow. For that to happen, you need it to be impactful, precise, attractive and resonant. You do not only need to describe and shape a new possible future (remember it is a pure possibility), something much more than a predictable or somewhat improved future compared to the present. You must also express it with words full of energy so that, when remembering, reciting or reliving these sentences, they connect you to what matters to you and your *energizol* tank. Now, if you feel your emotional state to be appropriate, if you truly want and dare to do it, I shall offer you some questions that will help you write down your vision about the life aspect you have chosen. Take your time, reflect on them, feel them and jot down what you find out.

Have you chosen the life aspect you want to work on? Take a minute to score your current satisfaction level in that wedge, from one to ten. Have you finished? Here come the questions!

What would a perfect future be like? How would you describe a ten score? Who are you in a ten score? What is happening there? What are you doing or saying? How are you doing it? How do you feel about doing it? What values are you living intensely? Who are you being? What skills are you applying? How do you react before difficult, stressful or challenging decisions? What effects do they have on your followers (players, relatives, helpers)? What are you daring to do in a ten score? What are you capable of there? How do others perceive you? What is possible in a ten score? What is your impact? How do you interact with others in a ten score? What is your behaviour like? What have you notably improved? How do you feel there? How is your mood? How connected are you to your purpose?

After gathering your answers, write down three or four powerful sentences that picture the future you hope for in this particular section, in six months, in one or two or five years ahead, whichever you think appropriate. Do it with vital and energetic words. Write in the present tense and in first person. Write with optimism and conviction, deeply feeling every word you write down on paper. Use your own language and forms of speech if necessary. Once you finished, read your text aloud. If you are not smiling, excited and pumped for your writing, cross out and erase whatever that does not resonate enough with you. Do it again. Write, synthesize, erase any empty words and go down to your essence. Swap out common verbs and adjectives for stronger and more heartfelt ones. Open up the dictionary, browse and search for synonyms until you find the appropriate words and feel it is right. You will know once you read it because you will feel deep inside. Remember that language makes up reality! Dare to shape a possible future for you! Think big now! Don't limit yourself! Just do it!

"Convers(a)ction" power

The Greeks, experts in matters related to sports and physical activities (they even invented the Olympics), believed that athletes needed to train and develop their four fundamental faculties to achieve plenitude by competing at their maximum level. These four faculties are: rational logic, physio-motor, ethical and emotional.

To explain it briefly and apply it to football, the "rational logic faculty" includes the capacity to read the game, and understand the tactics, strategy, models and systems, and master the technique. The "physio-motor faculty" includes everything related to the body, physical preparation, physiotherapy, recovery, nutrition and rest.

Until now, better or worse, all clubs work on these with more or fewer resources. An elite team will have ten or more professionals on their staff to divide all tasks, while a humble youth team in any anonymous village will rely on a for-all-jobs manager in charge of everything. We assume in both cases that working on these two faculties is fundamental for athletes to be fittest and offer their best performance. Athletes develop the other two faculties (emotional and ethical) less systematically and more intuitively. Or they simply do not do anything about them.

We could say that our *convers(a)ctions* accompany those we have the honor of leading, as we have presented throughout the book, and they also adjust to this Greek proposition by extending this four faculties model beyond the sports world and adapting it to any activity.

We have begun the journey exploring the "emotional faculty", since we will discover several things about those we have in front of us. Chiefly, what matters to them, what they truly want, what gives them energy and what takes it away, who they are, what they care about, what makes them jump

out of bed in the morning and what is inside their "acorn" that makes them unique and special. Their "saboteur" will appear here for the first time, to which we will listen to and overcome reducing their power and connecting them to their "true Self", who is much more than the tags they give them. Here they will visualize and feel who they could become if they dared to, and what these people could do from there on as they design a powerful and inspiring vision that drags them to the people they need to be and who they can transform into to deserve the extraordinary results that they are looking forward to accomplishing. By exploring this faculty, we will help them discover other ways of interpreting and explaining their reality. We will offer them different lenses to see new uncharted possibilities. They will learn to recognize and express their emotions. They will learn to change moods and will fully power up on the *energizol* to start their unstoppable transformation process.

Once I have chosen who I decide to be in the face of the situation or the challenge life puts before me, we move on to the "ethical faculty", where I declare my commitment, fully aware and responsible to live more connected to what I am. Inspired by the surprising and immense gift of looking inwards and discovering talents I did not even know we had until now, I commit to my essential values and true nature. I commit to living more connected to what I am and being much more aware of it in my decisions, answers, behaviors, relationships and life.

After declaring it and choosing what I say YES to and what I say NO to, we continue our journey through the four faculties. We reach the "rational logic", which involves incorporating our mind into the process (since our guts and heart had been the only protagonists until now) to design an action plan that allows me to begin my transformation and learning path. In this part of the *convers(a)ction*, we will define the objectives I want to achieve, the skills I want to develop and the goal or challenge to accomplish. We will think about what I need to learn or unlearn, my resources, who can support me, how much time I can spend on the tasks I decide to implement, how and when I am going to do it, and how I can check and prove I am reaching my goal, etc. We will organize and design our own CSMATA detailed plan.

Lastly, we only have to go over the fourth and decisive faculty, called "physio-motor" in the model. As we already know, the goal of any *convers(a)ction* is to take action, which is where the change, improvement and growth dwell. Einstein used to say, "the only learning is experiences. The rest is information". This is when the "saboteur's" voice resounds!

It starts talking to you in critical moments to persuade you from exposing and risking yourself. It tells you things like: "why would you do that", "you are going to ridicule yourself", "they are going to see you", "what will they think", "they will think you believe you are clever", "it is not worth it", "nothing is going to change", and similar stuff. You then stop and quit your plan, and your saboteur wins again.

It is similar to when you signed up to the gym at the beginning of the year with the best of intentions and, a month later, you realized you had not done what you had intended to, although you were certain you would when you decided to. Your "rational logic faculty" understood you needed to start exercising and taking care of yourself, but, when it came to taking action, the "saboteur" always appeared. Something similar happens with the desire to learn languages after the holidays. You think, "this is the last year" and you convince yourself, provide arguments regarding how important it is to speak Spanish and sign up for lessons. By the time Christmas arrives, you realize you have given up and quit attending it. You waste money and convince yourself you are not good enough! It is always the same. It is impossible. You are a disaster. You think, "I am like this". Once again, your "saboteur" has taken the reins and exposed your poor compromise's little worth.

Alfonso Alcántara (@Yoriento) states: "Whatever you think and feel, do what you must". If you have spent resources, time and effort developing a plan that brings you closer to someone, be it the athlete, manager or professional you want to become, and you feel it connects with what is important to you, you cannot let your "saboteur" stop you now. Keep going! Do whatever you must! Fulfill your plan! We will assess later what has happened, how it has been, what have you learnt, what has worked out, what you consider differently now, and how you feel. But do it!

Despite there being valuable discoveries in the "no-action", to reach the decisive moment with success possibilities and giving meaning to our *convers(a)ctions*, we need a previously done and excellent job exploring emotions and listening to the heart, which knows and feels but does not speak while we silence the mind that talks nonstop without knowing. When we stock up on *energizol* and manage to take action by fulfilling our plan, we complete a "virtuous circle", a complete turn of the four faculties. This circle brings us closer to our vision, to the person we are, someone more serene, aware, brave and wise. We keep completing circles because all processes of transformation and habit change need planning, time, effort and repetition. No way is it free, miraculous, easy, or immediate. But, when you are confident, you persevere, you remain enthusiastic and your commitment is authentic, the *convers(a)ction* power can be magical.

Making Pacts in 7 Pills

1. Making **P**acts is going from obedience, an obligation by fear of the consequences, to *commitment*, a personal decision that cannot be imposed nor demanded, and is discovered and strengthened in adversity. Committing is deciding and choosing what I say "yes" to and what I say "no" to.

2. Making **P**acts is cocreating the relationship you want to have with your followers. It is designing a space of *convers(a)ctions*, generator of new possibilities. It involves encouraging them to take responsibility for solutions and results. It is ceasing to impose and starting being an accomplice of a transcendental possibility, of what it is not yet, of what it could be with your help.

3. What we are, what we do and how we do depend on how we plan and design our CSMATA action plan (Challenging, Specific, Measurable, Achievable, Temporal and Attractive), so that we all advance, everyone at their own pace, in the direction our dreams tell us.

4. Leaders need to integrate minorities and give them a voice so that everyone feels listened to, understood and valued until all of them can answer affirmatively and without a doubt to the question: "can you live with this?". Making **P**acts is learning to take some decisions by consensus, which will make us trustworthy and deserving of the devotion of our followers.

5. *Purpose* is the compass that provides us with direction by replying to the reasons why we are here and giving meaning to what we do. The point is not having someone to aspire to, somewhere to get to or a goal out of our reach. Instead, everyone's purpose is already inside waiting to be revealed. We just need to awaken it, give it words and declare it.

6. *Vision* is the beacon that illuminates my path and the deepest expression of my desired future. It must contain, not only the objectives and goals I aspire to in sports, family or any other fields, but who I commit to achieving it from today. A truly powerful vision turns into "the *raison d'être*", a profound personal commitment to creating a new possible future.

7. Transformative leaders commit to, make promises to themselves and declare them publicly. Then they choose to create a new reality where there was only possibility in the past. Additionally, they set it in motion regardless of the current conditions. They realise commitment is a choice that does not depend on circumstances but only on their own decision.

YOUR COMMITMENT LETTER

"Commitment is an action in language that transforms a promise into reality. It is the word that speaks of our intentions with courage. Actions speak louder than words. Commitment is the material that builds character and is the power to change things. It is the daily triumph of integrity over scepticism".

JIM SELMAN

We have reached the end of the book, which hopefully will be the trigger of your transformation. It is a catalyzer that activates your new and improved version, a more aware and responsible one, with many new skills ready to apply immediately, acting like a leader at the service of those you have discovered you can and want to be. You are now connected to an inspiring purpose and you possess a defying vision of the new future you begin building today.

To finish this journey we have shared, I want to ask you to write a letter. A commitment letter. I challenge you to do it, put it in an envelope and send it to me by post (not email) to this address (Calle Arenal 5, Dpto 208. CP. 408005 Bilbao, Vizcaya, España). You will be the only one to read it. I will not open it, but I will guard it for six months and promise to returning it to you after that period. With this letter, I am asking you to make a promise to yourself and do it now, while you connect to your brave nature and your *energizol* tank, without letting your "saboteurs" hijack you in this decisive moment. They probably just appeared ("stop this nonsense!", "so stupid", "we don't need this", "close this book now!") and are trying to take over you "here and now". Ignore them! Smile and start writing. For the last time, I shall offer you the best I have to help you, questions!

*What is going to be different from now on? From today, what are you going to change radically? What are you going to do differently? What are you going to dare to do? What are you going to allow yourself that you are not right now? How are your behaviour and attitude going to change? Where, how and with whom are your relationships going to improve? How will your energy and enthusiasm be? What are you going to do to maintain them? How are your convers(a)ctions going to be from now on? How will you listen? What will your **Presence** be like? And your questions? How and with whom are you going to apply the "fruitful insight" and acknowledgement? How will it be for you to believe before creating? What tags are you going to remove from yourself? Where, when and with who will you do it? How will you apply the "sublime listening" and empathy? When and with whom will you express emotions and maintain them? What about transforming moods? To whom will you apply the "Wheel of Life"? How will it be to make **Pacts**, reach an agreement and pay attention to minorities? What will you do differently as a leader at the service of those you are responsible for and you can influence? Who are you becoming? Who will you be? How will you shine and be light for others? What will be possible for you now?*

You may only reply to the questions that impact you. You can also forget about them and write whatever comes from your inside. What you feel is "true" to you and generates enthusiasm, energy and hope ("life defending itself", as Julio Cortázar said) to start planning the small changes that will be the base to consolidate your great transformation. There can be issues referring to being and doing, but please, if you have come this far, make one last effort and search for the appropriate space and time to give yourself this extraordinary gift.

.....

You may move forward if you have written the letter. You know you have not done it yet.

.....

Go back! Read the questions! Feel them! Are you going to finish this book without daring to accept this challenge? Really? Take the chance! Write!

(Twenty minutes to write your letter)

Are you done? Reread it calmly. Wow! Exciting, isn't it? Congratulations!

Before folding it, I need you to reflect for a couple of seconds about what you are saying YES to and what you are saying NO to with this commitment. You know what I am talking about. You are choosing to open to new possibilities of being and doing while you give up on other habits, attitudes and behaviors you realize they take you away from the people and leader you want to be by writing the letter.

Now, draw a line under your letter's last sentence and write down three things you are saying YES and NO to with this commitment because it is finally a decision. Write down: "With this letter, I say YES to (x3)" and "(...) I say NO to (x3)".

There is only one task left for you before putting the letter in the envelope: declaring your commitment. Like a couple who only becomes married when a judge certifies it and the priest states "I pronounce you man and wife", or when someone is considered officially deceased when the coroner declares it, you also have to declare it to make it real. You need to declare it to go from the good intentions land to the action and authentic commitment land, where you begin your transformation, being and doing what you have written.

To declare it I ask you to face a mirror and tell yourself, speaking slow, loud and clear, what you are saying YES to and what you are saying NO to in this letter. Before doing it, you must feel it intensely and deeply. Take your time. This is the last thing I am going to ask from you.

If you accept the challenge of writing and sending me this letter, I assure you it will fulfill its special function as it did with many before you. Declaring your commitment is something that has character, power and magic in itself. You will soon forget about it, but when it comes back to you in six months, you will be surprised by the fascinating and unstoppable process of growth and transformation you have submerged in. From manager, father, boss, teacher to transformative leader. From an acorn to an oak tree. You will be who you want to be and I assure you that your brave commitment letter will be the prelude to your most daring actions. Enjoy the path, fulfill your promise and SHINE!

EPILOGUE

As a 14-year-old, my manager insisted on me having to learn how to kick the ball with my left foot. He even made me play as a left winger to force me to play with the "bad" leg because, as he repeated all the time, I had to be ambidextrous to be a good football player. I, in my logic-rational faculty, understood it perfectly, but I did not do it. It was a pain thinking of every touch and I tried my hardest not to do it. I did not dare to, I preferred not getting the ball. I wanted to be invisible. My "saboteur" harassed me with thoughts of the sort: "they will see you are terrible", "they will laugh at you", "you may break your leg again", "they will throw you out of the club when they see how bad you kick the ball", "you won't play again", "what an embarrassment", "you are going to ridicule yourself", "what will your *aita* (father) think about you" and similar thoughts. I was unable to take action. My *energizol* tank was empty and my "saboteur" roamed my mind freely while having total control over the situation.

Sometimes I imagine what would have been different if someone would have asked me at that moment: *what would it be like to kick it with your left foot? What sort of player could you become? What player do you admire a lot? What would he tell you? How would you feel if you dared to? What do you think is the worst thing that could happen? What would it be like to be brave? What would you be proud of? What would be different? What would your 'aita' think if he knew you are training to improve your left kick? How would he feel? How would it be to tell him you are going to do it? What would he say? What do you need from your teammates? What do you need from me? How may I help you? What could you do to start this week?*

Even now, just by thinking about this *convers(a)ction* and while I write it, I get the urge to start kicking it with my left foot and miss and keep hitting and missing. Not judging myself nor worrying nor being ashamed. Not punishing myself for my mistakes and learning from them. Trusting my body much more and feeling that I start kicking with my left foot effortlessly and without thinking. Coordinating better daily and keep wishing for the next training session to arrive so I could improve my stronger, longer and more precise kicks every day. Feeling a deep plenitude sensation for having had the bravery of doing it. That is precisely what I did and felt when I finally mustered the courage to face and defeat my eternal "saboteur"... 18 years later! I needed a whole life to dare to face it. What are you waiting for to shine?

ACKNOWLEDGEMENTS

This book, like the workshops and my role as a learning facilitator partner, it is based on and would not have been possible without the direct or indirect participation of many people whose contribution I want to thank.

The first and essential thanks are for Michelle Madeleine Kempton, simply because this book would have been impossible without her. Michelle is the creator of the original "7Ps" concept and co-designer of the seven workshops in their current format. If this was not enough, I profoundly thank her for also being my "woman of light", illuminating my path in so many shared workshops. It is a privilege to count on her as a coach, mentor, friend and partner in Incoade.

Thanks to Óscar Garro, Víctor García, Alfonso de San Cristóbal and Juan Ugarte for being Incoade co-founders, and for all the energy, laughs and enthusiasm we shared during those exciting times. They made it possible.

Thanks to María Alaña, my Incoade coach, coordinator and partner, for her limitless devotion, generosity, joy and availability, always and at any time. Thanks for being the "smile that makes you believe" to every one of our workshop pupils.

Thanks to Juan Carlos A. Campillo, my Incoade coach and partner, for his humility to share with me his valuable experience and deep knowledge in coaching and leadership.

Thanks to Susana Alonso and Natalia Márquez, co-directors of the IDDI at the *Universidad Francisco de Vitoria* in Madrid, for organizing the first edition of the Coaching and Sports Leadership Master in 2007 with the approval of the UFV, and especially for "forcing" me to being a facilitator.

They were the ones who helped me create this new reality I daily enjoy so much.

Thanks to Óscar Callejo, the secretary of the manager school at the RFEF, for his insatiable curiosity and eagerness to learn; for believing without success guarantees, and for the courage to dare to expand a new and transformative vision of how to lead people and teams through managers.

Thanks to Ricardo Leiva, COE Sports Director, for his limitless trust in Incoade, to the point of handing us national team managers, technical directors, managers and elite athletes, an invaluable gift I will never be able to return.

Thanks to so many teammates and managers with whom I spent twenty-five years of my life full of unrepeatable learning and experiences, shared values and dreams, sublime emotions, feelings and moments, eternal round trips in bus, friends forever, happy and sad moments and dinners. I have remembered you so often during these months, reliving those unforgettable times with sincere thanks and a smile.

Thanks to the teachers, coaches, facilitators and colleagues of every course, workshop and seminar I have attended as a pupil in the last decade, for their passion, commitment, humility and leadership in others' service. They have all been and are inspiring examples for me.

Thanks to all my clients and attending pupils at our workshops, for their bravery in sharing so many real things. Thanks for being open and vulnerable, for believing and trusting me, for their presence, generosity and joy, for their doubts, concerns and questions, for daring to self-transform, for showing me so much time and time again.

Thanks to Lucía Jiménez and Juan Antonio García Herrero, representing those who helped me with their comments regarding the book. Thanks for offering themselves to read my first versions and drafts, for spending their time correcting them, for giving me their honest opinion with so much love and for encouraging me to finish it.

Aside from the authors who have guided me in this journey, I would also like to show my appreciation to all the people who teach me daily. Some are well known and others not, whom I follow on my social media or read their blogs where they share their wisdom as valuable thoughts, quotes, reflections or articles. I comfort myself by thinking that so many brave pilgrims accompany me and dare to shine for me and others, and I feel happy for being able to do my bit, to them and like them.

Thanks to Marta Prieto and her publishing company Kolima for betting on our book in the context of total crisis in the editorial world. Thanks for making me feel like an author. Thanks for her serenity and a smile when dealing with all my thoughts, changes, suggestions and ideas.

Thanks to Ramón and Maritxu, my *aitas*, and my five siblings, my family. I feel blessed for belonging to it.

Thanks to Itsaso, Kattalin and Uxue, my beloved daughters and daily true teachers.

Thanks to Igone, my wife, my life's most crucial and best decision. Thank you for always believing in me. LQ+.

REQUEST AND OFFER

Before finishing this book, I have a last request for you. If you consider it appropriate and necessary, I would like to count on you to create a repository with examples of the different application possibilities of every one of the skills developed in this book, in as many fields, activities and contexts as possible. We would do this to make it available for everyone who wishes to consult it and be inspired by your courage and example to improve their leadership at others' service skills.

Then, when you have felt very present and connected in some *convers(a)ction*; when you have dared to ask powerful questions, give genuine acknowledgment, maintain awkward emotions, etc, when you feel any of these things have worked because the achieved objectives are different and better than the ones you achieved before applying one of your new skills, I would appreciate if you were generous enough to share your findings and learnings derived from your experience with my readers and me. If you dared to do this, I suggest using any of these communication channels to send me your comments:

Mail: imanol.ibarrondo@incoade.com
Web: www.incoade.com
Twitter: *@energizol*

On the offer side, I suggest you do this:

If you wish to live the "7Ps" transformative experience to continue and go deep in your coaching and leadership skills, you can check the Incoade web to know about the calendar with the following public onsite editions. If you are in charge of an institution or company and you wish to have a "7Ps in company" training workshop there, adapted to your job, business, staff and needs, do not hesitate to contact us at info@incoade.com

If you think we can help you and you wish to hire our services as speakers in conferences on leadership and influence topics, or as facilitators/inspirers for your staff, or if you are in charge of a team that you care about, in any field, and you want to trust us to accompany you in your transformation process toward the leader at the service you want to be, send us an email at info@incoade.com

REFERENCES

- ALONSO PUIG, Mario (2008), *Vivir es un asunto urgente (Living is an urgent matter)*. Ed. Aguilar.

- ALONSO PUIG, Mario (2010), *Reinventarse (Reinvent yourself)*. Ed. Plataforma.

- ALONSO PUIG, Mario (2013), *Ahora Yo (Now Me)*. Ed. Plataforma.

- ARTETA, Aurelio (2012), *Tantos tontos tópicos (So Many Fools)*. Ed. Ariel.

- ALCANTARA, Alfonso, Blog @Yoriento

- ALVAREZ DE MON, Santiago (2010), *Con ganas, ganas. (With desire, desire)*. Ed. Plataforma.

- AZKETA, María (2011), *Nubes grises para un autodefinido (Gray clouds for a self-defined person)*. Ed. Andar.

- BENNIS, Warren (1994), *Convertirse en líder (Becoming a leader)*. Amazon.

- BENNIS, Warren (2010), *Dirigir personas es como adiestrar gatos (Managing people is like training cats)*. Ed. R. Areces.

- BENNIS, Warren (2008), *Líderes: estrategias para un liderazgo eficaz (Leaders: strategies for effective leadership)*. Ed. Paidós.

- BLANCHARD, Kenneth, (2010), *Ejecutivo al minuto (Executive to the minute)*. Ed. Debolsillo.

- BOYATZIS, R., MCKEE, A., JOHNSTON, F., (2008), *Líder emocional (Emotional leader)*. Ed. Deusto.

- BUCAY, Jorge (2012), *Déjame que te cuente (Let me tell you)*. Ed. RBA.

- CABANE, Olivia Fox (2012), *El mito del carisma (The myth of charisma)*. Ed. Empresa Activa.

- CABY, François (2004), *El coaching (Coaching)*. Ed. De Vecchi.

- CAMPBELL, Joseph (1991), *El poder del mito (The power of myth)*. Ed. Salamandra.

- CARDON, Alain (2005), *Coaching de equipos (Team Coaching)*. Ed. Gestión 2000.

- CARLIN, John (2009), *El factor humano (The human factor)*. Ed. Seix Barral.

- COELHO, Paulo (2002), *El Alquimista (The Alchemist)*. Ed. Planeta.

- COVEY, Stephen (2009), *Los 7 hábitos de la gente altamente efectiva (The 7 Habits of Highly Effective People)*. Ed. Paidós.

- CSIKSZENTMIHALYI, M. (2011). *Fluir (Flow)*. Ed. Kairós.

- CUBEIRO, Juan Carlos, GALLARDO, L., (2010) *Liderazgo Guardiola (Guardiola Leadership)*. Ed. Alienta.

- CUBEIRO, Juan Carlos (2001), *Sensación de fluidez (Sensation of fluidity)*. Ed. Pearson Educación.

- CUBEIRO, Juan Carlos, GALLARDO L. (2008), *Liderazgo, empresa y deporte (Leadership, business and sport)*. Ed. LID.

- DE BONO, Edward (2007). *Seis sombreros para pensar (Six thinking hats)*. Ed. Paidós.

- DE BONO, Edward (2009), *Pensamiento lateral (Lateral thinking)*. Ed. Paidós.

- DILTS, Robert (2004), *Herramientas para el cambio (Tools for change)*. Ed. Urano.

- DYER, Wayne (2001), *Tus zonas erróneas (Your erroneous zones)*. Ed. Grijalbo.

- ECHEVERRÍA, Rafael (2006), *Ontología del lenguaje (Ontology of language)*. Ed. Granica.

- ECHEVERRÍA, Rafael (2000), *La empresa emergente (The emerging company)*. Ed. Granica.

- ECHEVERRÍA, Rafael (2006), *Actos del lenguaje. Volumen 1: la escucha. (Acts of language. Volume 1: listening)*. Ed. JC Sáez.

- ESPAR, Xesco (2010), *Jugar con el corazón (Play with the heart)*. Ed. Plataforma.

- FRANKL, Viktor (2007), *El hombre en busca de sentido (Man's search for meaning)*. Ed. Herder.

- GALLWEY, Timothy (2006), *El juego interior del tenis (The Inner Game of Tennis)*. Ed. Sirio.

- GLADWELL, Malcom (2011), *Fueras de serie (Outliers)*. Ed. Punto de lectura.

- GARCIA BUSTAMANTE, Santiago (2013), *El efecto Simeone (The Simeone effect)*. Ed. Plataforma.

- GARCÍA HERRERO, Juan Antonio (2012), *¿Somos un equipo? (Are we a team?)*. Ed. Círculo Rojo.

- GOLEMAN, Daniel (2006), *Inteligencia emocional (Emotional intelligence)*. Ed. Kairós.

- GOLEMAN, Daniel (2007), *La práctica de la inteligencia emocional (The practice of emotional intelligence)*. Ed. Kairós.

- GOLEMAN, Daniel, (2008), *Inteligencia social (Social intelligence)*. Ed. Kairós.

- GOLEMAN, D., BOYATZIS, R., MCKEE, A., (2009), *El líder resonante crea más (The resonant leader creates more)*. Ed. Debolsillo.

- GOLDSMITH, Marshall (2002), *La última palabra en desarrollo del liderazgo (The Last Word in Leadership Development)*. Ed. Prentice Hall México.

- GOLDSMITH, Marshall (2007), *Un nuevo impulso (A new impulse)*. Ed. Empresa activa.

- GOMÁ, Herminia, *Blog de coaching y liderazgo (Coaching and leadership blog)*.

- GRINDER, John (2010), *De sapos a príncipes (From frogs to princess)*. Ed. Cuatro vientos.

- GUARNIERI, Silvia, ORTIZ DE ZARATE Miriam. (2010), *No es lo mismo (From frogs to princess)*. Ed. LID.

- HUNTER, James C. (2007), *La paradoja (The paradox)*. Ed. Empresa activa.

- INCOADE (2009), *Guía del alumno del «Master de coaching y liderazgo deportivo» (Student's guide for the «Master in coaching and sports leadership»)*.

- INCOADE (2011), *Guía del alumno de las «7P para potenciar personas» (Student's Guide to the «7Ps to empower people»)*.

- JACKSON, Phil (2014), *Once anillos (Eleven rings)*. Roca Editorial de libros.

- MANDINO, Og (2011), *La Universidad del éxito (The University of success)*. Ed. Debolsillo.

- MARIAS, Javier (1994), *La felicidad humana (Human happiness)*. Ed. Alianza.

- MARINA, José Antonio (2006), *Anatomía del miedo (Anatomy of fear)*. Ed. Anagrama.

- MARINA, José Antonio, (2010), *Las culturas fracasadas (Anatomy of fear)*. Ed. Anagrama.

- MARTI, Eduardo. *Blog «Líder y liderazgo» («Leader and leadership»)*.

- MAS, Pere y NADAL, Toni (2011), *Sirve Nadal responde Sócrates (Serves Nadal answers Socrates)*. Ed. Debolsillo.

- MASLOW, Abraham (2009), *El hombre autorealizado (The self-actualized man)*. Ed Kairós

- MAXWELL, John C. (2006), *Líder 360 grados (Leader 360 degrees)*. Amazon.

- MAXWELL, John C. (2008), *17 cualidades esenciales de un jugador de equipo (17 essential qualities of a team player)*. Ed. Grupo Nelson.

- MAXWELL, John C. (2011), *Las 21 leyes irrefutables del liderazgo (The 21 Irrefutable Laws of Leadership)*. Ed. Grupo Nelson.

- NITOBE, Inazo (2010), *Bushido (Bushido)*. Ed. Tuttle.

- O'CONNOR, James (2005), *Coaching con PNL (NLP Coaching)*. Ed. Urano.

- PALLARES, Miquel (2008), *Coaching mental y fútbol (Mental Coaching and Soccer)*. Ed. Inde.

- PUNSET, Eduardo (2009), *El alma está en el cerebro (The soul is in the brain)*. Ed. Destino.

- PUNSET, Eduardo (2005), *El viaje a la felicidad (The journey to happiness)*. Ed. Destino.

- PUNSET, Elsa (2014), *Una mochila para el universo (A backpack for the universe)*. Ed. Destino.

- ROBBINS, Anthony (2010), *Poder sin límites (Unlimited Power)*. Ed. Debolsillo.

- ROBINSON, Ken (2009), *El elemento (The element)*. Ed Grijalbo.

- ROVIRA, Alex (2008), *Las palabras que curan (The words that heal)*. Ed. Plataforma.

- ROVIRA, Alex, (2009), *La buena vida (The good life)*. Ed. Punto de lectura.

- RUIZ, Miguel, (1998), *Los cuatro acuerdos (The Four Agreements)*. Ed. Urano.

- SANTANDREU, Rafael (2011), *El arte de no amargarse la vida (The art of not making life bitter)*. Ed. Oniro.

- SELLIGMAN, Martin (2005), *La auténtica felicidad (Authentic happiness)*. Ediciones B.

- SELLIGMAN, Martin (2011), *La vida que florece (The life that flourishes)*. Ç. Ediciones B.

- SENGE, Peter (2006), *La quinta disciplina (The fifth discipline)*. Ed. Granica.

- SHARMA, Robin (2001), *El monje que vendió su Ferrari (The monk who sold his Ferrari)*. Ed. Plaza & Janes.

- SKARMETA, Antonio (2012), *El entusiasmo (Enthusiasm)*. Ed. Debolsillo.

- STAMATEAS, B. (2012), *No me maltrates (Don't mistreat me)*. Ediciones B.

- TOLLE, Eckhart (2008), *El poder del ahora (The power of now)*. Ediciones Gaia.

- TOLLE, Eckhart (2009), *Practicando el poder del ahora (Practicing the power of now)*. Ediciones Gaia.

- TOLLE, Eckhart (2012), *El silencio habla (Silence speaks)*. Ediciones Gaia.

- TORAL, Gotzon (2009), *Liderazgo, un deporte de equipo (Leadership, a team sport)*. Editado por DFB.

- TRIAS de BES, F. y ROVIRA, A. (2004), *La buena suerte (Good luck)*. Ed. Empresa activa.

- UESHIBA, Morihei (2009), *El arte de la paz (The art of peace)*. Ed. Kairós.

- VALDANO, Jorge (2013), *Los 11 poderes del líder (The 11 powers of the leader)*. Ed. Conecta.

- VILASECA, Borja (2008), *Encantado de conocerme (The 11 powers of the leader)*. Ed. Plataforma/Debolsillo.

- WHITMORE, John (2005), *Coaching*. Ed. Paidós.

- WHITWORTH, Laura, KIMSEY-HOUSE, Karen y SANDAHL, PHILIP HENRY (2007), *Coaching Co-activo (Co-active Coaching)*. Ed. LID.

- WOLK, Leonardo (2006), *Coaching: el arte de soplar brasas (Coaching: the art of blowing coals)*. Ed. Gran Aldea editores.

ABOUT THE AUTHOR

 Imanol Ibarrondo was a professional soccer player for 12 years in first and second division teams. Already in 2005, after the founding of IN-COADE (Sports Coaching Institute), he began working as a coach for athletes and trainers, and for teams and national teams, as well as a trainer in coaching, leadership and team building skills.

Since 2010, he has collaborated with the COE (Spanish Olympic Committee) in the training of Olympic selectors, and for this reason, in 2016 he was part of the official Spanish delegation at the Olympic Games. During that time, he has collaborated with hundreds of athletes and coaches, with dozens of national and international clubs and Spanish teams of different sports such as field hockey or synchronized swimming.

More focused on the soccer itself, from 2015 to 2018 Imanol was part of the coaching staff of the Mexico soccer team and, just after the World Cup, he became part of the coaching staff of the first team of Real Sociedad de San Sebastian.

Imanol has expanded its scope of action to non-sports organizations, its specialty being working with people who seek to increase the impact and positive influence of their leadership, as well as the design and facilitation of thinking processes with groups from any field and sector of activity that want and need to become high performance teams.

KOLIMA
BOOKS